Game Theory in the
Behavioral Sciences

Game Theory in the Behavioral Sciences

Editors: IRA R. BUCHLER
University of Texas

HUGO G. NUTINI
University of Pittsburgh

University of Pittsburgh Press

Library of Congress Catalog Card Number:
LC 68–12727
Copyright © 1969,
University of Pittsburgh Press
Manufactured in the
United States of America

Reproduction in whole or in part is permitted for any
purpose of the United States government.

Contents

Figures

Tables

Preface

WITH the exception of Anatol Rapoport's "Games as Tools of Psychological Research," Bernhardt Lieberman's "Combining Individual Preferences into a Social Choice," and Kozelka's "A Bayesian Approach to Jamaican Fishing," the papers in this volume were originally presented at the Conference on Applications of the Theory of Games in the Behavioral Sciences, held at McGill University, Montreal, on August 15–17, 1966. The primary purpose of the conference was to explore, through formal reports of ongoing research and through informal discussions, potential areas for the application of game theory and related approaches in the behavioral sciences, with particular reference to problems of concern to social and cultural anthropologists.

Two basic, recurrent problems faced the organizer of the conference. Anthropologists expressed an interest in the utility of game theory as a "meta-language" in anthropological studies but disclaimed any knowledge of the formal apparatus of the theory; conversely, the mathematicians, economists, psychologists, and moral philosophers, who have made notable contributions to the theory of games, expressed delight at the prospect of becoming anthropologists for a few days but regretted their lack of command of the anthropological literature. It was decided, therefore, to broaden the substantive scope of the conference and to encourage anthropologists to explore potential domains of application within the areas of their particular interest and competence. The result is a rather heterogeneous collection of papers, ranging from Rapoport and Chammah's important and somewhat technical contribution to experimental games to Schelling's ingenious application of the meta-language of game theory to moral and legal concepts and the application of related mathematical models such as graph theory (Atkins and Curtis; Livingstone) and linear programming (Hoffmann; Buchler and McKinlay). For the most part, the papers in this volume are broadly concerned with anthropological topics: African tribal politics, brideprice, Melanesian and Jamaican economics, cultural rules, Kroeber's concept of cultural intensity, marriage systems, Mexican ladder systems, and the analysis of ethical systems.

Linear programming and graph theory, like the theory of games, depart from classical analysis (which is concerned with numerically measurable quantities and statistically determined effects), and are directed toward the consideration of sets of discrete entities and their structural relations (Rapoport 1963:495; Buchler 1966:2, 5, 39; Livingstone, this volume).* Many of the mathematical procedures used in this volume are deterministic in the sense of classical physics and should therefore be carefully distinguished from the probability models generally applied in anthropology and sociology, which more closely resemble the methods of statistical mechanics. They suggest a series of optimization problems and a variety of models for the study of interlinked decision processes that should be of interest to the anthropologist.

Aside from the frankly exploratory analysis of Moore (1957) and the general discussions of Lévi-Strauss (1953) and Fortes (1962), the only previous attempts to apply the theory of games to anthropological data are Barth's (1959) study of Pathan organization and Davenport's (1960) analysis of the minimax behavior of Jamaican fishermen. The former is a zero-sum (or constant sum) majority game; the latter, a two-person three-strategy, zero-sum game.

At this point, the reader may well pose the following query: Given the relatively limited interest in the theory of games (in terms of published research) within social anthropology, why devote a conference to this topic? Atkins and Curtis (this volume) have lucidly summarized the response that this query might elicit from the conferees:

> Game theory deals both with game rules per se and with rules for playing games intelligently. It has been rules of the latter sort, of course, which have claimed by far the larger share of the game theorist's attention—and quite properly so, given the motivations that guide most game-theoretic studies.
>
> By contrast, the historically dominant and still flourishing concern of the cultural anthropologist has been with the analogues, in culture at large, of game rules in the first or narrower sense—that is, with what might be referred to as "ground rules" that have more to do with structuring the basic cultural framework within which decision-making occurs than with guiding choices among the options that this framework may allow. Indeed, one major source of difficulty in finding immediate anthropological applications for game theory lies precisely in this difference of emphasis.

The intent of the conference, then, was to stimulate among anthropologists a greater interest in rules for playing games rationally and in rules that guide choices among the options that the cultural

*References are given with those for the Introduction.

framework allows. An increase in ethnographic accounts which formulate game rules, as well as game-playing rules, will make the anthropological applications that have appeared thus far seem comparatively trivial.

For their support of the conference, I am grateful to the Advanced Research Projects Agency of the Department of Defense and the Group Psychology Branch of the Office of Naval Research (the conference was sponsored under ONR Grant Nonr (G)–00042–66). I am deeply indebted to Richard Salisbury for handling local arrangements, to McGill University for providing facilities, and to the numerous secretaries and students who have, over the past two years, handled much of the correspondence and other work connected with this volume. The stimulus for this project derives from the intellectual insistence of Professor Claude Lévi-Strauss that the application to anthropological materials of mathematical methods that depart from classical analysis is a necessary tool as anthropology enters a mature stage of conceptualization.

IRA R. BUCHLER

Game Theory in the
Behavioral Sciences

Ira R. Buchler
Hugo G. Nutini

Introduction

IN these introductory remarks we shall briefly discuss three sets of related problems:

1. Some of the fundamental principles of conceptualization in the social sciences, with emphasis on the relationship between formal or analytical constructions and empirical phenomena—for the purpose of illustrating that the application of mathematics is a sine qua non to the solution of a series of problems, similar to those that were once a source of vexation to workers in the physical sciences;

2. Some implications of the game theorist's conception of strategy rules for various theoretical issues in social anthropology, with reference to the empiricit's conception of jural rules as absolute constraints on social behavior; and

3. Some of the mathematical relationships existing among the various departures from classical mathematical analysis that are considered in this volume.

THE EPISTEMIC CONDITIONS OF ANALYTICAL CONSTRUCTS

Bertrand Russell (1926:243) contends that it would be presumptuous to maintain that the universe embodies mathematical truths or that it reflects the analytic a priori nature of mathematics, but it is a fact that mathematics has become the most powerful tool in the conceptualization of the empirical world. In a sense we can properly say that modern science begins with the realization of the implications of this almost self-evident truth. Galileo was perhaps the first scientist to have understood fully that the business of science is to search for the correct mathematical strategy in harnessing empirical phenomena under the rubric of laws, thus disposing of the notion that simple statistical correlations of empirical facts will ever yield universal generalizations.

Nagel (1961:447–546), Reichenbach (1951), Northrop (1947), and other philosophers of science have argued that experimental laws in

1

most of what passes under the name of social or behavioral science are exclusively statistical generalizations and not universal in form. They maintain that the social sciences are to a considerable extent still in a pre-Galilean stage. Developments during the past twenty years, however, indicate that a Copernican revolution has been initiated in the social sciences, especially in psychology and economics. The explicit or implicit aim of this revolution is to break the deadlock into which these branches of knowledge, not unlike the physical sciences in the late nineteenth century, seem to have been led by the adherence of their practitioners to over-empirical methods of scientific explanation. This reaction implies, moreover, an intensive consideration of the quantitative aspects of behavioral phenomena. As some branches of mathematics became more and more qualitative, it was increasingly easier to apply them to predominantly qualitative behavioral empirical phenomena. It is by now perhaps accepted by the majority of social scientists that the secure establishment of a series of social science disciplines can be achieved only through the application of the qualitative branches of mathematics developed during the past two decades. Lévi-Strauss (1953) pointed this out for anthropologists nearly fifteen years ago, and he has since maintained that any successful conceptualization of social and cultural phenomena is directly proportional to the application of the correct mathematical tools.

Quantification is not new in the social sciences; several disciplines have been practicing it for the greater part of this century. But the quantification in which social scientists have engaged has been almost exclusively concerned with the application of statistical devices for the correlation of the raw facts of social and cultural experience. In this connection, Nagel's criticism (1961:504–10) that the social sciences have not hitherto devised sociological laws of a universal form is well taken. The main reason for this failure, he argues, is that social scientists have not been able to develop universally valid "laws" for "pure cases" against which, in terms of systematic discrepancies and departures from ideally formulated constructs, actual observational phenomena may be explained. It seems to us that in our search for the formulation of universally valid laws in the social sciences, finite mathematics (game theory, graph theory, linear programming, flows in networks, and so on) is an indispensable tool. Thus, if it is unrealistic to assume that the universe conforms to mathematical principles, then we must search for those aspects of the universe which admit of mathematical formulations. This is the approach that Nagel has in mind when he accuses social scientists of failing to apply the correct logical strategy in their conceptualizations.

Theoretical scientists and philosophers of science do not agree entirely regarding the theory and method of science. There are, however, some postulates of science on which there is agreement: (1) Modern science is concerned exclusively with process (method) and not with substance. (2) Modern science assumes that there is both "primitive" and "derivative" knowledge, and that it is the duty of the scientist to establish an order of priorities between an axiomatic set and its implications in order to accommodate the inductive and deductive elements always involved in a conceptual system. (3) Modern science involves the "bifurcation of nature" into the "immediately sensed" and the "postulated but not sensed," or into formal constructs and empirical reality. It should be the main concern of the scientist to develop the transformation rules that mediate between the analytical properties of formal constructs and the empirical reality of facts (Nutini, in press).

Social scientists often fail to realize the epistemic conditions for theoretical explanations—that is, the stipulation of a cognitive relationship between formal constructs (concepts, theories, models, etc.) and empirical data. The main reason for this failure is the fact that the logical and epistemological foundations of the theory and methods of the social sciences have never been carefully examined. Underlying a large number of unresolved problems in the social sciences are several fundamental concepts that must be thoroughly analyzed within a social, cultural, and psychological context before these problems can be solved. They are: (1) the establishment of "minimum vocabularies," or the delineation of primitive terms; (2) the concept of epistemological order; and (3) the construction of coordinative definitions (Nutini 1968:5).

The construction of minimum vocabularies is basically nothing more than the application of Occam's Razor: "Entities are not to be multiplied unnecessarily." The implication in our context is that it is best to conceptualize empirical phenomena (physical or social) on the basis of a minimum number of assumptions constituting an axiomatic set. We must be careful, however, in making inferences from minimum vocabularies. There are usually a number of minimum vocabularies for a given subject matter, and there is always the possibility that members of the same axiomatic set may themselves need to be demonstrated. In other words, the axiomatic set is an order of priorities established to accommodate the deductive elements that are always present in a conceptual system; this should enable social scientists to have uniform criteria for the classification of primary data, and such classification in turn becomes primary data for the construction of more inclusive constructs. Bertrand Russell (1946:14–15) developed the use of minimum vocabularies in his work on mathematical logic: during the past sixty years this work has become a cornerstone in the understanding of the structure of science (Nutini 1968:6).

The concept of epistemological order is closely related to the notion of primitive vocabularies, except for the fact that the former entails epistemological rather than logical priority, designed to accommodate the inductive elements in a conceptual system. This conception of science assumes that there is "primitive" and "derivative" knowledge, and that the main task of the theory-builder is to arrange what we know in a systematic order, starting with an axiomatic set of the empirical phenomena to which the system is supposed to apply. In addition, the criteria of priority must be conditioned by the axiomatic set, which must contain the rules establishing the correct relationship of theory to empirical data (Chisholm 1946:421–26). In social science terms, application of the concept of epistemology means simply the systematic design of the devices or transformation rules that must mediate between purely formal constructs, the models if you wish, and the empirical world of social, psychological, and cultural relations. The most important of these three notions, however, is the construction of coordinative definitions, which involve logical as well as epistemological considerations. Briefly, the notion of coordinative definitions has been developed by scientists and epistemologists in order to bypass the problem of the bifurcation of nature into the "immediately sensed" and the "postulated but not sensed" (that is, nature as sensed, and nature as conceived by scientific theory), which was introduced by Galileo and Newton, and which continues in modern science (Northrop 1941:171). To put it differently, coordinative definitions are constructions designed to solve the problems of applying a formal or analytical system to empirical reality—in our case, to social, psychological, and cultural reality, as the raw data of human experience. If this is not possible, the theory, model, or construct will remain analytical and in the realm of possibility, but inapplicable to the actual world. The indispensibility of coordinative definitions as links between theory and reality has been emphasized repeatedly by Reichenbach (1938:382–83; 1946:32–36; 1951:132–35). They have also been discussed by Carnap (1955) under the name of "semantic rules," by Bridgman (1927) as "operational definitions," by Nagel (1961) as "correspondence rules," and by Northrop (1947) as "espistemic correlations." Reichenbach (1946:32) puts the matter in perspective:

> We must distinguish between the *formal system* and its *interpretation*. . . . This may be illustrated by the example of geometry. An axiomatic construction of Euclidean geometry, such as that given by Hilbert, though fully listing all the internal properties of the fundamental notions, must be supplemented by *coordinative definitions* of these notions when the formal system is to be applied to reality. Thus physical geometry is derived from Hilbert's system by the use of coordinative definitions, according to which straight lines are interpreted as light rays, points as small parts of matter, congruence as a relation expressed in the behavior of bodies, etc. This interpretation is not a consequence of the formal system; and there are many other admissible interpretations. But these other interpretations do not furnish what we call *physical* geometry.

All scientific analyses include three distinctive contexts or stages: the axiomatic level, the level of experimentation, and the level of verification, each of which must be carefully distinguished in conceptualizing empirical phenomena. Reichenbach (1951:6–7) speaks of the "context of discovery" as the stage in which theories and general constructs are formulated with the aid of intuition, and the "context of verification" as the stage in which we experiment with empirical data and design verification procedures. Many social scientists, and especially anthropologists, confuse these levels of analysis, especially the axiomatic and the experimental levels, or the experimental and the verification levels, and we believe this is primarily responsible for our scant success in the correlation of data leading to generalization. Although social scientists are fond of speaking of empirical "verification"—that such and such arrangements of observational facts exist in the social, cultural, and psychological universe—this is not what verification means in science; verification is never the correlation of definition and observational facts, but rather the determination of whether a theoretical construct accounts for observational configurations of facts (Nutini, in press).

Our main concern in conceptualizing social, psychological, and cultural phenomena should be the devising of an appropriate methodology. It is necessary to have such a methodology in order to ascertain the strategic areas in which phenomena may yield the comparable relational and positional properties that go into the construction of theoretical constructs. In Nagel's words, we must develop the appropriate theoretical notions in order to indicate how universally valid laws for "pure cases" of social, psychological, and cultural phenomena might be formulated successfully.

Our brief excursion into the most salient tenet of the structure of science makes clear the all-important role of mathematics in the inductive-deductive conduct of scientific inquiry in dealing with human affairs. In a more immediate and restricted sense the application of the qualitative branches of mathematics, perhaps especially game theory and related approaches, should be of much help in solving the difficulties (sometimes artificially created) that seem to exist in the conceptualization of human affairs in terms of their sociological and psychological components. A single example will suffice to make our point.

Since the beginning of the century, when Durkheim staunchly postulated that sociology and psychology must be kept strictly separated, little has been done to bring about an approach (social psychology to the contrary) to the conceptualization of human affairs in which their sociological and psychological components are handled within the framework of a single integrated theory. A point discussed in some detail in the following section will illustrate what we believe to be a serious shortcoming of social science theory.

Game theory makes a distinction between the rules that structure the game and the individual options of the actors playing the game, or, as game theorists formally put it: ground rules and strategy rules. Social scientists, and especially anthropologists and sociologists, are aware of the distinction when they speak of cultural norms or jural rules, on the one hand, and statistical deviations from these norms or rules, on the other. They know that permanently organized groups of human beings have rules (ideal standards if you wish) according to which their societies are structured, and also that these rules are broken. More often than not, however, they fail to realize that in describing and explaining social phenomena, both the rules and the deviations from the rules are inextricably interconnected, and that one of these conceptual systems without the other will give only a partial account of the situation. To put it differently, ground rules may be termed mechanical (deterministic) models or ideal paradigms of what people *should* do, while strategy rules are statistical (stochastic) models of what people *actually* do. At the heuristic level, we would like to point out in this connection that much of the work done by anthropologists and sociologists suffers seriously because of the overwhelming concern of the former with ideological behavior and of the latter with actual behavior. Until social scientists become fully aware of the complementarity of deterministic and stochastic models, they shall continue to present lopsided descriptions and explanations of social phenomena.

The question here, however, is: How can the new mathematics, and especially game theory, help us to combine the sociological and the psychological aspects in conceptualizing human affairs? First, it seems to us obvious that the ground-rules level—or ideological level—is primarily sociological, that is, it has to do with consensual action; while the strategy-rule level—or stochastic level—is to a considerable extent psychological, that is, it has to do with private and group options and is the level at which decision-making takes place. Secondly, since it is assumed that these two levels cannot be separated, the thresholds where sociology and psychology become causally efficient must be regarded as strategic areas of conceptualization. These thresholds, we strongly believe, can only be adequately formulated in terms of mathematics, by which the proper components are brought to the fore. Failure to comply with the procedure here envisaged will result in either unrealistic assumptions about the nature of social behavior— witness the case of the functionalists—or a dogmatic and heuristically unworkable psychological reductionism, as exemplified by various forms of psychological anthropology.

GROUND RULES AND STRATEGY RULES

The theory of games is concerned essentially with games of strategy, in which the outcome depends on the interlinked decision processes of players, and, in this sense, may be usefully contrasted with games of chance, in which the outcome is determined solely by random events.[1] One of the central concepts of the theory of games is the notion of strategy, which is a complete plan that specifies the behavior of the players for all possible circumstances and contexts that become relevant during the course of play. A solution of a game may be defined as the set of strategies which are prescribed to players or, as in the case of Southwold's paper in this volume, to coalition formations, such that the outcome satisfies intuitive notions of rationality or rational behavior. An outcome of a game is, generally speaking, the

best that each player could achieve "given the rules of the game and
the constraints resulting from the strivings of all the other players to
achieve their goals" (Rapoport, this volume).

When a player has complete control of the outcome of a game, and
when the rank order of the players' preferences for various outcomes
is known, the construct rational decision is "defined obviously as
the choice of action which leads to the most preferred outcome"
(Rapoport, this volume). Decision theory is concerned with the problem of arriving at a decision after all the relevant facts are known.
Decision theory is not concerned with the factual (cultural) knowledge
that a player has about a given situation, or with formulating a theory
to explain how such knowledge is obtained. It is here that the theory
of statistical decisions, game theory, and related approaches on the
one hand, and cultural anthropology on the other, which seem in certain respects to be so far apart, complement one another. This point
is well made in the distinction made by Atkins and Curtis (this volume) between the anthropologist's interest in ground rules, which
structure the cultural framework within which decision-making occurs,
and the game theorist's interest in strategy rules, or rules for playing
games intelligently, which guide choices among the options which the
cultural framework allows.[2] Just as the anthropologist often ignores
strategy rules and the context in which various moves may be employed, the mathematical game theorist and the experimentalist[3] often
ignore, in the name of experimental control, the rules that structure
the framework within which decision-making occurs.[4] Many important theoretical problems in social anthropology exemplify the importance of this distinction and the necessity of considering both types of
rules in ethnographic and ethnological studies.

Consider, for example, Needham's (1962) notion of "prescriptive
marriage systems."[5] Rather than prescribe certain strategies to
categories or groups of players, Needham defines a class of societies in
which there are certain ground rules that have prescriptive entailments.
These entailments, we are told, are of an ideological nature. By bifur-
cating social organization and ideology, Needham ignores, in a most
consistent and dogmatic fashion, the options that the basic cultural
framework allows. This class of societies is then contrasted with another type of society in which the ground rules relevant to marriage
and alliance are preferential; i.e., they have no ideological entailments.
Needham, then, at least on an ideological plane, is led to the absurd

conclusion that there are two types of societies: one with ground rules, the other with strategy rules. This conclusion is clearly unacceptable. The point is not to classify societies in terms of types of rules, but rather to determine the contexts in which the ground rules provide options and the manner in which these options are utilized.

This situation has its analogue in the similarly unacceptable cognatic/unilinear distinction, which is also essentially a distinction between strategy rules and ground rules. The genetic argument in social anthropology, construed on either a logical or historical level, that social structures may be usefully regarded as the "statistical outcome of multiple individual choices rather than a direct reflection of jural rules" (Leach 1960; cf. Murdock 1960 and Leach 1961b), or the converse proposition, may be decoded, on a more basic level, as meaning that either ground rules or strategy rules are prior in some fundamental sense. This, too, we consider an arbitrary and unproductive formulation (cf. Buchler and Selby 1968a; Buchler, in press).

So much, at this point, for the anthropological significance of the distinction between ground rules and game or strategy rules. In our view, this distinction underlies numerous significant theoretical issues in anthropology and suggests the mutual relevance of ethnology and the theory of games.

Professor Rapoport's paper on "Games as Tools of Psychological Research" (this volume) is a lucid review of the various types of games of potential interest to psychologists and anthropologists, of the logical structure of the situations that they simulate, and of the decision processes underlying these situations. Rapoport clearly illustrates the distinction between zero-sum games and the dilemma games such as Prisoner's Dilemma, Chicken and Leader (Rapoport and Chammah 1965 and this volume), which belong to the class of non-zero-sum games in terms of a hierarchy of decision problems. In the case of the zero-sum-games, in which the outcomes are completely determined by the choices, it is clear, once the decision principle is understood, that it is the rational one; in the case of dilemma games, the concept of rationality becomes ambiguous.

As an example of an early application of zero-sum-game theory in cultural anthropology, let us consider Davenport's analysis (1960)[6] of the "minimax behavior" of a group of Jamaican fishermen. Fishermen set fish pots, which are drawn and reset, three regular fishing days a week. The captain of a crew is ostensibly confronted with a two-choice situation, as the fishing grounds are divided into inside and outside banks. The distinction between inside and outside "is made on the basis of the strength of the currents which flow across them" (1960:4). The inside banks are almost fully protected from the currents; the outside banks are not. Consequently, there is a good deal of unpredictability associated with setting pots on the outside banks, since the pots may be lost or damaged or the fish may be killed. However, the quality of the fish caught on the outside banks is higher and the quantity is greater. Wear and tear on canoes is also an important consideration. In fact, three alternative strategies are considered: (1) inside, (2) outside, and (3) in–out.

The essential economic facts for a fishing month are summarized by the following matrix (payoffs are in British pounds):

	Current	No-Current
Inside	17.3	11.5
In-out	5.2	17.0

If the village as a whole is regarded as one player and the environment as the other, the essential conditions for a two-person, two-strategy, zero-sum game are satisfied (Davenport 1960:8). Although no one in the village fishes entirely outside, Davenport (1960:8) computes "estimates of what incomes might be derived from this alternative." The complete matrix is:

		ENVIRONMENT	
		Current	No-Current
	Inside	17.3	11.5
VILLAGE	In-out	5.2	17.0
	Outside	−4.4	20.6

This changes the model to a two-person, three-strategy, zero-sum game. This 2 × 3 game is reduced to a series of 2 × 2 games, eliminating one strategy when another is dominant over it. A zero proportion is assigned to the eliminated strategy. "Since the maximum-of-the-row-minimums (5.2) is equal to the minimum-of-the-column-maximums (5.2), the in–out alternative is dominant over the outside alternative, and a proportion of zero is assigned to the outside strategy" (Davenport 1960:9). Or, 5.2 > −4.4. Thus, 5.2 = maximin, and 5.2 < 20.6, so 5.2 = minimax.

Neither of the remaining strategies is dominant over the other—the maximin is not equal to the minimax—so the theory predicts mixed strategies, or 5.8 in–out (33 percent) to 11.8 (67 percent) inside, and 5.5 current periods (31 percent) to 12.1 no-current periods (69 percent). Davenport (1960:9) gives:

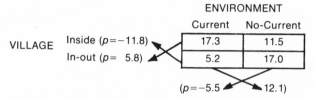

By shifting the unit of behavior from the total strategy of captains to the placement of individual fish pots and maintaining the same level of analysis—village/environment—Davenport (1960:10) predicts the proportion of pots set on the inside bank (0.811) and the proportion of time the current will run (0.30).

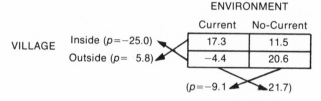

The predicted proportion may now be compared with the observed

	Observed	*Predicted*
Outside strategy	00%	00%
Inside strategy	69%	67%
In–out strategy	39%	33%
Current periods	25%	31%
No-current periods	75%	69%
Pots set inside	0.790	0.811

The group effect of the distribution of fishing behavior is a utility which approaches minimaximization. Davenport (1960:10) states:

If this kind of function is characteristic of groups or patterns in which choice is permitted, then the naïve assumption of complete conformity which certain structure-functionalists make about groups and patterns must be taken under further advisement.

With this we are in complete agreement, but this position certainly does not impel us to accept Murdock's non sequitur (1960:9) that "jural rules are best regarded as the outcome of a statistical trend in individual choice." (See also Sahlins 1963:44). As we have already indicated, a more balanced approach is provided by certain formulations which derive from the theory of games. This, of course, includes non-zero-sum as well as zero-sum games, games of collaboration and mutual dependence as well as games of pure conflict, and fixed-sum as well as bargaining games (Schelling 1963).

Any theoretical position that is derived from the assumption that jural rules absolutely constrain individual choice behavior, or that systems of jural constraint are an outcome of statistical trends in choice behavior, is likely to produce arbitrary interpretations. It is far more productive to assume that fields of individual choice behavior (strategic options) are defined by the structure of the basic system of cultural constraints, and that neither one nor the other is prior in a developmental or historical sense. Although one need not make naïve assumptions of complete conformity about groups and patterns, it is perfectly reasonable to assume—subject to experimentation—that degrees of appropriateness in strategic action are measured by their relationship to the options provided by the basic cultural framework.

A fundamental theoretical obstacle to acceptance of Davenport's analysis is readily discerned: One cannot reasonably assume that nature is a rational player, nor that the decision processes of "nature and culture" are cyclically reinforced (Luce and Raiffa 1957:279; cf. Buchler and McGoodwin 1968; Buchler, in preparation). If the behavior of nature is neither rational nor, by definition, strategic, then the theory of games is not the most appropriate formal language for the problem that Davenport poses. A re-analysis of Davenport's problem—using a language that does not assume that nature is a rational actor (Bayesian analysis)—is provided by Kozelka in this volume.

GAME THEORY, LINEAR PROGRAMMING, AND GRAPH THEORY: MATHEMATICAL RELATIVES

The two applications of the theory of games in anthropology that appeared prior to this volume are both zero-sum (Barth 1959; Davenport 1960). The anthropologist, psychologist, or sociologist, who is not familiar with the variety of departures from classical analysis in modern mathematics, may well be interested in the relationship of game theory to approaches such as linear programming and graph theory, with particular reference to the applications in this volume. We think that it is of some importance, particularly to the anthropologist, to grasp on an elementary level some of the relations among these approaches.

Every two-person, zero-sum game problem can be computed by converting it into a linear programming problem, and every linear programming problem can be converted into a skew-symmetric game (Dorfman, Samuelson, and Solow 1958:446–64; Luce and Raiffa 1957; Gale, Kuhn, and Tucker 1951).

Any linear programming problem is concerned with minimizing or maximizing something—this something or quantity—called an "objective function." There are always certain conditions that prevent the analyst from making this objective function infinitely small or large. The mathematical equations which express these conditions are called constraints (or restraints). For example, in the paper by Buchler and McKinlay (this volume) the constraints are

$$\sum_{i=1}^{m} x_{ij} \leq 1 \qquad j = 1, \cdots, n \tag{1}$$

which means that no individual can hold more than one cargo, and

$$\sum_{j=1}^{n} x_{ij} \leq 1 \qquad i = 1, \cdots, m \tag{2}$$

which means that no cargo is held by more than one individual. The problem of assigning individuals to cargos becomes one of maximizing the objective function

$$F(x) = \sum_{i=1}^{m} \sum_{j=1}^{n} q_{ij}, x_{ij} \tag{3}$$

Hoffmann's paper (this volume) is concerned with minimizing a cost function which expresses the amount of time needed to provide nutrients for one's family. The array of linear constraints expresses, in various forms, the fact that economic activities cannot occur in a negative number of hours.

There are also choice variables, "the numbers which are chosen so as to minimize (or maximize) the objective function and to satisfy all the restraints" (Dorfman et al. 1958:29). It is of importance to note that "the whole structure, social, economic, and technical, in which the deciding unit is embedded is involved in the practical identification of the choice variables, the processes, and the restraints, which specify the field of choice open to the unit of decision" (Dorfman et al. 1958:30).

In the zero-sum game discussed by Davenport (1960), the village, as a player, could regard the problem of finding an optimal mixed strategy as a standard linear programming problem (cf. Dorfman et al. 1958:446–47). Consequently, any ethnological or ethnographic problem in which the group effect of a behavioral distribution is a utility which approaches minimaximization can be computed into a related linear programming problem.

Consider the choice of strategy represented in the following payoff matrix (Dorfman et al. 1958:421).

Strategy of Player 1	Strategy of Player 2			
	1	2	3	$\cdots n$
1	a_{11}	a_{12}	a_{13}	a_{1n}
2	a_{21}	a_{22}	a_{23}	a_{2n}
3	a_{31}	a_{32}	a_{33}	a_{3n}
.				
.	$\cdots$	$\cdots$	$\cdots$	$\cdots$
.				
m	a_{m1}	a_{m2}	a_{m3}	a_{mn}

A mixed strategy for Player 1 (P1) will mean[7] a set of probabilities $X_1, X_2, \ldots, X_m$; each denoting one of the choices open to P1. When played against P2's strategies, any mixed strategy has a determinate expected value. The expected value of the mixture $X_1, X_2, \ldots, X_m$ against P2's strategy 1 is

$$E_1 = x_1 a_{11} + x_2 a_{21} + \cdots + x_m a_{m1} \qquad (1)$$

and the expected value of this mixture against P2's strategy j is

$$E_j = x_1a_{1j} + x_2a_{2j} + \cdots + x_ma_{mj} \qquad j = 1, 2, \cdots, n \qquad (2)$$

If we let V denote the smallest of the expected values against P2's n strategies so that

$$V = \min (E_1, E_2, \cdots E_n) \qquad (3)$$

P1's problem, then, is to choose $X_1, X_2, \ldots X_m$ so as to maximize V; "in other words, Player 1 seeks the mixed strategy for which Player 2's most advantageous strategy gives him (Player 1) as large an expected payoff as possible" (Dorfman et al. 1958:437).

If P1 has the choice variables $X_1, X_2, \ldots X_m, V$, and his objective is to make V as large as possible, then he is restricted or constrained by the above equations, which may be rewritten as

$$x_1a_{1j} + x_2a_{2j} + \cdots + x_ma_{mj} \geq V \qquad j = 1, 2, \cdots, n \qquad (4)$$

P1 is further restricted by the fact that $X_1, \ldots, X_m$ must be probabilities: They are non-negative. And if V must be as great as the maximin of the payoff matrix, and if the maximin is non-negative, so is V. The maximizer's problem is to choose numbers $X_1, X_2, \ldots X_m, V$, so as to maximize V subject to certain linear constraints: This is a linear programming problem.

Atkins and Curtis (this volume) provide an ethnographic application of Berge's (1962:58, 220) graph- and set-theoretic formulation of game rules. Berge also (1962:225) demonstrates that, as in the preceding discussion, a mixed strategy is simply a problem in linear programming.

In order to illustrate in a very partial and incomplete manner some of the relations between the theory of games and the theory of graphs, let us consider a classical linear programming problem formulated as a problem in graph theory. Consider a problem closely related, once again, to the optimal assignment model used by Buchler and McKinlay (this volume): maximum flow in a transport network.

Berge (1962:71) defines a transport network as a finite connected graph without loops. Associated with each arc u of such a graph is a number $c(u) \geq 0$; this is referred to as the capacity of the arc u. In such a graph (1) there is one and only one vertex X_0 (such that $\Gamma^{-1}x_0 = \phi$); this vertex is the source of the network; and (2) there is one and only one vertex z (such that $\Gamma z = \phi$); this vertex is the sink of the network. Berge (1962:72) poses this problem:

From a group of n towns, $\bar{x}_1, \bar{x}_2, \ldots \bar{x}_n$, buses run to a single destination $\bar{y}$; if ($\bar{x}_i, \bar{x}_j$) is a road connecting the two towns $\bar{x}_i$ and $\bar{x}_j$ let t_{ij} be the time required to go from $\bar{x}_i$ to $\bar{x}_j$ by this road, and let c_{ij} be the number of buses which can use it per unit of time (if there is no such road, $c_{ij} = 0$); let c_{ij} be the number of buses which can be stationed at $\bar{x}_i$, and let a_i be the number of buses originally at $\bar{x}_i$.

The problem is to schedule the buses so that as many as possible will arrive at $\bar{y}$ in a given time interval θ. The problem of maximum flow is therefore one of determining an *optimum schedule*, which is the same as finding numbers ξ_i^i so that the objective function

$$\sum_{i=0}^{n} \xi_{n+1}^i$$

is maximized. Rather than using the simplex method of linear programming, Berge (1966:73–74) uses algorithms for the problem of the maximum flow.

As Livingstone (this volume) suggests, graph theory is directly applicable to a variety of basic problem areas in social anthropology. For example, in his "Structural Study of Myth" Lévi-Strauss[8] (1963: 227–28) orders the Hopi myth of the origin of Shalako in terms of the following structure:

(Masauwu : x) $\simeq$ (Muyingwu : Masauwu) $\simeq$

(Shalako : Muyingwu) $\simeq$ (y : Masauwu)

which is identical with his ordering of the Keresan variants:

(Poshaiyanki : x) $\simeq$ (Lea : Poshaiyanki) $\simeq$

(Poshaiyanki : Tiamoni) $\simeq$ (y : Poshaiyanki)

He goes on to say:

This logical framework is particularly interesting, since anthropologists are already acquainted with it on two other levels—first, in regards to the problem of the pecking order among hens, and second, to what this writer has called *generalized exchange* in the field of kinship. By recognizing it also on the level of mythical thought, we may find ourselves in a better position to appraise its basic importance in anthropological studies and to give it a more inclusive theoretical interpretation. (Lévi-Strauss 1963:227–228).

The chapter on tournaments in Harary, Norman, and Cartwright's important study (1965:289–317) of directed graphs complements Lévi-Strauss' call for a more inclusive theoretical interpretation. If the logical framework that Lévi-Strauss derives on the level of mythical thought and generalized exchange is mathematically regarded as a tournament (cf. Buchler and Selby 1968b), then the theorems developed

by Harary, Norman, and Cartwright are directly relevant to a variety
of problems in anthropological studies. Consider a rather trivial
example. Although models of generalized exchange systems are invariably transitive, relations on the ground are often more produc-
tively defined by the notion of "degree of transitivity." Every
tournament is a nontrivial complete asymmetric diagraph, and every
strong tournament has at least three points (Harary et al. 1965:290).
Every model of a generalized exchange system also has three points,
is complete and asymmetric. Consequently, the degree of "transitive
triples" in any generalized exchange system may be calculated according to the following theorem (Harary et al. 1965:299).

Theorem. The number b of transitive triples in a tournament T with
score sequence $(S_1, S_2, \ldots Sp)$ is

$$b = \sum_{i=1}^{p} \frac{s_i(s_i - 1)}{2}$$

The relevance of the Harary, Norman, and Cartwright text on
directed graphs for a series of interrelated areas in social anthropology
can scarcely be overestimated. For example, the fact that asymmetric
exchange systems are empirical structures that satisfy the axioms of
digraph theory means essentially that the theorems developed for a
class of digraphs known as tournaments are valid assertions about
these structures. The theorems allow us to draw conclusions, which
are invariably nontrivial, about other properties. But there are, of
course, a rather large class of anthropological problems that cannot be
reasonably conceptualized within the framework of the mathematical
models that are applied in the papers that follow. Related approaches
such as flows in networks (Ford and Fulkerson 1962) and information
theory (cf. Buchler and Selby, in press) deserve more serious attention
than they have received thus far from anthropologists. Part of the
problem, we think, may be traced to an almost obsessive interest in
such low-level theoretical concepts as types of descent groups, resi-
dential groupings, and so on. As soon as anthropology is prepared to
turn in a more systematic manner to a consideration of decision processes, information processing, optimization problems, and transfor-
mations we will immediately be in a position to utilize the powerful
machinery of modern mathematics.

This collection of papers is not intended to be an introduction to
the variety of mathematical approaches of relevance to anthropological

problems. In connection with various other publications in this area (Kay, in press), it represents a tentative and somewhat primitive step in the development of a field that might, at some point in the future, be worthy of the label "mathematical anthropology."

NOTES

1. Shubik (1964) and Rapoport (1960) provide lucid elementary introductions to some of the basic concepts of the theory of games; Dresher (1961) also provides a useful introduction, and Blackwell and Girshick (1954) discuss the relevance for decision theory of certain aspects of game theory—the minimax theorem, the utility theorem, and so on. Braithwaite's (1963) essay merits more critical attention from anthropologists than it has received thus far, and Luce and Raiffa's introduction to *Games and Decisions* (1957) is of fundamental importance.

Aside from the early studies of Tylor (1879, 1896), John M. Roberts and his associates (Roberts, Arth, and Bush 1959; Roberts and Sutton-Smith 1962; Roberts, Sutton-Smith, and Kendon 1963; Roberts, Hoffmann, and Sutton-Smith, 1965; Sutton-Smith and Roberts 1967) have made the only important contribution to our understanding of games in culture. Games are viewed as expressive models and player involvement is explained by a conflict-enculturation process.

2. See Buchler and Selby (1968a) for a discussion of the utility of this distinction in "lineage theory."

3. Rapoport and Orwant (1962) provide a useful review of the literature on experimental games.

4. The so-called "ethnoscience" approach is concerned, to a certain extent, with these problems.

5. The classic study of Lévi-Strauss (1949) is the most important work on marriage systems in anthropology; he has also developed important modifications (1956 and 1963). Schneider (1965) provides an interesting review of the literature.

6. Cf. Barth (1959).

7. This section closely follows Dorfman, Samuelson, and Solow (1958:436—38); a more rigorous statement of the argument is developed in Sec. 16-1–16-6.

8. See Lévi-Strauss (1964, 1966); Leach (1961a).

REFERENCES

Barth, F. 1959. Segmentary Opposition and the Theory of Games: A Study of Pathan Organization. J. of the Royal Anthropological Inst. 89:5–21.

Berge, C. 1962. The Theory of Graphs and Its Applications. New York: Wiley.

Blackwell, D. and M. A. Girshick 1954. Theory of Games and Statistical Decisions. New York: Wiley.

Braithwaite, R. B. 1953. Theory of Games as a Tool for the Moral Philosopher. Cambridge: Cambridge U. Press.

Bridgman, P. W. 1927. The Logic of Modern Physics. New York: Appleton Century.

Buchler, I. R. in press. Rules, Laws, and Probability in Social Anthropology *in* Research Methods in Contemporary Social Anthropology. Paris: Mouton.

————. in preparation. Mathematical Anthropology. New York: Holt.

Buchler, I. R. and J. R. McGoodwin. 1968. Mathematical Programming and
  Economic Anthropology. Technical Report No. 1, Group Psychology
  Branch, Office of Naval Research.
Buchler, I. R. and H. A. Selby. 1968a. Kinship and Social Organization. New York:
  Macmillan.
————. 1968b. The Formal Study of Myth. U. of Texas (Multilithed).
————. in press. Animal, Vegetable, or Mineral? in Festschrift for Claude Lévi-
  Strauss, ed. J. Pouillon and P. Maranda. The Hague: Mouton.
Carnap, R. 1955. Foundation of Logic and Mathematics (International Encyclope-
  dia of Unified Science, Vol. 1, No. 3). Chicago.
Chisholm, R. N. 1946. Russell on the Foundations of Empirical Knowledge in The
  Philosophy of Bertrand Russell, ed. P. A. Schilpp. Evanston: Library of Living
  Philosophers.
Davenport, E. 1960. Jamaican Fishing: A Game Theory Analysis in Papers on
  Caribbean Anthropology (Yale U. Publications in Anthropology Nos. 57–64),
  pp. 3–11.
Dorfman, R., P. A. Samuelson, and R. M. Solow. 1958. Linear Programming and
  Economic Analysis. New York: McGraw-Hill.
Dresher, M. 1961. Games of Strategy: Theory and Applications. Englewood
  Cliffs: Prentice-Hall.
Ford, L. R., Jr., and D. R. Fulkerson. 1962. Flows in Networks. Princeton:
  Princeton U. Press.
Fortes, Meyer. 1962. Introduction in Marriage in Tribal Societies, ed. M. Fortes.
  Cambridge: Cambridge U. Press.
Gale, D., H. Kuhn, and A. W. Tucker. 1951. Linear Programming and the Theory of
  Games in Activity Analysis of Production and Allocation, ed. T.C. Koopmans.
  New York: Wiley.
Harary, F., R. Z. Norman, and D. Cartwright. 1965. Structural Models: An
  Introduction to the Theory of Directed Graphs. New York: Wiley.
Kay, P. ed. in press. Explorations in Mathematical Anthropology. Cambridge:
  M.I.T.
Leach, E. R. 1960. The Sinhalese of the Dry Zone of Northern Ceylon in Social
  Structure in Southeast Asia, ed. G. P. Murdock (Viking Fund Publication in
  Anthropology No. 29). Chicago: Quadrangle Books.
————. 1961a. Lévi-Strauss in the Garden of Eden: An Examination of Some
  Recent Developments in the Analysis of Myth. Transactions of the New York
  Academy of Sciences 23:386–96.
————. 1961b. Pul Eliya: A Village in Ceylon. Cambridge: Cambridge U. Press.
Lévi-Strauss, C. 1949. Les Structure Élémentaires de la Parenté. Paris:
  Presses Universitaires de France.
————. 1953. Social Structure in Anthropology Today. pp. 524–53, ed. A. L.
  Kroeber. Chicago: U. of Chicago Press.
————. 1956. Les Organization Dualistes Existent-Elles? Bijdragen tot de Taal-,
  Land-en Volkenkunde 112:99–128.
————. 1963. The Structural Study of Myth in Structural Anthropology. New York:
  Basic Books.
————. 1964. Le Cru et le Cuit. Paris: Plon.
————. 1966. Du Miel aux Cendres. Paris: Plon.
Luce, R. D. and H. Raiffa. 1957. Games and Decisions: Introduction and Critical
  Survey. New York: Wiley.
Moore, Omar Khayyam. 1957. Divination: A New Perspective, American Anthropologist 59:316–27.

Murdock, G. P. 1960. Cognatic Forms of Social Organization *in* Social Structure in Southeast Asia, ed. G. P. Murdock (Viking Fund Publications in Anthropology No. 29). Chicago: Quadrangle Books.

Nagel, E. 1961. The Structure of Science. New York: Harcourt, Brace & World.

Needham, R. 1962. Structure and Sentiment. Chicago: U. of Chicago Press.

Northrop, F. S. C. 1941. Whitehead's Philosophy of Science *in* The Philosophy of Alfred North Whitehead, ed. P. A. Schilpp. Evanston: Library of Living Philosophers.

———. 1947. The Logic of the Sciences and the Humanities. New York: Macmillan.

Nutini, H. G. 1968. On the Concepts of Epistemological Order and Coordinative Definition. Bijdragen tot de Taal-, Land- en Voldenkunde 124:1–21.

———. in press. Lévi-Strauss' Conception of Science *in* Festschrift for Claude Lévi-Strauss, ed. J. Pouillon and P. Maranda. The Hague: Mouton.

Rapoport, A. 1960. Fights, Games and Debates. Ann Arbor: U. of Michigan Press.

———. 1963. Mathematical Models of Social Interaction *in* Handbook of Mathematical Psychology, eds. R. D. Luce *et al.* New York: Wiley.

Rapoport, A. and A. M. Chammah. 1965. Prisoner's Dilemma: A Study in Conflict and Cooperation. Ann Arbor: U. of Michigan Press.

Rapoport, A. and C. J. Orwant. 1962. Experimental Games: A Review. Behavioral Science 7:1–37.

Reichenbach, H. 1938. Experience and Prediction. Chicago: U. of Chicago Press.

———. 1946. Bertrand Russell's Logic, *in* The Philosophy of Bertrand Russell, ed. P. A. Schilpp. Library of Living Philosophers, Evanston: Northwestern U. Press.

———. 1951. The Rise of Scientific Philosophy. Berkeley and Los Angeles: U. of California Press.

Roberts, J. M., M. J. Arth, and R. R. Bush. 1959. Games in Culture. American Anthropologist 61:597–605.

Roberts, J. M. and B. Sutton-Smith. 1962. Child Training and Game Involvement. Ethnology 1:166–85.

Roberts, J. M., B. Sutton-Smith, and A. Kendon. 1963. Strategy in Games and Folk Tales. J. of Social Psychology 61:185–99.

Roberts, J. M., H. Hoffmann, and B. Sutton-Smith. 1965. Pattern and Competence: A Consideration of Tick Tack Toe. *El Palacio* 72:17–30.

Russell, B. 1926. Our Knowledge of the External World. London: Allen & Unwin.

———. 1946. My Mental Development, *in* The Philosophy of Bertrand Russell, ed. P. A. Schilpp. Library of Living Philosophers, Evanston: Northwestern U. Press.

Sahlins, M. 1963. Remarks on Social Structure in Southeast Asia. J. of the Polynesian Society 72:39–50.

Schelling, T. C. 1963. The Strategy of Conflict. New York: Oxford U. Press.

Schneider, D. M. 1965. Some Muddles in the Models: Or How the System Really Works *in* The Relevance of Models for Social Anthropology (ASA Monograph No. 1). London: Tavistock Press.

Shubik, M. 1964. Game Theory and the Study of Social Behavior: An Introductory Exposition *in* Game Theory and Related Approaches to Social Behavior, ed. M. Shubick. New York: Wiley.

Sutton-Smith, B. and J. M. Roberts. 1967. Studies of an Elementary Game of Strategy. Genetic Psychology Monographs 75:3–42.

Tylor, E. B. 1879. On the Game of Patolli in Ancient Mexico and its Probable Asiatic Origin. J. of the Royal Anthropological Inst. 8:116–29.

———. 1896. On American Lot-Games as Evidence of Asiatic Intercourse Before the Time of Columbus. Internationales Archiv für Ethnographie 9:55–67.

PART **I**

APPLICATIONS

CHAPTER 1

Martin Southwold

A Games Model of
African Tribal Politics

THE argument of this paper is in large part
derived from *The Theory of Political Coalitions* (1962) by the political
scientist William H. Riker. Riker presents a model of political
behavior based on the theory of *n*-person games, which I have tried
to use in illuminating some conclusions about tribal politics in pre-
colonial Africa. My analysis diverges to some extent from Riker's,
and I have made some modifications to his terminology. I have noted
these changes, but I have not attempted to give a complete account of
Riker's own theory independently of my development of it.

Riker says that the subject studied by political scientists is decision-
making (Riker 1962:10), and that his theory will be confined to one
very important kind of decision-making process. I have termed this "the
contestive procedure."

[When a decision-making group is to make a decision, it is confronted with several alternatives or options among which a choice is
to be made. The members of the group sort themselves into subsets,
each supporting one option; in other terms, each option is supported
by a coalition of members. The decision is then taken by the contest,
a procedure by which the relative strength or weight of each coalition
is measured. If any coalition attains the weight necessary for decision,
as defined by rules, then that coalition is recognized as having won,
and the option it supported is ipso facto chosen as the decision of
the group, binding on all members.

For complete generality it is necessary to refer to the relative weight
or strength of coalitions. In many situations, the effective weight of
each individual member is standard—for example, as a result of a
"one man, one vote" rule—and here the weight of a coalition is a
direct function of the number of its members. In such cases, analysis

23

can be conducted with direct reference to the size of coalitions, and I shall generally do this, since such reference makes the argument easier to follow.

Familiar examples of decision-making groups operating by the contestive procedure are legislative or deliberative bodies such as the U. S. House of Representatives or the General Assembly of the United Nations. A matter for decision arises when some member or set of members proposes a motion, and another set opposes it; often other options are produced as other sets of members propose amendments. Coalitions are formed as the supporters of each option recruit further members in support of their stand. At some point the issue will be resolved by a contest, which in these cases takes the form of a vote. If the decision-rule employed is a plurality one, specifying that the largest coalition wins, a decision must result; under majority rules, there may be either a decision or a stalemate. It is easy to see that this model also fits national elections, where the decision-making group is the electorate, and the contest a poll or ballot. It is slightly less obvious that the model is also applicable to rebellions, revolutions, civil wars, international wars, cold wars, confrontations, and so forth.

It should be evident from this account that the crucial element in political activity is coalition-building, since the result of the contest is determined by the relative sizes of coalitions. And as Riker observes, there is a convenient model for coalition-building in the theory of n-person games. More specifically, the model Riker uses is the n-person zero-sum game with side-payments permitted and with rational players having perfect information.

So far, I have described the contestive procedure as if it were a device employed by groups in order to reach decisions, and as if the discrimination of winning and losing coalitions were merely a means to this end. But this description is false to the subjective perception and motivation of the actors: for them, winning is rather the object of the exercise, and the various options that are presented are little more than devices to seek support in coalition-building. In many contests indeed, and particularly in those with which this paper is concerned, the options are simply whether A shall win, or B, or C. Whether or not this is an unduly cynical view of political behavior, it is an axiom in Riker's model, since he defines rationality in terms of winning: "Politically rational man is the man who would rather win than lose, regardless of the particular stakes" (Riker 1962:22).

Up to this point, I have simply analyzed the way in which one decision is reached. I intend, however, to employ the dynamic model, which assumes a succession of decisions and contests as a continuous process within an enduring decision-making body. Here, strategic considerations are somewhat more complex, since behavior over any one decision is influenced by the result of previous contests and by the expectation of future contests. I shall assume that the winner of a contest remains in control of the group until it is defeated in some later contest. Hence at the time of any contest the participants can be distinguished as the party in power (the winner of the previous contest) and the party or parties out of power.

Some of the technical terms used in this analysis are defined below.

1. The *decision-rule* is the rule defining the minimum size (or more generally, weight) that a coalition must attain in order to win. The following varieties may be distinguished:

a) *Plurality rule:* The largest (or weightiest) single coalition wins.

b) *Simple majority rule:* To win, a coalition must include more than half the total members (or total weight) of the group. In another version, it is only half the total of members participating in the contest that must be exceeded, but since abstention or neutrality is irrational in a zero-sum game, I shall ignore this distinction.

c) *Two-thirds majority rule:* To win, a coalition must include or exceed two-thirds of the total members (or weights), or to state it otherwise, a winning coalition must be at least twice as large as its complement (the losing coalition or coalitions).

d) other specified majorities required.

Noted that while there is always a winner (and therefore a decision) under a plurality rule—and under a simple majority rule as well, except in the rare event of a dead heat—under more restrictive majority rules it often happens that no coalition wins. However, there is no decision-rule that allows more than one coalition to win the same contest.

I maintain (though Riker does not) that there is no such thing as a plurality rule, given rational players of a zero-sum game. For, if a coalition is about to win with a plurality which is not a majority but a minority, then the complement, the prospective losers, must amount to a majority and could win if they united into one coalition. Since it is contrary to the rationality condition to prefer a losing strategy to a winning one, they *must* join forces; therefore, no coalition can win with less than a majority, and all decision-rules (in the model) are majority rules.

2. A coalition large enough to win under the applicable decision rule is a *winning coalition;* if it is barely large enough and would cease to be winning on the subtraction of one member, it is a *minimum winning coalition.* Wherever, in a group, a winning coalition has formed, any other coalitions are *losing coalitions.* Where the decision rule allows a coalition that is not large enough to win yet large enough to prevent the formation of any other winning coalition, this will be termed a *blocking coalition.* Riker limits the term "coalition" to those subsets which have formed in the stage of coalition-building immediately prior to the contest: that is to say, when either a winning or blocking coalition has formed.

3. Subsets that have formed in the earlier stages of coalition-building Riker terms *proto-coalitions.* The terms "party" and "faction" may be used for proto-coalitions and coalitions.

4. A structure of so many disjunct subsets or factions Riker terms a *partition* (1962:37). Thus "the 4-set partition" means the structure where the group is divided into four factions.

5. *Decision-making* involves first a stage of coalition building, then the contest, and finally the stage in which the winning coalition harvests and shares the fruits of victory. In the ongoing process of political life these three stages constitute a unit for which it is convenient to have a term: I have chosen the word *colluctation,* partly because it sounds impressive, partly because its obsolescence makes it easy to assign a new and specialized meaning to the word. The history of a political group is a series of colluctations, each centering on a contest.

In the tribal politics of pre-colonial Africa, the major contests did not take the form of votes under an authoritative constitution, as in the examples we have considered, but rather of rebellions and civil wars within tribes or nations, and wars between them. Even outwardly peaceful decisions were taken on the basis of the threat of force. Such decision-making groups I shall term *combative.*

Winning in combative contests certainly requires coalition-building. The outcome of a battle depends partly on luck and partly on good generalship. Except insofar as the latter is a generally known and calculable factor, we shall treat these as randomizing factors, or "noise," and say that generally the weightiest coalition wins—or, as Voltaire put it, that "God is always on the side of the big battalions." Equating coalition weight with size certainly seems legitimate for tribal Africa, where "one man, one spear" parallels our familiar "one man, one vote."

Hence, we might suppose that in combative decision-making groups the decision-rule, or at least its functional analogue, requires a plurality—which is to say a simple majority. But here we must take into account a characteristic of such decision-making groups: The occurrence of contests is not exogenously determined, but depends on the initiative of some coalition—that is, a contest is provoked by a coalition which expects to win it. In order to have a reasonable expectation of winning despite the chances of battle, a coalition needs to have substantially more than a simple majority.

Where war is very destructive or expensive, even a minority can sometimes win a contest by threat of battle. My informants in Buganda told me that men relished war in the old days, and this seems to me very likely. Under such conditions, a party is likely to be coerced by the threat of battle only when defeat seems almost certain. Probably, then, something approaching a two-thirds majority would be required to win by threat of battle.

I have alluded above to an important distinction: that concerning the occasions for contests. In the United States, national elections occur at fixed intervals, and their timing cannot be altered by any coalition. In Great Britain, the party in power chooses the date of an election, though its freedom to postpone is limited by law; the out-party has an indirect, but sometimes significant, ability to affect the timing of a contest by its conduct as the Opposition. In a combative decision-making group, the position is almost the opposite: The occasion for contest is chosen by an out-party, and the in-party cannot easily do more than slightly hasten or retard developments. Obviously, the reason is that the out-party has much to gain if it can win a contest; but less obviously, the in-party is likely to be worse off even if it wins a contest that it has itself initiated. For, as the in-party, it is already a winner, and its only object in freely initiating another contest would be to win still more. But in doing this it would run a grave risk of eliminating the losers altogether, and, as we shall shortly see, in a zero-sum game the value of such a crushing victory is nil. Since the party which chooses the occasion for contest naturally seeks to choose an occasion most favorable to its own prospects, this would seem to imply an advantage to out-parties. Just as the British system is notoriously conservative, since it tends (other things being equal) to favor the retention of power by those who already have it, so the structure of combative decision-making bodies would seem to favor reversals of fortune. Riker seems to consider that this is true of decision-making bodies in general: "The relationship of forces maintains pressure towards a decision. And once a decision is taken, its dynamic is to encourage the repetition of the process" (Riker 1962: 147), and "to say that this model lacks equilibrium is to say that the social processes it purports to describe are also unstable—that the political society itself is in fact unstable" (1962:148).

As I remarked earlier, Riker's model is based on the theory of n-person zero-sum games with side-payments permitted and with rational players having perfect information; this necessarily implies that colluctations are significantly similar to such games. Since this similarity is by no means incontestable, Riker finds it necessary to produce some arguments in its support. He is evidently disturbed about the rationality condition, since he argues at some length that the imputation of rationality (in the technical sense) to at least a sufficient number of the actors in political affairs is plausible.

The assumption that colluctations can be treated as zero-sum is much more difficult to justify. There are eight separate passages in which Riker glances at the problem without ever tackling it thoroughly, a fact that suggests that the problem remained unresolved for him. The first difficulty that arises is that it is doubtful whether any real-life situation is simply zero-sum: There are always positive-sum elements also involved. Riker deals with this by remarking that in making the zero-sum assumption we are singling out the elements of conflict in social situations and ignoring the elements of common advantage (1962:29); whether this distorts reality too severely may be decided by seeing whether or not the theory is usefully predictive.

More serious difficulties arise from the definition: "The zero-sum condition is the requirement that the gains of the winners exactly equal in absolute amount the losses of the losers" (Riker 1962:28). As Riker remarks (1962:15), "this . . . assumes that gain and loss can be quantified and measured." It seems to me very difficult to quantify, except in a purely arbitrary manner, such political gains as glory, or the death of an opponent, or such losses as one's own death. Worse, the zero-sum condition seems necessarily to involve the interpersonal comparison of utilities, with all the pitfalls that this notoriously unhappy comparison entails.

We can partly avoid these difficulties if we recognize that the zero-sum game will be a suitable model of behavior if the actors perceive their situation as zero-sum—or very similar to zero-sum, irrespective of what the situation may be objectively. Since the zero-sum game is a model of direct and absolute conflict, wherever people suppose themselves to be in direct and absolute conflict, they will act like zero-sum players. This, however, would not be sufficient grounds for the principal deduction that Riker goes on to make; his analysis requires that the gains of the winners should be dependent on the losses of the losers, so that if there are no losers, there are no gains.

This requirement will be met, at least sufficiently, wherever, and to the extent that, political decisions involve the reallocation of such scarce resources as wealth, power, and prestige. (Indeed any allocation of power or prestige is inherently zero-sum, since for any man to hold power at least one other must possess no-power; the same is true, in a rather similar way, of prestige. Admittedly, these considerations are partly weakened by the fact that some people actually prefer no-power to power, and believe that the meek are blessed.) Further, as Riker remarks, victory itself is a prize, and "to speak of victors implies the existence, or previous existence, of the vanquished" (1962:31).

But Riker's most valuable observation is one which, oddly, he does not explicitly relate to the present point: "Policy changes," he says (1962:106), "are valuable only when they are controversial, only when they involve the satisfaction of one interest at the expense of another. In a sense, the value of policy is a function of a kind of scarcity, namely, a scarcity of beneficiaries." This implies, as I read it, that the very fact of the contestive procedure entails zero-sum factors, since people would not trouble to align themselves in support of an option unless they expected to gain from its adoption, and others would not oppose it unless they expected to lose by it. This factor is intensified by the fact that it is usually necessary to offer side-payments in order to build up a winning coalition: for the ability to give such side-payments implies that the profits of victory must be substantial, so substantial that they could hardly be realized except at the expense of others. Hence I conclude that, in general, contests will have sufficient zero-sum factors to justify the theory, even though an exact numerical demonstration of the zero-sum condition cannot be attained.

The games model also assumes that all players have perfect information—in a technical sense. That is, every player must know at every stage of coalition-building, what factions every other player has joined (Riker 1962:78). (Accurate information about the weight of every player is also required; but since in the cases we are considering it is assumed that each player has one and the same standard weight, we may take this for granted.) It must be acknowledged that real-life situations are rarely, if ever, characterized by systematically perfect information. However, the modification of rational strategy imposed by imperfection of information can be simply stated, and in the political model of Riker's theory, perfection of information is treated as a condition which is approached asymptotically. I will explain shortly what this involves; here I shall note briefly some of the factors which influence the degree to which information approaches perfection.

Information is likely to be more nearly perfect when:

1. *The membership of the decision-making body is small.* It is easier to discover what a few people are doing than what many are doing.

2. *The members are in close contact.* We might expect information to be best when political bargaining takes place in one room, and to decline in quality as the setting expands to an entire building, a city, a nation, a continent, a planet. Of course, the employment of such devices as the telephone tends to counter the effect of mere physical distance.

3. *The issues and the anticipated consequences of various decisions are clear-cut.* If you can clearly see where another man's self-interest lies, and can assume that he will see it too, then you can predict how he will behave and can dispense with reports of what he is actually doing.

4. *The actors are bound to act with quasi-permanent factions whose memberships are public.* An Englishman is fairly certain to side with England in a war, and a member of the Tory party is fairly certain to vote with the Tories.

5. *It is unlikely that actors will abstain or remain neutral.*

6. *The effective boundaries of the decision-making body are clearly known.* Until quite recently, for example, European powers were uncertain whether or not to reckon non-European powers as possible participants in their international quarrels.

From analysis of characteristic functions, and from other arguments, Riker (1962:32), deduces, persuasively if not rigorously, that:

In n-person, zero-sum games, where side-payments are permitted, where players are rational, and where they have perfect information, only minimum winning coalitions occur.

He then translates this proposition into "a descriptive statement, or sociological law, about the natural world," and calls it the size principle:

In social situations similar to n-person, zero-sum games with side-payments, participants create coalitions just as large as they believe will ensure winning and no larger.

This formulation (Riker 1962:32–33, also 47) allows for the fact that information in the real world is hardly ever perfect. Let us suppose, by way of illustrating the imperfection of information in the real world, that a leader knows the percentage of his coalition in the decision-making group within an error of plus or minus 5 percent. In the case of a simple majority rule, such a leader would be unwise to aim at an objectively minimum winning coalition of 50 percent, since the result would be that he would lose almost as often as he would win, and the advantage of winning with a coalition that is only somewhat larger than 50 percent would be far outweighed by the disadvantage of losing. He should therefore aim at a coalition of 55 percent of the decision-making group. In this event, he will find that his coalition approaches 60 percent as often as it does 50 percent. Uncertainty will be still greater when there is doubt about how many actors will participate in the contest; here, in order to judge whether a leader has a winning coalition, he needs also to estimate the size of other coalitions, which must be subject to a still larger margin of error. In the real world, then, it is necessary to aim at larger than minimum winning coalitions in order to insure against uncertainty.

This situation might seem to render the size-principle of little value to analysis of real-life politics. However, one can suggest "a static relationship of covariation in coalition formation": the worse the information, the more often will winning coalitions actually exceed the minimum; the better the information, the more often will they come close to the minimum (Riker 1962:88–89). Riker refers to this hypothesis as the information effect. If we accept it, the following holds true:

1. If we can estimate the quality of information (for example in terms of my six criteria above), then we can predict the approximate size of winning coalitions.

2. Conversely, if we have information about the actual sizes of winning coalitions, then we can make deductions about the quality of information, and hence about the conditions governing its quality.

It may be objected that we have produced only hypotheses—even though Riker offers some significant evidence in support of both the size principle and the information effect—but the production of interconnected hypotheses deduced from reasonable axioms, of which the social sciences stand in great need, is a major object of this analysis.

The size principle may be expected to operate at two distinct stages of a colluctation: first, as the above account implies, at the stage of coalition-building prior to the contest and, second, in the stage following the contest when the winners are dividing the spoils. The principle is likely to operate much more effectively at the second stage: (1) because people actually engaged in realizing payoffs are likely to be most aware of the shape of characteristic functions; (2) because information is very good at this stage (after a contest you tend to know who fought for you and who against you); and (3) because leaders have finer control over the membership of their coalitions at this stage, since by denying someone a share of the spoils they are, in effect, denying his membership. Hence we should expect that when a winning coalition happens for any reason to be much larger than the minimum, its leaders will set about shedding surplus members, either directly, by expelling them, or indirectly, by neglecting their interests. Riker produces evidence to show that this does happen in reality.

Some of the verbal arguments in favor of the derivation of the size principle from analysis of characteristic functions are:

1. If the prizes of victory are substantially constant, then the fewer the winners, the larger the share of each.

2. If, so to speak, the payment per head by losers is restricted, then the fewer the winners, the more the losers, and the greater the pool to be divided. Both these arguments are offered by Riker (1962:33), though he does not seem to make explicitly what I think is a still more decisive point, namely:

3. There will generally be some minimum payoff that any member will require if he is to support a coalition. Hence, the more members a winning coalition has, the larger the total sum of gains it needs to realize. But, by the zero-sum condition, these gains must be paid for by the losers. Since the total membership of the group is fixed, the more

winners there are, the fewer the losers, and the larger will be the share of the total payment that each loser must contribute. The joint effect is that, as the winning coalition increases in size, the payment per head required of the losers increases hyperbolically; and at some point one is likely to kill the goose that lays the golden eggs. Specifically, if losers are overtaxed, they will be tempted to secede, for by leaving the decision-making group they drop their status as losers and so annul their debts. But since, according to the zero-sum condition that the gains of the winners depend on the losses of the losers, by this maneuver the winning coalition is left in possession of the field and of nothing else: If the winning coalition drives out the losers, it drives out its own potential gains. Obviously, this outcome must be avoided. (This is why it is dangerous for the party in power in a combative decision-making group to initiate a further contest.)

Even apart from the information effect, there is a serious limitation on the size principle that Riker has not made fully explicit. He points out (1962:182–83) that under plurality and simple majority rules there is a very strong, almost inevitable, tendency for a system of two quasi-permanent factions to develop. Once a winning coalition has formed in one contest there are clear incentives for seeking to hold it together for action in future contests. Since it is always difficult to build up a winning coalition, one obviously has a poorer chance of achieving it if he throws everything into the melting pot and starts again from scratch, than if he preserves those elements that have already demonstrated a winning capacity. Moreover, Riker argues, the nature of important kinds of side-payments entails some expectation of or advantage in permanence. Then the best chance the losers have of averting continual and repeated losses must be to unite and attempt to attract dissidents from the in-party; and similar arguments indicate the value of quasi-permanence for this faction also.

The pressures toward bipolarity in contests can be shown also without reference to the tendency toward permanence. Contests are inherently bipolarizing, since it is their function to distinguish just two conditions—winning and losing; and the effect of this situation must be expected to work through into the organization. Consider the 3-set partition—similar arguments apply a fortiori to partitions with larger numbers of sets. Assuming a simple majority decision-rule, information must be extraordinarily imperfect for the members of more than two proto-coalitions to suppose that they amount to winning coalitions. At least one set must know it is certain to lose if it remains independent, and ought therefore to seek to coalesce with another. If both the others are (erroneously) confident of winning alone, such an offer may be rejected; but after the contest, only one coalition can regard itself as winning. The losers then ought to coalesce, both in order to hold down as far as possible the exaction of payment and still more with a view to victory in a future contest.

If, then, there are strong reasons why all contests are likely to be between two coalitions only, the size-principle predicts not only that contests will be won by minimal winning coalitions, but also that they will be lost by maximal losing coalitions. In other words, every winner will have a rival almost equal to it in size. But there are reasons why any winning coalition will tend to erode with the passage of time. It is virtually impossible to distribute the spoils so as to satisfy every member; also, in the kind of group we are considering, the winning coalition forms the government, and it is impossible for governments not to make enemies and to lose prestige on account of failures due to human frailty or the intractability of the environment (cf. Gluckman 1955, ch. 2), though it is possible to attract new supporters to replace losses. It would seem to follow that the more nearly equal in size the winning and losing coalitions are, the shorter will be the interval after victory before the gap is closed—and indeed opened in the opposite direction. Once former losers have overtopped former winners, they have every incentive to provoke a contest by which their advantage will be registered in victory. The occurrence of minimal winning coalitions, then, should result in frequent contests, each normally reversing the previous decision. But this result shows that it is not rational to aim at minimal winning coalitions, since the relatively small advantage these offer over larger coalitions is offset by the fact that the fruits of victory will not be enjoyed for long.

This does not demolish Riker's theory; rather, it makes the model more complicated. While Riker spoke of a relationship of covariation between (1) the size of winning coalitions and (2) the quality of information, I would add two more covariant factors: (3) the frequency of contests and (4) the facility of maintenance of quasi-permanent factions. These four factors are interrelated in complex ways. We might note, for example, that both frequent contests and the existence of quasi-permanent factions will each tend to improve the quality of information.

This complication of the model might seem to reduce its utility, since it is now more difficult—but not impossible, if sufficient data are collected—to make specific predictions capable of testing. On the other hand, there is the advantage of wider theoretical articulation. Two other factors are relevant to the model: (5) how much of a variety of side-payments is available? I would suggest that the more complex a society and the richer a culture, the easier it is to produce a variety of side-payments to satisfy winners and thereby to retard the expected erosion of a winning coalition. Similarly, (6) the more favorable the natural environment, and the more adequate the technology for handling it; and again, the more dominant a group (such as a nation) is in its political environment, then the easier it is for a government to prosper and to avoid the failures and humiliations which cause it to forfeit support.

It is particularly important, however, to underline the relevance of yet another factor: (7) the facility of secession for losers. In the political groups in which we participate, it would normally be so nearly impossible for a losing coalition to break away from the group that we make no allowance for secession in our calculations. But in tribal Africa the situation was quite different (as it is to a large extent in modern Africa). These were small scale societies, in which most of a person's interactions and dependencies were confined to a small area; primary political loyalties were usually confined to quite small local groups, of which, moreover, the membership was largely permanent. When these became gathered into larger states, the factions that engaged in national contests tended to be based on such local groups, which were economically autarkic, and only weakly bound together because of poor communications. It was, therefore, exceedingly easy for losing coalitions to secede. Often this involved no more than a mere declaration of independence, but even when it entailed moving away (as among the seceders from the Zulu nation), the move was facilitated by the relative lack of fixed capital investment.

The relative ease of secession under these conditions would be expected to have three effects relevant to the model:

1. Stakes should be kept low—one would not, for example, expect losers of rebellions to be executed or savagely persecuted.

2. Actually a special case of (1)—winning coalitions ought to be minimal, since, as we have seen, the burden on each loser increases as a hyperbolic function as the size of the winning coalition increases. This, in isolation, should lead us to expect frequent contests.

3. Tendencies towards quasi-permanent dual factionalism should be counteracted. Since a losing coalition can so easily become a separate nation, its organization ought to be broken up before the break occurs. I do not call to mind direct evidence that this policy was followed in tribal Africa; but the marked reluctance of modern African governments to tolerate the existence of a strong organized opposition party may be called in evidence. If this analysis is correct, the result should be to retard the frequency of contests—that is, it counteracts the effect of (2) above.

I became interested in Riker's theory when I was studying the political history (mainly pre-colonial) of the kingdom of Buganda. It is clear that the principal concern of politicians must have been the incumbency of the throne, since virtually all other offices (and most sources of wealth) were held at the pleasure of the *Kabaka* or king, who could freely dismiss incumbents, and appoint those in his favor to almost any office he pleased. Contests for the throne took two forms: the choice of a successor when a king died, and rebellion. Rather to my surprise I found that these were not very distinct, and had to be treated as variants of one process (for evidence, see Southwold 1966). Only a prince could hold the throne; but as eligible princes were defined as the sons or sons' sons of a former king, and polygyny was practiced, there was usually a wide choice. No prince was allowed to hold any chiefship or political office apart from the throne itself. Princes thus had no forces of their own with which to fight for the throne. A prince was attached to his mother's (patrilineal) clan, which was a commoner clan. He could count on the support of the chiefs, and to some extent, of the ordinary men of this clan, but as there were two dozen or more clans, and at least half of these were politically prominent, this support was not sufficient to insure the throne. Victory, as there is evidence to show, required a coalition of chiefs of various clans, who of course expected to be rewarded if their prince became king. The main difference between rebellions and the peaceful choice of successor is that rebellions were usually (but not always) decided by battle, whereas, in the latter case, the threat of battle was usually decisive.

Riker's theory should also be relevant to the analysis of the internal politics of other African kingdoms and chiefdoms, and of their international relations. Indeed it seems likely that the theory should fit such situations even better than it does those to which Riker himself applied it (international relations and the politics of the United States).

For several reasons, the zero-sum nature of politics in tribal Africa should have been very marked:

1. Politicians were (I suppose) single-mindedly concerned with gaining offices; and as offices are inevitably scarce, competition for them must be intense.
2. The major source of wealth was people: and since control over people is essentially a political matter, political contests tended to determine the greater part of the allocation of wealth. Other institutions for the allocation of wealth, such as the market, were commonly ill-developed: a politician who was a failure could not compensate by diverting his energies to commerce.
3. Wealth was absolutely scarce, and its marginal utility probably was greater than with us.
4. Whereas with us, genuine issues of policy are occasionally involved in contests, and on these issues consideration of the welfare of the group sometimes dilutes factional self-interest, this situation was probably rarer in Africa, since technological and cultural poverty restricted the range of options.

There was probably a higher level of rationality than there is among politicians in our society. In the first place, there were usually no unrealistic ethical religions to distract men from hard-headed maximization. Secondly, these societies were relatively simple, so it was easier to obtain a sound grasp of issues and strategies. Thirdly, the societies were relatively static, so that the fruits of experience accumulated over generations and remained relevant. From proverbs and traditions, and still more from his father and grandfather, if they had been active politicians, an intelligent man could gather an impressive treasury of political wisdom.

In general, one would expect information to have been exceedingly imperfect, owing to the notoriously inadequate communications, but this was not necessarily so. In many of these kingdoms—and Buganda is an excellent example—important chiefs were required to spend much of their time in the capital, thus narrowing the relevant arena of politics and improving the quality of information.

Deduction from the model would lead us to expect contests, the cultural form of which was rebellion and civil war, or threat thereof, concerned principally with control of the national government, represented by the throne. There would have been a series of such contests. This is what Gluckman has described a number of times (notably Gluckman 1963a and 1965) as "repetitive rebellion" or the "rebellious cycle."

It might seem of course that it is no great achievement for a theory to predict a simple well-known fact. This idea would be a mistake. It is most important to have an axiomatic theory from which to deduce verified statements about the real world. The model indicates that contests (and notably civil wars) are a mechanism by which de jure power (authority) is reallocated and that they work by registering the strength or de facto power of factions or sections of the nation. The contestive procedure—in this case civil wars—can be seen as a mechanism by which the distribution of de jure power is continually readjusted to fit the distribution of de facto power (which normally shifts over time). This is a vital, even necessary, function.

Gluckman (1963a:38) writes that, among the Zulu, the average interval between rebellions was about fifteen years, and suggests that this pattern may have been a more general one (1965:279). This is broadly consistent with the evidence I have examined for Buganda (see Gluckman 1965:149), though the interval between civil wars among the Bemba seems considerably longer (Gluckman 1963a:14). Even fifteen years seems long when considered against the model, and the time span tends to suggest that information was so imperfect that winning coalitions were normally much larger than the minimum, and/or that quasi-permanent dual factionalism did not develop. One African kingdom—the Shilluk (Evans-Pritchard 1948)—was divided into two enduring political factions, largely as a result of its linear configuration along the bank of the Nile. I do not know of direct evidence of the presence or absence of quasi-permanent dual factionalism in other kingdoms, and suspect that it would be difficult to obtain, since such factions, if they existed, might well not be specifically named. In Buganda, for instance, it has been suggested that there was enduring rivalry between clans of a southeastern or lacustrine bloc, and

those of a northwestern or *Nyoro* bloc. This theory could be tested only
if one could determine which clans belong to which bloc, and the
requisite information has not been published in English.

Gluckman's theory that civil war might tend to preserve national
unity was strongly attacked by Schapera (1956, especially pp. 175–76),
who observed that, in southern Africa, rebellions, so far from maintaining national unity, typically led to the secession of the losers. He
shows that in this area the typical political history was one of repeated
segmentation and resegmentation of political units. This is predictable
once losers secede; the zero-sum condition implies that the winners
no longer have any gain, and can achieve it only by means of another
contest producing losers from among themselves. But the causes of the
secession of the first losers must be expected to lead also to secession
of the new losers, until eventually every group must fragment into
minimal, and subpolitical units. That political history nevertheless
continued is due to the fact that these processes of fission were
balanced by processes of fusion deriving from a more inclusive zero-
sum game. That is, the segments deriving from intra-tribal politics
became players, forming coalitions which were new kingdoms or
chiefdoms, in a supra-tribal game.

If we ask what might have determined the occurrence of what may
be termed Gluckman processes or Schapera processes, the model
suggests that the facility of secession should be a crucial variable.
In two cases at least—Barotseland (Gluckman 1965:146) and Buganda
(ibid.:151)—it is plain that secession occurred rarely, if at all, because
political factions were based not on local segments but on dispersed
groups. Although in Barotseland this was probably in large measure
a result of the unusual economic differentiation of that nation, no
such factor applies in Buganda. There, the clans (if we may trust
Baganda traditions) were originally localized, and only gradually became dispersed as the sovereignty of the king encouraged internal
migration. Clearly the enduring unity of Buganda cannot wholly be
explained by a factor which presupposes it. We see then that the kings
were able to unite and hold together the kingdom originally because
its environment was dominated by the more powerful adjacent kingdom of Bunyoro. We may guess from this what has in fact been frequently remarked—that the stability of national units was related to
their international status. In an international game each unit had
approximately the status of a blocking coalition, since, if it amounted

only to a losing coalition, it would have been conquered or reduced
to ruin. Now if a blocking coalition divides into two, it is almost certain that one, more likely both, will amount to losing coalitions, and
will eventually be destroyed unless potential conquerors are under-
going similar dissolution. At first sight this would seem disadvanta-
geous to losing coalitions in the national game, since they would lose
the possibility of secession. But losing coalitions might still threaten
to secede, as long as their rivals were equally certain to be ruined in
the international game. Suicidal threats can be effective in politics,
particularly when made by those who have less to lose against those
who have more to lose (cf. Schelling 1963). Losing coalitions, then,
might well have a firm bargaining position, which they could use to
insure that stakes are kept low. (Such a situation might well facilitate
quasi-permanent dual factionalism.)

The connection between the height of the stakes and the perils of
secession points to the relevance of Gluckman's analysis of the development of the law of treason. Such a law is not found in relatively
primitive states, nor is participation in rebellion treated as a crime.
It would raise the stakes considerably, and this would be dangerous
wherever the threat of secession has substance. Gluckman (1963b:
1538) has related the development of the law of treason in England
in the latter half of the fourteenth century to "the kind of 'organic
interdependence' in which the division into territorial segments would
be countered by the integrating effects of a more differentiated economic system"; this is entirely concordant with the present analysis.
Additionally, it would appear that a similar development might result
from other factors than economic differentiation.

The pre-colonial period of Buganda history falls into three quite
sharply distinguished periods (see Southwold 1966). In the second of
these, successful rebellions were relatively frequent; in the third there
were no successful rebellions, and unsuccessful rebels and even potential rivals were butchered ruthlessly. During the second period, more
particularly its earlier part, Buganda was under strong military pressure from her rival Bunyoro, whereas the third period opened with an
impressive Baganda victory at the expense, indirectly, of Bunyoro,
which at that time had entered on a period of relative weakness. In the
second period Buganda was a blocking coalition which dared not risk
secession by raising the stakes, and consequently had to tolerate rebellion; whereas in the third period she was almost a winning coalition

from which internal losers would be sorry to depart, and in which internal winners did not greatly fear secession, so that stakes could be pushed up. On the other hand, it must be said that by her victory at the beginning of the third period Buganda had probably expanded beyond her limits of sure control, and there would seem to have been real danger that the newly acquired province would break away; in terms of my analysis this condition should have led to a lowering of the stakes.

It might be said that my analysis has dealt only with well-known facts, and insofar as it has gone beyond them has merely raised questions without answering them. This may well be true, but no theory in the human sciences can be expected to keep abreast of the richness and complexity of the facts in which we are properly interested. What a theoretical model, even such a simple one as this, can do is to articulate conclusions, to clarify issues, and to point to questions for further investigation. As Luce and Raiffa (1958:115) observe, "a case can be made for studying simplified models which are suggested by and related to the problem of interest. The hope is that, by analogy, their analysis will shed light—however dim and unreliable—on the strategic and communication aspects of the real problem."

Rather than end on an unduly modest note, I should like to outline a computation which might be made on the basis of this theory. I cannot in fact make the computation with the data from Buganda, as these are too sparse; but as sufficient data for a similar computation might well be obtainable for literate societies, and certainly would be for contemporary contests, I am not offering mere speculation.

I have noted above that contests in Buganda were decided between coalitions of chiefs. The armies that these chiefs mustered may have been drawn partly from the men of various clans of the districts they governed, and partly from their normally dispersed clansmen. To know which of these was the principal source of recruitment would radically affect our notion of the kind of political system this was. Now Kaggwa (1953), the Buganda historian, gives names, or rather titles, of some of the leading chiefs on both sides in a number of contests. Let us suppose he had given us complete lists for a dozen or more contests. The title of a chief tells us what district he ruled over; and Kaggwa normally tells us the clan affiliations of the chiefs. We should need to know the populations of districts and clans, preferably more accurately than by projecting back from their current levels.

Let x be the proportion of the men of his clan that a chief led into

battle, and y the proportion of the men of his district. We shall
assume that individual differences canceled out, and that it is mean-
ingful to work with average values of these proportions. Then the
contribution of a chief to a coalition can be expressed as the adult
male population of his clan times x, plus the adult male population
of his district times y. By addition we obtain the total strength of
each of the two coalitions. We assume that the winning coalition was
the larger, and that this difference is best expressed by a multiplicative constant, z. The result of each contest can then be expressed by
an equation in the form:

$$ax + by = z\,(cx + dy)$$

where a, b, c, and d are all known numbers. With three such equations we could solve for our unknowns x, y, and z; and from each set
of three contests we could derive further independent solutions. So
long as these solutions were reasonably consistent, we could have
some confidence that we had found out what we wanted to know.
Suppose for example that x ranged between 1/4 and 1/10, while y
ranged between 1/40 and 1/70; we should conclude that clan allegiance
mattered much more than local allegiance. From such figures we
might also conclude that only a small proportion of men took an
active part in contests, that these were more like coups d'état than
civil wars; and this might be taken as supporting what I have supposed on other grounds: that this was a system of politics of the
palace and the capital. Our solutions for z would show us to what
extent contests were won by minimum winning coalitions; and since
our raw data would tell us about the frequency of contests and the
extent of quasi-permanent dual factionalism, we should be in a position to make a deduction about the quality of information available
to the actors. If their information appeared to be good, this fact would
tend to support our conclusion that there was a system of politics
of the capital; if it appeared to be poor, we should look for further
explanation; we might then discover, for example, that treachery and
double-dealing were highly developed arts.

No doubt, in practice, if one attempted such a computation one
would encounter numerous and possibly fatal snags and pitfalls.
Nevertheless, this illustration, idealized as it is, is sufficient to demonstrate that games theory may suggest computations by which we
could derive facts from data that do not transparently indicate them.
Such promise is a major reason for seeking further to develop the

applications of games theory. The naïveté of my model and the inadequacy of my data make the above illustration an exercise in science fiction—but it is the kind of science fiction that may be only a short pace ahead of science fact.

REFERENCES

Evans-Pritchard, E. E. 1948. The Divine Kingship of the Shilluk of the Anglo-Egyptian Sudan. Cambridge, England.
Gluckman, M. 1955. Custom and Conflict in Africa. Oxford, England.
———. 1963a. Order and Rebellion in Tribal Africa. London.
———. 1963b. Civil War and Theories of Power in Barotseland: African and Medieval Analogies, Yale Law J. 72:1515–46.
———. 1965. Politics, Law and Ritual in Tribal Society. Oxford, England.
Kaggwa, A. 1953. Basekabaka be Buganda. Kampala and London.
Luce, R. D., and H. Raiffa. 1958. Games and Decisions. New York.
Riker, W. H. 1962. The Theory of Political Coalitions. New Haven and London.
Schapera, I. 1956. Government and Politics in Tribal Societies. London.
Schelling, T. C. 1963. The Strategy of Conflict. Cambridge, Mass.
Southwold, M. 1966. Succession to the Throne in Buganda in Succession to High Office, ed. J. R. Goody (Cambridge Papers in Social Anthropology No. 4). Cambridge, England.

CHAPTER **2**

T. C. Schelling

Some Thoughts on the Relevance of Game Theory to the Analysis of Ethical Systems

When a man falls sick, his closest companions kill him, because, as they put it, their meat would be spoilt if he were allowed to waste away with disease. The invalid, in these circumstances, protests that there is nothing the matter with him—but to no purpose. His friends refuse to accept his protestations, and kill and eat him just the same.

. . . .

When the King of Scythia falls sick, he sends for three of the most reputable sooth-sayers, who . . . declare that such and such a person (whose name they mention) has sworn falsely by the king's hearth . . . . The man, of course, denies the charge, and makes a great fuss, whereupon the king sends for more soothsayers—six this time instead of three—who also bring their skill to bear. Should they convict the accused of perjury, he is beheaded without more ado, and his property is divided by lot amongst the first three soothsayers; if, however, the new six acquit him, more are brought in, and, if need be, still more again, and if, in the final result, the majority declare for the man's innocence, the law is that the three original ones should be executed.

. . . .

Abducting young women, in their opinion, is not, indeed, a lawful act; but it is stupid after the event to make a fuss about it. The only sensible thing is to take no notice; for it is obvious that no young woman allows herself to be abducted if she does not wish to be.

Herodotus, The Histories
(Aubrey de Selincourt, trans. Penquin Books, 1954, pp. 14, 217, 263.)

This chapter first appeared in article form in the *Journal of Conflict Resolution,* *XII*–1 (March 1968), pp. 34–44.

Among the Greeks, "Certain offenses which human law could not punish nor men detect were placed under divine sanction," according to H. D. F. Kitto. "Perjury is an offense which it may be impossible to prove; therefore it is one which is peculiarly abhorrent to the gods" (Kitto 1951:197).

Here we see a shrewd coupling of economics with deterrence: if divine intervention is scarce, economize it by exploiting the comparative advantage of the gods. If their intelligence system is better than that of the jurists, give them jurisdiction over the crimes that are hardest to detect. Let them, too, become witness to the truth: "May the gods strike me with a thunderbolt if I speak not the truth!" And be careful not to go partners with anyone who does not share your gods.

Kitto does not tell us—there was no need to in the passage quoted —why lying was bad and needed to be deterred or punished. Jean Piaget has asked some children about lying, and finds that though the littler ones associate lying with naughty words, which are bad merely because adults say they are bad, and slightly older ones find them bad because of what they lead to—the way clumsiness is bad because it leads to broken dishes—"The older children of 10–12 generally invoke reasons which amount to this: that truthfulness is necessary to reciprocity and mutual agreement . . . Deceiving others destroys mutual trust." On the purpose of punishment, "The little ones introduce an expiatory element into all their answers, whereas the older children are content to justify punishments by their preventive value" (Piaget 1962:170, 227).

In short, kids find truth socially useful; lying is bad because the children have freely and contractually adopted a rule against it; the purpose of punishment is both to deter and to reaffirm the rule. And the offense, if one lies, is to be judged by the intent behind it and not merely by the consequences it leads to.

If good is intended, perhaps the lie is no offense. In that case the children would represent what Joseph Fletcher calls "situation ethics." In this "new morality," Fletcher considers a lie told in the interest of good to be not merely an evil mitigated by good intentions but a positive obligation. "If a small neighborhood merchant tells a lie to divert some 'protection' racketeers from their victims, no matter how compassionately the lie is told, he has chosen to do *evil*" according to certain "intrinsicalist" ethics, though it may be forgiven as a "lesser evil"; Fletcher scorns this attitude. "It is not excusably evil, it is positively good. This is the fundamental point of the extrinsic position" (Fletcher 1966:11, 64–65).

But he points out that "moral choices need intelligence as much as they need concern, sound information as well as good disposition. To be 'good' we have to get rid of innocence." (1966:114–15). One must evaluate the consequences of an act, including the consequences on the behavior of others, and be personally responsible for evaluating those consequences. "It is possible that by learning how to assign numerical values to the factors at stake in problems of conscience, Love's calculations can gain accuracy in an ethical *ars major*. The temper of situation ethics is in keeping with the attempt to quantify qualities" (1966:118). Fletcher even credits game theory with helping already.

It may be too early to credit game theory with much help, but surely there is promise. Fletcher is saying, in the language of game theory, that situation ethics does not content itself with prescribing individual strategies but requires us to scan the entire matrix, evaluating each outcome, and attending to the preferences of others. It is not the deed, but its intended (expected) consequences by which morality is to be judged. Ignorance is no excuse; one must think through the consequences and evaluate them; if necessary, predicting the behavior of others.

Lying, after all, is suggestive of game theory. It involves at least two people, a liar and somebody who is lied to; it transmits information, the credibility and veracity of which are important; it influences some choice another is to make that the liar anticipates; the choice to lie or not to lie is part of the liar's choice of strategy; the possibility of a lie presumably occurs to the second party, and may be judged against some a priori expectations; and the payoff configurations are rich in possibilities, since a lie can be told for the good of the victim, the truth can be told to pave the way for a later lie, and a lie can even be told with the intention that it not be believed. Just in identifying the kinds of lies there can be, as a starting point for legal analysis or moral judgement, it may be helpful to draw the matrix of choices for both parties, their payoffs, what they believe about each others payoffs, what penalties or constraints they perceive on their own or each other's choices, and any available techniques for inducing credulity or establishing credibility. Somewhat as the logician needs a "truth table" for the analysis of sentences, the moral philosopher may need a payoff matrix for evaluating the consequences of truth and falsehood, credulity and skepticism, in the interaction of two parties to a lie.

A problem that Fletcher did not consider—perhaps because it is not strictly ethics—but that Piaget's children probably had to consider, is credibility where there is no penalty on lying. Every man, I suppose, appeals to situation ethics when his wife asks how he likes her new dress; the man who thinks he has cancer may prefer an "intrinsicalist" doctor who will tell him no lies for his own good. The Bible on which the witness places his hand, though it may discriminate against the virtuous who prefer not to offend God, is not merely a way of preventing lies but equally of permitting people to swear to the truth.

We are accustomed, in discussions of social contract or about the Prisoner's Dilemma, to think about those constraints that a man may wisely incur upon condition that others do likewise. As Mancur Olson's recent book points out, we may rationally vote to close the loophole that we take advantage of in our tax system, or vote mandatory dues in an organization that individually we would not support with voluntary contributions (Olson 1965). Piaget's children are clearly willing to restrict themselves with rules, in a reciprocal way, just as individual farmers are willing to decrease output on condition that all the other farmers do likewise. Each gains more by his fellows' abiding by the rules than he loses by having to abide by them himself. Equally interesting, though, are the cases in which some constraint is sought unilaterally. Nothing is more frustrating than being unable to convince skeptics of the truth.

How many ethical rules are of this sort—that it can be an unconditional advantage to be known to abide by the ethic? Is lying unique? No, breaking promises is much the same. If a corporation could not be sued, it could neither borrow money nor sign long-term contracts. Prisoners post bail voluntarily, and hostages are sometimes freely offered. Other constraints can help; in ancient times, eunuchs often got the best jobs because they could credibly deny themselves certain intentions.

What we are talking about—and it is here that something like game theory may possibly make a contribution to the study of ethical systems—are the social consequences of constraints on behavior. Constraints can come from religion, ethics, law, instinct, sentiment, taste, the nervous system and other parts of the human body, custom, the physical environment, and the contrivances we equip ourselves with. Game theory would be most pertinent to those constraints that affect peoples' expectations about each other, for working out the social-behavioral implications of different ethical systems. And in that process the difference between ethics and law, or ethics and instinct, may be less important than the similarities.

Konrad Lorenz's recent book, *On Aggression*, is full of what he calls "behavioral analogies to morality"—instinctive inhibitions that serve, among animals, some of the purposes that morality, law, custom, or discipline serve in human society (Lorenz 1966). The wolf obeys a "law" against attacking the very young. That he obeys it involuntarily makes it a different kind of law, but not wholly different, from human commandments against murder, incest, or the eating of flesh, which may have behind them both some instinctive and some acquired abhorrence as well as the authority of God and government. Lorenz points out "the correlation between the effectiveness of the weapons of an animal species and the inhibition preventing their use against other members of the species," thereby reminding us that ethics, custom, and law tend to be pertinent to the proclivities and capabilities of human beings. We have no need for commandments against the things that we will not or cannot do (1966:57–84; see also 109–38).

Instinctive reactions can even substitute somewhat for the Greek gods. Some of us cannot lie without blushing or otherwise giving ourselves away; and the polygraph shows that some kind of dissonance is generated by the mere consciousness of lying. It is not too fantastic to imagine that, were it useful in the preservation of the species, the dissonance might have been great enough to paralyze the vocal cords and make lying impossible, or to cause acute headaches that would punish lying instantly, or to make something like the blushing phenomenon so undisguisable as to give the alarm. Were that so, we might need no moral prohibition on lying, or legal sanctions on perjury, any more than we need a commandment that says a man may not eat his own flesh.

INDIVIDUAL ETHICS AND SOCIAL RESULTS

Game theorists have long been intrigued by the paradox that individual rationality may lead to social inefficiency. The exploration of Prisoner's Dilemma has such a long history now that most of us have forgotten where the accompanying story originated. Rapoport has been emphasizing for years that in some of these situations conscience may be socially superior to individual rationality (or, as I believe he would say it, conscience ought to be part of the definition of "rationality"), and that virtue, if reciprocated, can bring its own reward (1960:chs. 1–13; 1964:chs. 6–15). I have often tried to point out that conscience is but one of the forms that a useful constraint can take, and that military discipline and damage suits are oriented towards much the same problem (1965:367–79); now Lorenz comes along and shows us in how many ways natural selection has changed the payoff structure (or put some otherwise dominant strategies beyond reach) for the wolves that might eat their own young, or each other's.

Lorenz also shows us that certain kinds of aggressiveness can serve a purpose—for example in distributing economically over a food-producing territory the members of a species that, if they were nicer to each other, might be too concentrated for efficient utilization of the food supply. This suggests that a too-selfless ethic can be as socially harmful as a too-selfish ethic. And indeed we can turn the Prisoner's Dilemma matrix inside out and get the Altruist's Dilemma, as in the following matrix, where one player chooses row and receives the lower-left payoff in the cell chosen and the other chooses column and receives the upper-right payoff:

	0	−2
0		1
	1	−1
−2		−1

If each player tries to maximize his partner's payoff, he has a dominant strategy that leaves them both worse off than if they had minded

their own business and played selfishly for personal score. While it
is indeed socially inefficient for people to make small personal gains
at large expense to others, it can be equally inefficient socially to
make large personal sacrifices for the slight benefit of others. (People
may, of course, like the sense of virtue that goes with the latter kind
of social inefficiency, but then other people probably get a competitive satisfaction out of the former.)

An interesting question is suggested by the occasional incompati-
bility of individual rationality with social efficiency: Is there a corresponding paradox in the field of ethics? That is, might the most
attractive ethic that we could recommend to an individual, when we
generalize it to all individuals, prove to have undesirable results? The
role of selflessness mentioned above may suggest this effect, as might
the role of personal responsibility in Fletcher's "Situation Ethics."
The obligation to break a promise, to tell a lie, even to kill, in the
interest of some greater good (or greater love) has to be examined in
the context of its universal acceptance and of its universal anticipa-
tion. There can be no promises (except the promise to be good) if
everyone is obliged to disregard his commitments when abandonment
serves his (moral) purpose. Euthanasia, wisely administered, may
eliminate the needless suffering of the hopelessly ill, but it may also
cause acute anxiety among those who think themselves potential
victims. The demands on personal wisdom and judgment required by
an ethic that judges all deeds by their full consequences might make
life less predictable, less secure, possibly more guilt-ridden. And we
may still need some arbitarary laws, or some arbitrary focal points
for the convergence of a common definition, in order to tell where
abortion becomes infanticide, or neglect becomes murder.

We should also keep in mind that "ethical man" may be as much
of an abstraction as "economic man" or "rational man," and that to
judge an ethic by what life would be like in a world peopled exclusively by ethical men may be but a theoretical exercise. There are at
least three reasons for this:

1. People are not only motivated unconsciously in their actions, but
can be unconsciously motivated in their conscious reasoning about
values. In deciding whether to sterilize the socially incompetent, to
single out an invalid for mercy-killing, to forbid a teenage marriage,
or to suppress a defective birth, it may be humanly impossible to
recognize unconscious motives and to evaluate or disqualify them.

2. Like Lorenz's animals, we have instincts. Some serve essential purposes, and some are ill-adapted to our social and physical environment, which has changed more rapidly than our biological evolution can accommodate. Ethics can neither oppose the instincts nor take them for granted; it can no more oppose them than it can oblige a good man not to blush when he tells a white lie, or not to love his own children more than he loves other people's children. Ethics cannot take instincts for granted because much of the business of ethics is to moderate our natural tastes and instincts and to harmonize the tastes and instincts of people who impinge on each other. Perhaps, for example, Fletcher disparages too much (1966:79 and 115, for example) both romantic love and sentimental love; these may be the instinctual bases of the less personal "good will" that he wants us to find compelling or attractive. And perhaps certain kinds of selfishness are the empathetic basis for the sense of pity or concern that might motivate men toward some good ethic.

3. "Ethical man" may need knowledge and intelligence of as unrealistic a kind as the corresponding knowledge and intelligence required to be a rational consumer or business executive. The best of us may not be very good at quantifying our own selfish payoffs, particularly when dealing with uncertainty; we may be no better at it when trying to quantify the components of justice. Fletcher is right in insisting that we have to try, but where we think we are terribly fallible, we might be wise to settle for an arbitrary rule instead. Surely there are some among us to whom situation ethics should not be recommended. Just as a child may not pass junior lifesaving until he is twelve, vote or marry until he reaches majority, or be sent to an adult prison until he has reached 16 or 18, we might have to decide at what age a child is to solo as his own ethicist.

One implication of this last point (3) is that in thinking about an ideal ethic, we must recognize that not everybody can follow it, and that only some of the people will participate in a satisfactory ethic. This means that an ethic based on a kind of social contract must take as a premise that not everybody will sign the contract.

It is fascinating to consider how different most ethical thinking would have had to be if biological evolution had not given mankind a pretty clear definition. The rights and duties of animals get little attention in ethics—mules go to war without representation in parliament. Children are treated as equal because eventually they will grow up; racial differences are minute compared with the differences between man and other species; male and female are physically, intellectually, and temperamentally alike enough to permit some doctrine of equality to underlie most of the religions and ethics that gain our respect. Most of us no longer believe that God wants us to destroy the infidel. But just suppose that species differentiation were not discrete but continuous, so that in several directions man blended into other creatures the way, say, adults blend into children. The whole idea of a universalist ethic might have to be dropped. For the fundamentalist, this is a meaningless speculation; but for those to whom man is a product of biological evolution, and who consider this particular world not the only world that might have emerged—and especially to those who could combine ethics with science fiction—it may be fruitful to consider what biological premises underlie a particular ethic.

Had something like the Rh factor been so widespread that few males and females could be fertile together, sexual promiscuity would have been a biological necessity. And if conservation of some nutrients required that human flesh not be wasted on scavengers but consumed within the species, some presently abhorrent dietary practices would be our way of life. And if we depended on biological symbiosis with some intelligent creatures who for biological reasons could not share our ethics, ethical coexistence would bring real problems.

THE POTENTIAL CONTRIBUTION OF GAME THEORY

In considering what game theory can do for the study of ethics, three kinds of contributions are worth distinguishing. First, there are the ethical problems to which game theory has already addressed itself, and about which there are some theorems or results ready at hand. These tend to be ideas that game theorists have found interesting, not problems posed by people whose main interest is ethics.

Second, there is the possible use of game theory or some of its conceptual apparatus by those whose main concern is ethics. This would correspond to the use that could be made of game theory by legal scholars, sociologists, strategists, and others.

Third, there are some ethical issues that tend to be raised by the methodology of game theory itself. One can ask whether game theory supposes a certain ethic, or has some stated or unstated ethical assumptions or implications of its own. One can even inquire what kinds of ethical issues can be formulated within the domain of game theory and what kinds cannot. If game theory has limitations in this regard, those very limitations may correspond to some ethical distinctions and game theory may provide an operational way of identifying them.

Among the ethical problems with which game theory has knowingly coped, one relates to collective decision processes, and is involved in both welfare economics and the theory of democracy. I have in mind the work on whether a "community preference" can exist, explorations of the majority-voting paradox, etc. (see Luce and Raiffa 1957:ch. 14; see also Buchanan and Tullock 1962). Another is typified by Braithwaite's little essay, *The Theory of Games as a Tool for the Moral Philosopher*, John Nash's work on bargaining games, and Howard Raiffa's on arbitration.

The second kind of contribution is typified in the ethics of "deterrence." The problem arises in capital punishment, in international threats of military retaliation, and more generally in the whole realm of rewards and punishments. There has been some discussion of the ethics of a doctrine of massive retaliation (or any retaliation against noncombatants) as a means of deterring or influencing an adversary. Beginning with the notion that actual reprisal against noncombatants is abhorrent, one can still inquire whether and when the threat of such reprisals is an abhorrent method of coercion. The difficulty arises because threats, when they succeed, need not be carried out, and the conditional readiness to engage in something abhorrent need not be correlated with the likelihood that the event will actually be initiated by the threatener. The matrix might look like this:

	Behave	Misbehave
Punish	0 2	1 0
Not Punish	2 3	3 1

Since punishment presumably follows misbehavior and an effective threat must precede it, this matrix does not represent the game in its normal form. But we can suppose that column is chosen first, row second, and prior to column's choice there is an option to make a *conditional* choice of row to which one is firmly (or in some degree) committed. If the potential punisher has obliged himself to choosing row one in the event of misbehavior and row two in the event of good behavior; if all significant interests are represented in the payoffs; if the payoffs are known and both participants rational; we can conclude that column does not misbehave and row does not inflict the punishment, though he was ready and even obliged to as a result of his prior threat. The ethical question—rather *an* ethical question—is whether, if the punishment is bad, the threat of punishment is bad.

I do not intend to find an answer to the question for anybody else, or to propose that one can determine an answer with the help of game theory. My point is merely that this somewhat game theoretical formulation may help to pose some of the right questions. And one of the first questions is, does it matter? There may be an important distinction between those ethical systems or beliefs to which the occurence or likelihood of actual punishment is relevant, and those to which it is irrelevant. Some of the character of an ethic may be discovered by distinguishing a threat from its fulfillment and inquiring whether, if fulfillment is abhorrent, the threat itself necessarily is.

Other questions arise—whether row's effort to influence column is itself moral, and whether that in turn depends on the morality of column's prospective behavior. Are people to be punished for *doing* evil or for *being* sinful, should the sinful be allowed to escape punishment by merely abstaining from bad deeds? Is the mere making of threats, with a willingness to fulfill, corrupting even if it is ethical? A law providing capital punishment may be so successful that nobody is ever executed; whether or not it is immoral, it may be bad, but it is important to identify whether it is bad because it is immoral or bad in spite of being moral.

Fletcher's hypothesis about lying to the racketeer, so that he cannot find his victim, poses this kind of question. Instead of disguising the whereabouts of his victim, one might threaten the racketeer with retaliation if he carried out his unsavory enterprise. If the lie is a positive good because of the consequences, then perhaps the threat is a positive good because of its consequences—as long as we have considered all of the consequences. The key point seems to be that the consequences depend on what one expects others to do, even on how one expects others to react to one's own behavior. Therefore the full matrix of payoffs and the prediction of the final outcome—matters that look rather like game theory—are the determinants of morality. Declining to rescue a cripple who, in desperation, will at last exercise his muscles and not only save himself but cure himself, as occurs at the climax of so many dramatic stories, is presumably judged moral or immoral according to one's intentions and one's confidence in the predicted outcome.

Evidently we are dealing with something a little like the problem of liability at law. The strategy of rules against confession, wiretapping and self-incrimination, or in favor of secret ballots, have to be evaluated through the incentives they provide and the behavior of victims or adversaries under different rules. The very notion of criminal negligence depends on some reasonable assessment of how people can be expected to behave.

ETHICAL PREDILECTIONS OF GAME THEORY

Does game theory make, customarily or necessarily, any particular ethical assumptions?

One can surely put ethical premises into a particular game. The usual treatment of Prisoner's Dilemma, to pick a familiar example, ignores any obligation to confess or to speak truth, or to cooperate with the law, or any loyalty to one's partner, and has the man try only to minimize any legal penalties he might incur. But if we eliminate the little story we eliminate those ethical premises. We can reinterpret the matrix with another little story and have quite a different set of ethical premises.

The question is whether there is anything about game theory as a method of analysis that gives it a bias toward a certain ethic or makes it incapable of accommodating certain ethics. Does the abstractness of game theory itself—the elimination of the story and reduction of the situation to some kind of payoff matrix—have ethical implications? Do the explicit and implicit characteristics of rational decision restrict the ethical scope of game theory?

The most common argument to the effect that game theory makes ethical assumptions, or is ethically biased, is that the decision maker is assumed to be interested—even advised to be interested—exclusively in his own payoffs. He is to take others' payoffs into account in his decision, but only to anticipate their choices, not to attach his own value to the others' payoffs. Rationality seems to be identified with selfishness.

This argument, I think, is not usually valid. There is no need to suppose that the payoffs reflect selfish interests. They reflect the player's valuation of the outcomes, and he can surely value them selfishly, altruistically, or in terms of justice or welfare. If a game reflects a lawyer's choice of strategy, the lawyer can be playing to maximize his fee, to get an innocent man acquitted, or to establish a precedent that he believes to be in the interest of justice. He may do this out of fun, pride, or ethical obligation, or to get revenge on an opposing attorney. It is so convenient to talk about money stakes in a game, or personal "utility," that in the examples we choose and in the informal language of analysis we often make the man sound selfish although we need not.

The motion that it is selfish not to take an adversary's or a partner's payoffs into account may apply in an economic "game" played with a deserving partner;* it will not apply in a "game" with the Ku Klux Klan in which the life of an innocent person is at stake. To take the other party's preferences into account may merely be to compromise one's ethical principles. If the payoffs in each cell represent one's complete evaluation of the outcome represented by that cell—his evaluation of all the consequences, including the welfare of the other player (or the ethical obligation to punish him)—then all the ethics are accounted for, and further compromise would be a denial of one's principles.

LIMITATIONS OF GAME THEORY

If game theory is not committed to a particular ethic, the question can still be raised whether its method is limited to a class of ethics. Game theory at present is limited in the ethics it can handle, but identifying its limitations can help to clarify some ethical principles, and perhaps to enlarge game theory in order to explore some of the ethics that it is not presently equipped to handle.

*As I tried to emphasize in "Strategic Analysis and Social problems," cited earlier, the social utility of a "cooperative" ethic depends on what the cooperators are up to. Robert L. Cunningham (1957) points out that a conscience-inspired willingness to cooperate in a two-person or n-person Prisoner's Dilemma situation permits competitive sellers to collude in restraint of trade, to the disadvantage of consumers and, if generalized to all possible oligopolists and oligopsonists, possibly to everyone's disadvantage.

Consider someone who is to make a choice in which he has no
personal selfish stake (or in which he is prepared to renounce any
personal stake) and who says that his only interest is in making the ·
right choice—a good or moral or ethical choice. He has no interest in
the consequences, he just wants to do the right thing. Game theory
will not be much help; it deals with the relation of consequences to
choices. We may, with game theory, clarify the character of this ethic
and distinguish it from other ethics. Fletcher's "situation ethics" is
oriented toward consequences; familiarity with game theory may help
to distinguish situation ethics from other ethics.

Consider another case. Suppose we represent the personal payoffs or interests of the participants by numbers in the cells of the
matrix and superimpose as an ethic that each is exclusively interested
in the other's payoff. This interest can be love or hate, a desire to
maximize or to minimize the other's payoff; the point is that each is
exclusively concerned with the outcome to the other. Can game
theory handle this?

It depends a little on what we mean by "handle." Surely we can
let each participant attempt to maximize or to minimize the payoff
numbers for the other player that we have already put in the cells. In
fact, we can just as well interchange the payoffs, with a change of
sign if necessary, and deal with it as an ordinary game. But this begs
the interesting question: If your sole aim in life is to make me happy,
and mine to make you happy, am I to maximize your payoff or to
help you to maximize mine? Alternatively, if we are ethically obliged
to punish each other, do I successfully punish you by reducing your
payoff or by frustrating your true ambition, which is to keep me
from maximizing mine? What we have is something a little like a
game involving the scoring system that is to go into the game we are
to play.

Here is where the work like Valavanis' becomes especially pertinent
to game theory (1958:156–69). Whenever one participant is affected by
the welfare of the other, there is a problem to be solved within each
cell of the matrix before our game is well defined. Depending on the
interaction of utilities (or payoffs or welfares), there may or may not
be a unique pair of definable payoffs to put into the game. If the
more interactive payoffs are discrete rather than continuous, there
may be no solution. That is to say, the functions relating the welfare

of one to that of the other may be incompatible, or may result only from some dynamic psychological process.

Look at one more implication of focusing on "choice and consequences." It eliminates motives from the strategy of decision. One player is interested in the other player's motives only in so far as they determine his choice; and his motivation is assumed to be reflected in the payoffs. Suppose, though, that I am interested not in what choice my partner will make but in why he made it (or will make it): I want to reward him for a good choice and punish him for a bad one. If the matrix takes a particular shape, this may be easy; there may be a single strategy for me that yields him a high payoff (reward) if he chooses in my favor and a low one (penalty) if he does not. But a matrix can take many shapes, and may confront me with a dilemma. Let me give an illustration.

Take the familiar Prisoner's Dilemma matrix and suppose that both of us want to reward cooperators and to punish noncooperators; and suppose that that interest outweighs the personal payoffs reflected in the original numbers. The situation now has two equilibria. If we both cooperate, each is rewarded for his cooperation, each has rewarded the other for cooperating, indeed each has (properly) rewarded the other for rewarding oneself for being good . . . and we are happy all down the line. But if we both decline to cooperate, and "lose" in the usual sense, each of us is, superficially, content. I have punished a noncooperator by my refusal to cooperate. So has he. But this equilibrium lacks the infinite convergence of the other. I have punished him for refusal to cooperate; should I have rewarded him for punishing me for my refusal to cooperate? But then he failed to reward me for punishing a noncooperator, and perhaps deserves to be punished . . . . But then if neither of us is really much concerned with the original numerical payoffs, nobody has either cooperated or failed to cooperate!

I am not solving the problem, I am introducing it. The way game theory has managed to cope with the infinitely reflexive problems of "he thinks I think he thinks I think . . ." may provide a model for handling some interactions of motives. I find it difficult even to define this problem without some of the conceptual apparatus of game theory.

For what I have called "motives," we can sometimes substitute "ethics," systems of rules or systems of valuation. We can then study the interaction of two different ethics between two different people, or the interaction of two players who share the same ethic. My hunch is that it is worth while to explore a wide variety of ethics, not merely those that appeal to us. For learning about the subject, studying the perverse may be as fruitful as studying the virtuous. Studying the interaction of the perverse with the virtuous may be expecially interesting. If I like to fight, does the Golden Rule say I may pick a scrap with someone? What does it then say to him? If I desire virtue, must I demand that evil obtain in my universe, so that I can combat it? If I believe in sacrifice or mendicancy, can I believe in it for everyone else or must I demand that there be a class of *gentiles*? What are the "multiplier effects" of rules that demand of each more than he receives? Economists discovered that thrift might lower the GNP, just as the slaying of predators causes deer to starve.

One of the ways to study ethical systems is to look at their interactive implications. Another is to investigate what changes in payoffs and constraints make particular rules unnecessary or essential. A third is to examine the social implications of coexistence between two radically different ethics. There are others, of course; and for some of them the conceptual apparatus of game theory can evidently help.

REFERENCES

Buchanan, J. M. and G. Tullock. 1962. The Calculus of Consent. Ann Arbor: U. of Michigan Press.

Cunningham, R. L. 1967. Ethics and Game Theory: The Prisoner's Dilemma, *in* Papers on Non-Market Decision Making, II. Richmond: U. of Virginia, Thomas Jefferson Center for Political Economy.

Fletcher, Joseph. 1966. Situation Ethics: The New Morality. Philadelphia: Westminster Press.

Kitto, H. D. F. 1951. The Greeks. Baltimore: Penguin Books.

Lorenz, Konrad. 1966. On Aggression. New York: Harcourt, Brace & World.

Luce, R. D. and H. Raiffa. 1957. Games and Decisions. New York: Wiley

Olson, Mancur, Jr. 1965. The Logic of Collective Action. Cambridge, Mass: Harvard U. Press.

Piaget, Jean. 1962. The Moral Judgement of the Child. New York: Collier Books.

Rapoport, Anatol. 1960. Fights, Games and Debates. Ann Arbor: U. of Michigan Press.

———. 1964. Strategy and Conscience. New York: Harper & Row.

Schelling, T. C. 1965. Strategic Analysis and Social Problems. Social Problems 12 (Spring 1965) 367–79.

Valavanis, Stefan. 1958. The Resolution of Conflict when Utilities Interact. Journal of Conflict Resolution 2 (June 1958) 156–69.

CHAPTER 3
Walter Goldschmidt

Game Theory, Cultural Values, and the Brideprice in Africa

In this paper, I shall examine what seems to me to be the greatest single problem in the cross-cultural use of game theory and suggest that if we turn game theory upside down, perhaps its logic—if not its mathematics—may be helpful in surmounting one of the major obstacles to our understanding of culture.

Game theory may be described as a kind of algebraic formula that determines within the rules of the game, by means of probability statistics, the strategy most likely to maximize the attainment of the goals of each of n participants. Being algebraic, i.e., using no culturally defined units for either persons, rules, strategies or goals, the system is, or presumes to be, fundamentally culture-free. The matter requires some examination.

We have isolated four elements which deserve our attention: persons, rules, strategies, and goals. The first of these may readily be determined as creating no cross-cultural problem. Game theory recognizes person in both the individual and the corporate sense, so that whatever the social units of significance are—individual, clan, age-set, etc.—they may be entered into the equation.

The rules of the game also vary from situation to situation. What anthropologists make the primary subject of their normal discourse, game theory calls the rules of the game. That is, the ethnographies are essentially the explicit depiction of the total rules for the game. For instance, I have recently written a detailed ethnography of Sebei law. Quite clearly, my task was to set forth the legal rules delineating the permissible in Sebei action—though I hasten to add that a great deal happens which is not permissible (in spite of the pronouncement by my interpreter, who said: "It is *very* impossible for a man to sleep with his neighbor's wife."). This does not render suspect the universal anthropological assumption that every culture does have rules of the game; indeed, rules could not be broken if they did not exist. Game theory does nothing to help us discover what the rules of any particular society and situation are, but it does not in any way violate the principle of a culture-free formula. It is worth considering, however, that our strategy always involves the possibility of breach of rules.

By and large, anthropologists have given precious little attention to the matter of strategy in non-Western culture; they tend not to think in these terms. This was particularly true of those earlier anthropologists who wrote under the dominance of what I call "the theory of culture as custom." Early anthropology, and particularly Boasian anthropology, was dominated by this orientation. Alfred Kroeber was in the audience several years ago when I presented a paper (Goldschmidt 1951) on social interaction among the Yurok and Hupa of northwestern California. He graciously accepted the general character of my analysis, but on one point he was entirely negative. He could not see how, even in these highly litigious societies, a person could advance his social position. After Europeans came in and money could be earned, yes; but not under native conditions. The dead hand of custom lay heavily on Kroeber's anthropological thought. The social anthropologists have done better. The notion of diverse strategies within the rules of the game seems to be entirely in accord with universal ethnographic fact and does not run afoul of social theory.

When, however, we turn to the matter of goals, the situation is not so clearly culture-free. Von Neumann and Morgenstern in the classic work that brought game theory into the limelight, after some hemming and hawing, say quite simply that "we shall assume that the aim of all participants in the economic system, consumers as well as entrepreneurs, is money, or equivalently a single monetary commodity" (1964:8). Later (1964:605), they face the issue implicit in cross-cultural extrapolation:

> Our general method to ascribe a value to every possible coalition of players is essentially dependent upon the numerical nature of utility and we are at present not able to remedy this.
> We have pointed out before that the hypothesis of the numerical nature of utility is not as special as it is generally believed to be. . . . Besides, we can avoid all conceptual difficulties by referring our considerations to a strictly monetary economy. Nevertheless it would be more satisfactory if we could free our theory of these

limitations—and it must be conceded that the possibility of doing this has not been established thus far.

Things had not progressed along these lines when J. D. Williams (1954:21) wrote:

One of the conceptual problems, a critical point in Game Theory so far as its application to real-life conflict situations is concerned, is reached when we try to fill in the boxes with the values of the payoff. While there will be individual cases in which the requirements are less severe, in general we have to assume that the payoff can, in principle, be measured numerically; that we in fact know how to measure it; and that we do measure it, with sufficient accuracy. Further, the units of measurement must be the same in all boxes, and the units must be simple, dimensionally; that is to say, we are not prepared to cope with dollars in one box, grams of uranium in another, and lives in another—unless of course we happen to know exchange ratios between these items and can eliminate the heterogeneity of units of measurement. If the payoff in each box contains several numbers representing disparate items—which may be some dollars, some uranium, and some lives, say—we are still in trouble, except in special cases. This difficulty can arise in ordinary games; consider, for example, a two-person game between master players; the stakes may be sums of money and prestige. *Unless we are prepared to adopt an exchange ratio between prestige and money, our analysis is likely to be in trouble.* (Italics added.)

Shubik, in his introduction to a book of selections on game theory (1960:14), recognizes the diversity of values, but does nothing to resolve the problem:

Although our wants and aspirations may change over the years, for many purposes it is desirable to assume that over some range of time an individual has a valuation scheme whereby he can evaluate the worth of any prospect with which he is confronted. The outcome of a game presents a prospect which must be evaluated. It results in an allocation of resources or a distribution of posts and honors or, in war, in a distribution of casualties and destruction.

Now this is the essence of the anthropological problem, for it is the anthropologists who have pointed out that cultures vary in terms of their values, and that values are the central and focal element in culture. Certainly if we are to apply game theory cross-culturally we must assume that payoff = values—that is, we must face the issue that von Neumann and Morgenstern raised.

I have at hand only three anthropological studies using game theory. One (Moore 1957) is the utterly charming demonstration of the efficacy of scapulimancy in hunting; it is useful because it randomizes behavior and thus deprives the prey of the ability to anticipate human actions. This work does not raise the question of values, because it relates to man's basic need to eat—nobody can reasonably doubt that the payoff to a primitive hunting expedition is to bring home a bag of kill (although this need not be the payoff for hunting expeditions in our society).

The second study is Davenport's impressive demonstration (Davenport 1960) that the fishing behavior of Jamaican villagers fits the mathematical model supplied by game theory. But here, again, we are not transported to cross-cultural values, for these Jamaicans are engaged in a commercial enterprise; the payoff is in pounds sterling.

It is worthwhile here, however, to note an aspect of Davenport's paper that he fails adequately to appreciate. Being a good anthropologist, Davenport notes other cultural values associated with what he calls in-out fishing, i.e., the prestige of the better boats and participation in a major sport. What is particularly interesting is that his data fit expectations without regard to the prestige value of the behavior. If game theory analysis really fits a pure economic model and does not have to concern itself with other motives such as prestige, the implications are that prestige goals are not themselves relevant to the generality of behavior within a cultural situation, though they may still relate to the question as to what type of person (i.e., by personality type or other situational factor) will choose one strategy over another. Needless to say, we are not about to abandon the sociological importance of prestige on the basis of $n = 1$, but the point is worth noting.

The third work is Barth's Pathan analysis (Barth 1959). Here again, there is in these political alignments a set of values in the form of direct power relationships with their attendant economic payoff. It must be stated that in this instance, Barth's analysis does give us some remarkable insights into Pathan social organization.

Let me summarize this first section by saying that while game theory presumes to be an algebraic formulation which can apply cross-culturally, the fact is that one term in the equation is explicitly culture bound, and that existing cross-cultural studies because of their specifically economic character, have not demonstrated that these theoretical approaches can be used generally in other cultural contexts.

I want to illustrate the problem inherent in cultural values by an explicit contrast. The Hupa-Yurok of northwestern California and the Indians of the northwest coast culture area share certain aspects of culture which are significant to our purposes. In both, things of great social importance are possessed, and they lend prestige to the individual associated with them. It is quite clear from ethnographic accounts that normal members of these tribes spend much of their time in the manipulation of these goods which are heavily laden with symbolic import. A naïve person might well say the Californians and the northwest coasters share a prestige-wealth complex and therefore that they share the same values. This is not the case.

In northwestern California, each individual endeavors to accumulate as much property as he can. Such property, which has ceremonial use, gives its owner prestige and power in the community. All men (except slaves and bastards) are free to seek such goods, and every proper father brings up his son with the ideals of behavior that will enable him to choose such strategies as will further his aim. This is a litigious society, and the arena for these games, therefore, is the law court—or more accurately legal confrontation—rather than the marketplace. I am quite sure that minimax considerations operate in this arena. Where there are so many regulations, a person must have many opportunities to engage in legal disputes, and he is not held in personal contempt for furthering every personal advantage. His success, however, depends ultimately on his potential fighting strength, and this in turn is dependent upon several factors, one of which is the validity and propriety of his claim. Thus each individual must calculate whether, in a given instance, he will be supported in his demand, or in the event that his associates withdraw support from what they consider to be an outrageous demand, what level of the demand he can sustain without loss of backing. I have, as a matter of fact, used this very situation in a dramatic form to demonstrate the strategies of everyday life in the context of a set of ethical game rules (Goldschmidt 1952).

I described Hupa actions at some length in a very different idiom but to the same general purpose long ago (Goldschmidt and Driver 1940). Hupa society is characterized by a highly individualistic pattern of behavior; each individual is free to seek status as best he can. This status is measured in the ceremonial goods he accumulates, which (aside from inheritance) are usually acquired through litigation. Each individual normally has certain alliances with his family and other groups, but he is not bound by these ties and makes both firm and fleeting alliances as he sees fit. In making these alliances, he uses his wealth to establish obligations. It is important to appreciate that the litigations that play so important a role in the accumulation of wealth take place without benefit of a government or formal courts. They rest upon the force that each party to the controversy brings to bear on the ultimate sanction. It follows that the patterns of alliances are crucial for the furtherance of a man's claim. But it should also be noted that as the alliances are not binding, an individual may find that his support diminishes if he makes an untenable claim. He is therefore compelled to manage his affairs so that his claims are justifiable. We do not have the data on aboriginal Hupa life that would enable us to determine just how these calculations work out in fact, but the rules and strategies are clear. The major ceremonials, incidentally, are expressions of alignments, for although rich men lead the ceremonials at will, others lend them additional ceremonial paraphernalia (the wealth that confers status) according to their current sentiments. These ceremonials, therefore, are public expressions of the sociograms of social alignments, reaffirmed or changed each biennium that the major ceremonial—the White Deerskin Dance—is performed.

Though the idiom is different, the Hupa pattern of behavior is closely parallel to our own in that wealth confers status; wealth is privately and individually held; and a person's wealth is enhanced by operations of a system of exchanges that depend upon the astuteness of the individual.

It has been popular to examine the potlatch in similar terms. Efforts have been made to calculate interest and to assume that the Kwakiutl operate in terms similar to the Yurok and the Hupa (and, of course, ourselves) in trying to maximize personal goods. But if we look at the manifest behavior of these peoples, we find that this is not what they are doing. Owning the blankets, coppers, etc., is useful only as a means to other ends—namely, the accumulation of prestige and the acquisition of titles and their enhancement in a society of presumptively set statuses. Efforts made from time to time to see the potlatch in terms of investment and interest have not been convincing because these attempts miss the essential goal of the potlatch game. A recent analysis by Drucker and Heizer (1967) leaves no doubt that this is the case.

Game theorists would say: "Well and good! The Californians want things, the northwest coast people want prestige, and all we need to do is to quantify the goals. Then we can determine strategies if we are armed with the rules of the game." But once we know the goals, knowledge of the strategies is already in hand and game theory has nothing to offer us.

The fact is, we demonstrate the goals by an examination of the strategies. We are able to say that the Tlingit values are not the same as those of the Hupa and Yurok, because we have seen that their strategies are different. The Tlingit or Kwakiutl Indians giving a pot-latch destroy goods—an act quite literally repugnant to the Californians. A Tlingit can choose between two strategies with respect to a notable copper he possesses: He may give it to his chief rival or he may destroy it by breaking it and throwing it into the sea. If he does the former, he may reasonably expect in the future two coppers in return; if he does the latter, he will have no coppers. Manifestly, if our astute Tlingit game player is in the copper-owning business, his strategy is to give a copper to his rival; if he is in the prestige-getting business, he shows his disdain by the second strategy. Since a truly important man will choose the strategy of destruction, we learn that the true payoff is not the possession of these goods, but the demonstration of prestigious status.

This leads to what I think may be the real contribution to game theory in cross-cultural studies, that is, to provide us with a way of looking at human behavior so as to find what the goals are. Put another way, game theory assumes the goals to be known and with this knowledge calculates the strategies. Social anthropologists examine the strategies and through these calculate the great unknown in exotic cultures: the values. Though this process can be stated in algebraic terms, the fact is that these are not calculations, but modes of reasoning. They are, however, modes of reasoning that are rarely made in anthropology. Therefore game theory as an approach, rather than as arithmetic, may reasonably be of use to those of us who want to arrive at cross-cultural understandings of human behavior. Perhaps, where adequate data are made available—admittedly a difficult condition—it will even be possible to indulge in some calculations.

I come now to the matter of brideprice in Africa. A controversy of long standing exists as to whether the payment of goods (usually livestock) that a man makes to his bride's family should be called brideprice, bridewealth, or some other euphemism; that is, should the transaction be analyzed as an economic phenomenon or should it be treated merely as an earnest expression of sentiment—a "prestation" comparable to the gift of a diamond in our own society. The controversy is scientifically meaningless, and is merely a reflection of our own cultural values, of our moral revulsion at commercialization of sentiment, especially sexual sentiment. Anthropologists became involved in the controversy because missionaries were trying to undermine the practice as morally reprehensible and demeaning to womanhood, whereas anthropologists knew that it was deeply embedded in the texture of native life and that it did not have the psychological implications that these well-meaning people assumed it to have.

The question as to whether the transfer of cattle and other goods from the family of the groom to that of the bride should be treated as an economic transaction has been cogently raised by Gray (1960). Gray believes that the refusal to recognize the market aspect of these transactions deprives us of significant aspects of the analysis of the relationship. He makes an exceedingly good case for the fact that among the Sonjo (whose society he has himself analyzed) the transactions for wives are indeed essentially commercial; his case becomes somewhat thinner when he extrapolates this behavior to a selected set of other cultures where goods are also transferred from the family of the groom to the family of the bride.

Let us now consider this practice in terms of a general formula for game theory: "Persons, using strategies available within the rules of the game, reach goals." In this instance our ethnographer will give us the persons, rules, and strategies, with which we should be able to calculate the goals.

It might appear to the culturally naïve that, as the purpose of bride payments is the acquisition of wives, the goals would always be women. This is by no means obvious. In this exchange situation an individual might, aside from wives, seek to maximize cattle (or other wealth used in exchange), children, sexual outlets, prestige and power, peace and harmony, or many other valued conditions or things, to all of which he may attach values of varying intensity.

We must remember also that in game theory, the goals of the contestants must be the same, or must be such that the gain for one can be expressed as the negative of the gain for another. Blue wants to maximize profits; Red to minimize losses; Red wants to win the battle; Blue wants not to lose the battle, etc. (The fact that this is not always the case has been best demonstrated in nonscientific terms in that charming document, *The Mouse That Roared*.) We are to assume, with all game theory, that the goals can be stated in common terms for all participants, so that if it is the immediate goal of a person to acquire a wife for cattle, these must be seen as interchangeable. This does not create any difficulty in bride bargaining; if wives are acquired through the transfer of goods, then the transfer of a daughter (who by the rules of the game cannot be a wife) makes goods available with which wives may be purchased. Contrariwise, the acquisition of a wife makes possible the production of daughters, by which more cattle can be obtained.

Among the rules of the game are those forbidding incest: To gain a wife or sexual outlet, one must not utilize one's own children or family, but must obtain one from outside. One does this by exchanging valued goods with the father or parents or clansmen that "control" the woman. There will be rules determining other proprieties, but they vary from culture to culture. It is clear that in a basic sense, wives, sexual outlets, and the probability of having children are all mutually interrelated. Furthermore, women are exchangeable for goods. Therefore it would appear that these goals are interchangeable. Certainly there is nothing in the strategy of the bargaining situation, in which the groom endeavors to minimize the payment and the bride's father to maximize it, which will tell us where the payoff lies. To do so we must look at some of the other strategies employed.

The Sonjo situation suggests that the payoff is, in fact, in wives. The reason that this should be so is quite straightforward: Women among the Sonjo are a scarce commodity. This comes about from a particular situational factor. The Sonjo are a rather impoverished group living among the warlike and aggressive Masai. The Masai are always willing to pay the hundred goats that a Sonjo wife costs, and their demand for wives appears to be unlimited—apparently there is no concept of marginal utility among them with respect to women. Furthermore, they appear to be willing to make such a payment regardless of the bride's age. Depreciation and obsolescence are disregarded. It is in this context that we must examine the strategies of Sonjo men.

The one advantage Sonjo men have in securing a wife is that the bargain is made in advance, when the woman is a mere girl. Gray does not say why, but we may well imagine that the reason the Masai would be unwilling to make an arrangement with a delayed payoff would be the difficulty of collecting from a strange tribe and lack of pressure to make such an investment in "futures." Therefore the first strategy employed by the Sonjo is to make a deal with the father of a young girl. The rules of the Sonjo arrangements are that the risks lie with the purchaser; the goats are transferred and the girl becomes the future wife, provided she survives the vicissitudes of life on the high plains. But as we all know, cute little girls do not always grow into lovely wives. If the husband finds his wife unsuitable, he may do one of two things: He may exchange her outright for another woman (paying or collecting the difference in the value established by the original transaction) or he may sell her outright for goats. He does not thereby lose all (but he does lose the natural increase of the goats originally transferred, as well as a tax if there is a sale rather than an exchange) and can exchange his woman for a wife of his choice. We know, further, that his interest in the matter is the wife, and not her potential for reproduction, because Sonjo men will transfer rights to a woman who has already borne children, even though the Sonjo rules clearly indicate that these children remain with the mother and he loses all rights to them. If we had sufficient case material on what actual Sonjo have done, as opposed to the generalities supplied by Gray, we might be able, by counting the ratio of strategy choices, actually to calculate the relative importance of wives and children to Sonjo men. We could thereby establish a hierarchy of values.

When we turn to the Sebei of Uganda, matters are different. They too exchange cattle (and other secondary goods) for wives; the incidence of polygyny is somewhat higher. As with the Sonjo, the bargaining is treated as such, with the groom's family endeavoring to minimize the cost and the bride's to maximize the return. As an aside, it should be noted that these exchange activities demonstrate certain characteristic market phenomena. For instance, as a result of British pacification and disease control, there has been a long-term secular increase in cattle population and consequently a steady climb in brideprice. Again, some Sebei areas are devoted largely to farming and little livestock is available, while others have small populations and larger herds. In the former there is a high ratio of women to cattle; in the latter a low one. The Sebei say that women marry to the east; that is, they tend to move from the area of dense population to the area of larger herds. It would appear that the old supply-demand ratio of economic behavior can appropriately be applied to transactions in wives, suggesting considerable cross-cultural viability of older economic theory.

The Sebei rules and circumstances are different from those of the Sonjo. There is no artificial scarcity created by a guaranteed export price as among the Sonjo, though the higher incidence of polygyny makes women rather difficult to acquire. The rules do not provide that a man may sell his wife; he may divorce her only with cause. Sebei children remain with the father (genitor) and are a part of his agnatic group. It is against the rules to divorce for barrenness.

No doubt a man endeavors to minimize payment, the girl's father to maximize it but, again, there is nothing in the bargaining situation that tells us whether the groom seeks a wife or a sexual outlet, or sees the exchange as a means of maximizing his herd through the reproductive potential of the woman. Some of the strategies are, however, diagnostic. If you ask Sebei men whether they prefer male or female children, they will opt for the former, though they want both. Clearly, if their strategy was directed at maximizing cattle, they would want girl children, for a houseful of daughters would lead to a kraalful of cattle. (It does not matter from our viewpoint that they cannot actually do anything about this strategy; the choice is still diagnostic even if it cannot effectively be utilized.) This aspect of Sebei behavior suggests that cattle are not the primary goal of marriage, but that children are. Again, while the Sonjo are puritanical with respect to extramarital relationships, the Sebei are not—nor do they condemn their women for such acts, though they may punish them. This suggests that the payoff is not in sexual outlet. The importance of children to the agreement is suggested by the fact that my case records indicate that a man will divorce his wife for child neglect, repeated inducement of abortion, etc., though he may not do so for reasons of barrenness. Another point is that a woman's value is not reduced as a result of having had intercourse, but it is if she is older (in a second marriage, for instance) so that her period of fertility has been reduced. Furthermore, a man will not reclaim all his brideprice if his wife has borne him children, for to do so would endanger the lives of these offspring. Finally, though the Sebei are not notably generous to their sons, they will endeavor to help them with the brideprice—even for second marriages, when there is no moral compulsion to do so.

These elements of Sebei strategy suggest that the payoff to the Sebei is neither cattle, wives, nor sexual outlet but rather, children. More accurately, it is male progeny or, in broader terms, the strengthening of the agnatic kin group. Other aspects of Sebei behavior—strategy choices in other Sebei games—strongly support this conclusion. The treatment of murder cases indicates that the underlying motivation is in preserving or reestablishing the strength of the patrilineal kin group.

It is of interest that the overt behavior of the Sebei in everyday life does not lead an observer to focus much attention on the clan. There are no regular clan ceremonies to reinforce sentiments, no clan gatherings except when action is necessary as a protective measure, and no real expression of clan solidarity and harmony. To be sure, every man recognizes his clan affiliations as a primary orientation to the social world; this aspect of Sebei life is not covert. But it is in no sense self-evident among the Sebei that clan considerations are fundamental motivations in human action. When we examine the immediate neighbors of the Sebei, their close cultural relatives who have preserved the pastoral mode of life to which their culture was a basic adaptation, we find many evidences of the clan as the manifest unit for social action. Among the Samburu, for example, each marriage must have the direct approval of the two clans involved (Spencer 1965).

These conclusions do not exhaust the possibilities inherent in the exchange of women. Hart and Pilling (1959) discuss the exchange of women among the Tiwi of Australia. Here, for quite other reasons than among the Sonjo, women are also scarce, and a man has difficulty in obtaining a wife. Hart and Pilling indicate clearly that the exchange strategies were designed to maximize individual influence and power in the community.

Game theory approach succeeds in altering the basic question of brideprice by freeing us from the semantics of the sentiment versus commercialism controversy, and allows us to examine behavior in terms of the diverse ends to which persons direct their attention. Brideprice retains its rationale and the matter of exchange is not obscured, but the rationale itself varies according to the pattern of cultural values. The strategies employed in the exchange of women therefore tell us where the payoff lies.

While for the most part I have implied that there is a single dominant value, the fact is that there may very well be a hierarchy of values operative in any single situation. It is not impossible that one could establish, through game theory calculations, the relative importance of such diverse values, though we have no examples with adequate data to demonstrate this possibility.

In this paper I have tried to make two major points:

1. Game theory, as developed by economists and military strategists, assumes a set of established values and is not culture-free as it appears to be; therefore it can be used cross-culturally only in the limited area of explicit economic ends.

2. The general conceptual apparatus of game theory is useful, however, as a mode of determining what the values actually are in a given society. By examining the strategies that the ethnographer finds to be regularly employed, he can determine where the payoff is, and what the values are.

Game theory leads to this mode of analysis because it makes a most important distinction with respect to the character of social life between rules of the game and strategy choices. Cultural anthropologists have been too much concerned with the former; social anthropologists too much with the latter. The relationship between the two has not been adequately explored.

Yet I am not sure just how much game theory as a formal system actually offers us. The conclusions regarding the cultures examined in this paper were not derived from any formal use of game theory. They were made independently, in terms of my own theoretical approach, but I think that they fit the logic of game theory, and that this logic may help others in formulating a basis for the analysis of cultures.

One further point deserves consideration. In my *Comparative Functionalism* (Goldschmidt 1966) I have developed an approach that suggests an ultimate unity in human motivations, operative within the rules provided by cultures and the matrices provided by societies. This set of assumptions suggests that there may be a level of generalization about motives that is transcultural and which, therefore, could serve as content for the ultimate payoff in the gamesmanship of life, wherever it is lived and whatever the rules may be. There appears to be a certain common denominator to all the diverse cultural payoffs I have discussed, though it is not easy to give it a name. If, for instance, we dig deeper into the motivation of Tlingit prestige drive, we find that it relates directly to the control of basic economic resources, as Garfield (1947) makes quite clear, while the neighboring Kwakiutl use the potlatch as a means of preserving their integrity and authority over certain similar rights, if I read Codere (1950) correctly. The matter is made even more explicit by Drucker and Heizer (1967). Similarly, the Sebei concern with clan welfare relates to the pattern of mutual help in a pastoral society and both protection against physical injury and loss of cattle. Hupa and Yurok property relates directly to the authority the individual has in the community and his access to resources. The case is straightforward among the Tiwi. I am not sufficiently versed in Sonjo culture to relate marital strategy to such a generalized goal. What I am suggesting is that perhaps the outlook toward culture provided by game theory and the examination of strategies to find the nature of the payoff may lead us to a means of uncovering generalized human motivations that are in fact transcultural and universal.

REFERENCES

Barth, Frederik. 1959. Segmentary Opposition and the Theory of Games: A Study of Pathan Organization. J. of the Royal Anthropological Inst. 89:5–21.

Codere, Helen. 1950. Fighting with Property: A Study of Kwakiutl Potlatching and Warfare, 1792–1930. (American Anthropological Society, Monograph 18).

Davenport, William. 1960. Jamaican Fishing: A Game Theory Analysis. (Yale University Publications in Anthropology No. 59).

Drucker, Philip and Robert F. Heizer. 1967. To Make Thy Name Good: A Reexamination of The Southern Kwakiutl Potlatch. Berkeley and Los Angeles: U. of California Press.

Garfield, Viola. 1947. Historical Aspects of Tlingit Clans in Angoon, Alaska. American Anthropologist 49:438–452.

Goldschmidt, Walter. 1951. Ethics and the Structure of Society: An Ethnological Contribution to the Sociology of Knowledge. American Anthropologist 53:506–524.

———. 1952. Ways of Mankind. Boston: Beacan Press. (See script entitled "The Case of the Sea-Lion Flippers" by Lister Sinclair.)

———. 1966. Comparative Functionalism: An Essay in Anthropological Theory. Berkeley and Los Angeles: U. of California Press.

Goldschmidt, Walter and Harold E. Driver. 1940. The Hupa White Deerskin Dance. (U. of California Publications in American Archaeology and Ethnology, Vol. 35, No. 8).

Gray, Robert F. 1960. Sonjo Bride-Price and the Question of African "Wife Purchase." American Anthropologist 62:34–57.

Hart, C. W. M. and Arnold R. Pilling. 1959. The Tiwi of North Australia, Case Studies in Cultural Anthropology. New York: Holt.

Moore, Omar Khayyam. 1957. Divination: A New Perspective. American Anthropologist 59:69–74.

Shubik, Martin. 1960. Game Theory and Related Approaches to Social Behavior. New York: Wiley.

Spencer, Paul. 1965. The Samburu: A Study of Gerontocracy in a Nomadic Society. Berkeley and Los Angeles: U. of California Press.

Von Neumann, John and Oskar Morgenstern. 1964. Theory of Games and Economic Behavior, 3d ed., Scientific Editions. New York: Wiley.

Williams, J. D. 1954. The Compleat Strategyst: Being a Primer on the Theory of Strategy. New York: McGraw-Hill.

CHAPTER 4

Richard F. Salisbury

Formal Analysis in Anthropological Economics: The Rossel Island Case

THE present study attempts to demonstrate the utility of formal analysis in anthropological economics, by making sense of a body of reported data,[1] which a "substantivist" analysis (Dalton 1965) and a more traditional economic analysis (Barić 1964) discard as inconsistent. Anthropological economics, as I expound at greater length in a forthcoming work (Salisbury, in press), takes as its aim the demonstration of the logic of choice used for resource allocation—that is, it accepts the aims of economics—but, using empirical data of the kind familiar to anthropologists, it studies those sectors of social behavior to which the classical analysis of traditional economics does not apply. It assumes that choices are made logically, even if the logic is not that of maximizing immediate returns of material goods by "higgle-haggling," which substantivists appear to view as the only form of rationality. Choices logically designed to produce optimum results over a long term can be expected to differ markedly from choices made on a short-term basis. Where there are different degrees of uncertainty about environmental conditions or about the actions of other persons, different magnitudes of inherent risk, different degrees of seriousness of the consequences of failure, the logical pattern of choice should not coincide with the short-term rational choice. To put these statements in game theory terms, classical economics formally analyzes the consequences that would ensue if everyone employed a maximax strategy of concentrating on the activity giving him the greatest comparative advantage in a non-zero-sum game with a large number of players. Anthropological economics concentrates on other strategies, other payoff matrices, and other game situations. In these terms a formal analysis of nonclassical, non-Euclidean economics is possible (Salisbury 1962b:71). The present paper seeks to show that such analyses are productive.

The game theory approach also clears up much of the confusion that exists in cultural descriptions of other economic systems. When describing a game, one must specify formal rules to which all participants must subscribe or be considered "outside the game." One finds similar economic rules, usually phrased as existential statements such as "there are one hundred cents to a dollar," with which all actors in an economic system agree. On the other hand, in a game there are many alternative strategies that different actors describe as "*the* way to play the game," or to which they ascribe moral qualities, arguing that "everyone *should* play the game in this way." Such strategy statements appear culturally as maxims, such as "A penny saved is a penny earned." The strategy statements can be related to the rules as logical extensions of them, if one makes certain assumptions about the risks involved in the game, about the consequences of failure, or the rewards of winning. But what is immediately apparent, and what would be a source of confusion if one attempted to write a consistent cultural description of Western economics, for example, is that there are alternative strategies and alternative cultural maxims. "Penny-wise, pound-foolish" is the obverse of Franklin's doctrine of frugality. It is also clear that the alternative strategy-statements are equally logical, under different views of the economic situation. Using different strategies may be equally logical if the true risks are unknown, or when the situation may change from time to time. The stock market exemplifies this clearly. Sellers, who believe stocks will drop, can find buyers only if others believe stocks will rise. Economic behavior thus demonstrates admirably what is coming to be recognized in other areas of cultural behavior (Salisbury 1959, Wallace 1961:29–42), namely, that complete consensus makes interaction impossible and that cultural diversity, within a framework of agreement on a few formal rules, is essential in human society.

Such a position demands that a straightforward ethnographic report on a social system of resource allocation (an economy) should contain a number of formal rules about which all informants are agreed, a series of strategy statements (usually of highly inconsistent natures) often explicit formulated by numbers of informants as maxims, and enough information about the nature of the game being played to render the different strategies comprehensible. Specifically, information

on numbers of players (the population), their different roles, the
risks and limiting situations in the society (its ecology and technology),
and the quantities of goods and services being allocated are required
as a minimum. By these criteria, Armstrong's description of Rossel
Island (Armstrong 1928)[2] stands out as a classic of ethnography; its
main defect is the ethnographer's attempt to interpret large bodies of
data in terms of a single strategy (the taking of interest), which ob-
scures somewhat the view of Rossel Island. Beside it, Malinowski's
account of the Trobriands appears as naïve sensational reporting; it
cites few figures, obtrudes the author's own feelings about what should
be the single strategy governing allocation (reciprocity), and, by not
citing the differences in informants' views, makes it difficult to say
which views are Malinowski's and which are Trobriand views. Unfortunately, Armstrong treats only one aspect of Rossel Island economics
at length—shell money. This has the compensating advantage, however, that it is possible to use the topic as a concise illustration of the
nature of anthropological economics and the ethnographic reporting
it demands.

The case is also useful in illustrating the methods of the anthropological economist. His basic data are quantitative descriptions of
transactions and the series of explanations given by people to justify
their behavior. His task is to construct the rules of a game in which
players would be expected to behave in the ways observed and to present their explanations of their own behavior as logically derivable
from the least number of assumptions about the rules and the conditions of the game. In many cases the classical economic game, and the
assumption that every player is trying to maximize his short-term
material gains, provides an adequate basis for analyzing the observed
behavior. In other cases, as Foster (1965:293) has shown, the assumption that all persons are playing a game in which the rewards are so
limited that one man's gain exactly balances another man's loss (i.e.,
a zero-sum game) is the most parsimonious explanation of observed behavior. In yet others, strategies of minimizing the possibility of loss
(minimax strategies) may be seen as underlying observed behavior of
apparently cautious, unadventurous types.

It may be empirically untrue that economic life is a zero-sum game,
since increases in aggregate yield are possible; it may be that, empirically, conditions are inappropriate for minimax strategies. The investigator must seek to establish what the empirical conditions are.

But merely by establishing the apparent logic behind people's actions, he can make predictions about their other actions under the same conditions, and can extrapolate their actions under changed conditions.

In more complex situations the investigator is confronted by individuals apparently using different strategies, or even playing different games, even though each one's behavior is contingent on the behavior of others.[3] This occurs particularly when the true payoff matrix is not widely known or is unknowable, or where people are in different power positions, make different evaluations of long-term security and short-term gains, or are exposed to different risks. The investigator can then follow the game theorist's technique of following through the implications of long series of interactions (plays) in which players adopt different strategies. If he has also established the objective conditions of risk, payoff, etc., he may later be able to predict the future outcome of series of plays, should those conditions be changed. The Rossel Island material does permit at least a tentative analysis up to this point.

ROSSEL ISLAND SHELL MONEY

Rossel, situated at the extreme eastern end of the New Guinea archipelago, is perhaps the remotest of all the islands in the archipelago. On the island small shell discs (*ndap*) are given in exchange for goods or services in most transactions where men are involved, from the purchases of craft goods to weddings. Other shells (*nko*), also used in transactions, are said to be female shells, but these will not be discussed here—largely because Armstrong's information about these shells is quite spotty. The Rossel use of a single term for all male shells indicates that they are considered a single logical set, contrasting with female shells. The set of *ndap* is differentiated into twenty-two named types (1928:61) ranked in an order that Armstrong numbered from 1 (low) to 22 (high). Each type or denomination is appropriate to a particular set of transactions. High denominations, particularly No. 18 and No. 20 are appropriate to only one or two types of transaction (No. 18 for weddings or pig purchases, No. 20 for cannibal feasts or purchase of ceremonial canoes); lower denominations are appropriate to a longer series of specific transactions—No. 4, for instance, buys a basket, lime stick, or lime pot (1928:85). The various denominations have a qualitatively different value, although each represents a quantitatively different level of prestige. The relationship between the prestige levels of adjacent denominations of shells is a complex one, which Armstrong tried to analyze in oversimplified terms of "compound interest," as if the difference in value were a matter of the time for which a shell is loaned. The evidence is incomplete but it would seem that in Rossel thought a shell of denomination n is equated with the shell of denomination $n-1$ (its *ma*), plus a consecutive series of up to ten lower ranking shells (the *dondap* of the *ma*) (1928:71–73). There are special terms for each member of a consecutive series starting from the principal *(yono)* down to the first *(wo)* (1928:79). Lending and borrowing of *ndap* is common, with the loan of one denomination being returnable by a higher ranking shell, with the rank difference varying roughly with the length of the loan (1928:72–73). Armstrong gives examples of loans of short low-ranking series (e.g., No. 3 plus No. 4, which presumably immediately equate with No. 5) being repaid after a few days by a single higher value (No. 6), and of loans of single high-ranking shells repaid by the same shell plus a series of lower ranking shells *(dondap)* (1928:67). It is also possible to obtain the loan of a shell *(ma)* by depositing the next higher ranking shell as a security *(tyindap)* with the lender; presumably in such a case the return of a shell of the *ma* value, in exchange for the original *tyindap,* eliminates all indebtedness.

Stated in formal terms the complex manipulations of Rossel Island money appear as a game in which the object is to maximize the volume of services received from others in exchange for shells. At any one time, different people want different services. Some individuals possess shells but temporarily do not want services. The system regulates the demand for a complex of goods and services, and the existence of shell money equivalents motivates other individuals to provide those goods and services.

Thus far the formal description relies almost entirely on Rossel Island terminology, clearly stated by Armstrong and about which there is no argument among informants (although Armstrong, from a short stay, could not fully work out the complex relationships of *tyindap, ma,* and *dondap* for all denominations and times). Other aspects of the shell money exchanges appeared to Armstrong as unclear, inconsistent, or illogical, and he mentions disagreements among informants as well as disagreements among parties to exchanges. I propose to interpret these obscurities or disagreements as the expression of diverse strategy statements, formulated by informants with different interests to maintain, which Armstrong, given his old fashioned Malinowskian idea of uniform cultural homogeneity, was unable to include in his explanation. As an ethnographer who has repeatedly listened to such conflicting strategy statements, I respect Armstrong's work all the more because he had the intellectual honesty to admit doubts and confusions. Let us, however, attempt a series of formal analyses of the Rossel Island system and so arrive at the nature of strategy disagreements deductively. We may then return to the empirical evidence, to show the fit between it and the formal analyses.

Armstrong's own formal analysis is that of a classical economist: Although the time and percentage indices are unclear, the Rossel system is a system of compound interest. For the person owning a *ndap* the interest gives him an incentive to lend his shell, and penalizes him with the interest loss, should he hoard it. For the person desiring services the interest constitutes a cost against which he can measure the value of the services at the present moment. It motivates him to provide services to someone else in advance, and so avoid the obligations of debt, or to return the loan as soon as possible. The strength of the incentive/sanction is provided by the interest rate, and Armstrong tries to calculate this, estimating that the expectation is that loans will be repaid in about three weeks.

The analysis has considerable merit. It predicts the high velocity of circulation of *ndap* through loans, and suggests that individuals could make a living by lending at high rates (i.e., forcing speedy repayment) and borrowing at low rates (i.e., delaying repayment of others) (1928:66). It suggests that the individual who has clear ownership of a shell (whose stock possessed, plus loans due and minus debts owing, is a positive number) has a claim to a constant supply of services from others. Those without shells must constantly supply services at a certain rate; only if they supply a larger number in a given time period can they acquire clear title to shells, and thus accumulate claims to future services from others. Those with claims to services are those who own shells and are chiefs (*limi*); upward mobility is achieved initially by providing services and acquiring shells, but is then dependent on "playing the market." This is a common situation elsewhere in Melanesia (cf. Salisbury 1966).

It is not a very powerful analysis, for it assumes that *ndap* exist in large quantities, and that there is ready convertibility or subdivision of *ndap* into other denominations. It assumes that individuals can switch immediately from being lenders to being debtors, and that each position is simply the reverse of the other. None of these assumptions is entirely true, though the assumptions may be approached in relation to the low-ranking shells and the goods and services which they buy.

Let us consider other assumptions in turn, and the analyses they lead to. Firstly let us take the relative inconvertibility of *ndap*, and the equation of each denomination with a specific set of services. This means that an individual, A, requiring a specific service must seek out not only an individual, B, who is prepared to provide that service, but an individual, C, who can lend him the appropriate denomination shell, and an individual, D, who will accept yet other services from A, and so enable him to repay C. It may sometimes occur that A has the correct denomination himself and a simple purchase occurs, or that B and D turn out to be the same individual and the transaction becomes one of delayed exchange of qualitatively different services. Normally, however, a simple desire for services from others sets in motion a complex series of relationships, involving at least four parties.

On the other hand the position of a shell possessor is relatively simple. He has to seek out only one individual, the man who wishes to borrow his shell; or, having once lent the shell he is simply preoccupied in insuring its return with interest as quickly as possible. The relative inconvertibility of *ndap* complicates his position in that a possessor who envisages becoming in the near future a buyer of the specific services his shell will obtain may wish to hold onto his shell until that time arrives, in order to avoid the complications of being without the shells to obtain the services. This complication would not concern shell possessors who took either a short-run view of matters, and always lent out whatever they had, or a long-run view that shells are in constant circulation so that by lending one obtains a sequence of different services and shells and the eventual return of a shell of the same denomination. If each denomination changes into the next in three weeks, one could expect to have gone through seventeen changes in a year and have one's original shell back plus a No. 17 at that time. More realistically, an individual possessing two or more shells and loaning each one continuously could expect to have any particular denomination pass through his hands two or more times each year.

In short, one would expect to find three discrepant views of the system as a result of the relative inconvertibility of *ndap*. The service-desiring nonpossessor would describe it as a burdensome system of debts, putting him at a disadvantage with respect to the wealthy and

involving him in needless complications. This aspect is mentioned by
Armstrong (1928:67) especially as it applies to young men; the system
is seen as inefficient and demanding ten times as much lending as
would be required if a more convertible monetary medium were used
(1928:65). Dalton (1965:53) particularly stresses this aspect. The careful possessors of a few shells would tend to emphasize the purchasing
aspect of the system, and the specific services that can be obtained
with each denomination shell—"any commodity or service may be
or less directly priced in terms of them" (1928:59). They would tend to
see wealth in terms of concrete possessions. It would be expected that
such people would also tend to favor more or less direct exchanges of
services and/or shells, buying services when the right shell is at hand,
and reciprocating when the exchange partner needs services. Armstrong
(1928:88) describes in a puzzled footnote an apparent tendency for
reciprocity to occur in pig sales. The third group of shell possessors
includes both those who have only immediate gain in mind and those
who have many shells and long-run perspectives. Their tendency
would be to see the system as an open one, which rapidly circulates
goods and services, and which provides frequent feasts and ceremonials as loans are repaid and new obligations incurred. This group
would emphasize that it is a generous system, in which each man seeks
aggressively to lend valuables as soon as they come into his possession,
and in which one's well-being depends not on the number of shells he
owns but on the number that pass through his hands. Again Armstrong
cites (1928:74) the desire to touch *ndap* as they pass by, but interprets
this only as "evidently a witnessing of the transaction."

The rigidities of the system as a whole appear much less acute to
individuals who possess large numbers of *ndap*. To a Rossel Islander
these rigidities are more or less serious, depending on the numbers of
ndap of different values a man holds, on the size of the population
(and the likelihood of any one individual holding a shell of any particular denomination), and on the frequency of transactions involving
particular denominations. Theoretically, one could assign hypothetical
values to each of these factors and, by substituting them in a computer simulation of the Rossel Island exchanges, predict what strategies
would be most successful under different conditions. This is imprac-
ticable for present purposes, but Armstrong does give some of the
parameter values for 1920–21, and these may be used in a single sub-
stitution. The effects of population increase, the introduction of

European consumer goods, or the production of new shell currency
might then be predicted as departures from the 1920–21 state.

Rossel Island's population in 1920 was 1,415, including 406 adult
males, who lived in 145 "villages" (1928:230), 116 of which are mapped
by Armstrong as forming two rings around a rectangular island, half
of the villages fronting on the coast, and the other half backed by the
central mountains. The island perimeter is about sixty miles. The
villages are evenly scattered approximately a mile apart along the
coast and on the inland ring, but the two rings are more than a mile
apart. Armstrong obtained figures for the number of *ndap* of different
denominations as follows (1928:62–63): 7 × No. 22, 10 × No. 21,
10 × No. 20, 10 × No. 19, 20 × No. 18, 7 × No. 17, 7 × No. 16,
10 × No. 15, 30 × No. 14, 30-40 × No. 13, and larger numbers of all
lower denominations; No. 4 was "by far the commonest," with at
least 200. He estimated a grand total of less than a thousand *ndap*
altogether. The average adult male owned, therefore, slightly over
two *ndap*, but only seven *ndap* were present in the average village.

Armstrong does not cite frequencies of transactions, but the population figures would indicate about fourteen marriages and twenty-
eight funerals each year, assuming a stable population and a life
expectancy of about sixty years. Each No. 18 shell would thus be
needed roughly once every year and a half for a wedding; the number
of times each would be needed for the purchase of a pig at a feast
could vary widely, as the production of pigs increased or decreased,
but considerations of the size of pigs and the meat-eating capacity of
Melanesians suggest that five uses per annum was a ceiling, and probably one or two uses was usual. Cannibal feasts, construction of large
houses, or the sale of gardens, each requiring a higher value *ndap* as
yono but an No. 18 as part of the series, probably occurred highly
infrequently so that higher denomination shells were virtually im-
mobile, and a few No. 18's were involved as *dondap* in payments of
higher denomination shells.

The denominations between No. 17 and No. 14 appear to have cir-
culated mainly as *dondap*, when higher denominations were the *yono*
ndap, principally at pig feasts. This would have involved slightly
higher rates of circulation for No. 17 and No. 14 than No. 18, since
they were fewer in number. For the lower denominations it is impossible to calculate frequencies of use as, for example, No. 13 could be
used to compensate for three months of work; No. 13 was also the

yono ndap for small canoe purchases (1928:86). All others figured as members of *dondap* series *and* as *yono ndap*, and so were probably in virtually constant circulation.

Let us now consider the circulation mechanisms of shells of which less than thirty-five were in circulation, and of those with over thirty-five in circulation. An individual wishing to borrow one of the scarce denominations could not expect to find one available in his own village or the three neighboring ones—on the average there would be one for every five villages. He would have to expect to travel to distant villages to obtain the loan or would have to wait until a shell was paid'into his immediate neighborhood and then petition the possessor for a loan. Even if the network of relationships described by Armstrong (1928:31–37) and implied by the virilocality of residence and nonlocalized matrilineal clan system of the island would have spread contacts over wide areas, these factors would not have vitiated the need for travel beyond the local political unit to obtain the loan of scarce shells.

Rather than to travel at random to obtain shells, it would be more practical for prospective borrowers to follow the peregrinations of particular shells and to wait until a shell reached an individual with whom the borrower had a preexisting relationship. The borrower could then immediately ask for a loan. Armstrong discusses the fact that all coins above No. 12 rank are individually named (1928:62). Such names would play an important part in enabling people to follow shell movements. Shell movements would not only be traced, they would be anticipated. Pre-existing relationships would be cultivated with those individuals who were adjudged likely to be shell-recipients in the future. Stated the other way around, individuals likely to be shell-recipients would be the objects of cultivation by individuals in search of future loans. To establish a reputation of being a likely shell-recipient would be a major aim of a person seeking power. Such a person would try to establish a fiction (which other people would deny) that he was entitled by right to control shells. Armstrong (1928:60, 68) makes several rather vague comments linking possession of such shells with chiefship and the ownership of large canoes. Chiefs *(limi)* are presumably, if Rossel is similar to virtually every other area of Melanesia, men of ability who possess a minimum of inherited advantages, and who have achieved their positions by politicking and financial manipulations. In such a context it is reasonable to expect an investigator to report a variety of imprecise statements, such as "Chiefs are wealthy men," and "Wealthy men are chiefs by right," as well as statements complaining of the arrogance of wealthy upstarts. This would seem to be the situation Armstrong reports.

Yet the claims of chiefs to outright ownership have other consequences. Let us consider a hypothetical situation in which all twenty No. 18 shells are in the hands of individuals who have no debts to others; individuals, in other words, who can claim an unclouded title, or one held by right. Let us call these twenty men chiefs. A nonchief, X, wishing to obtain a wife for his son, or to buy a pig, would have to incur a debt toward one of the chiefs. To repay the debt he would have to approach another chief and also collect a series of *dondap* shells of low denominations. Otherwise, he would have to obtain the loan of a No. 19 of which there are only ten in circulation. Clearly, in view of the discrepancy in numbers of No. 18 and No. 19 shells alone, there would be a tendency for loans of No. 18 to be repaid by a return of the No. 18 and *dondap*, rather than by the higher denomination. Let us consider only the implications of direct payment of No. 18 shells, and further borrowing from one of the chiefs. Having first borrowed from chief A, individual X would remain permanently indebted, borrowing from chief B to repay chief A, and from C to repay B. Each time he would have to add low value shells as *dondap*. To liquidate the debt he would either have to marry off a daughter or sell a pig, or (less likely) manipulate loans until he could himself claim clear title to a No. 18.

The twenty chiefs themselves would have a vested interest in keeping the shells circulating among themselves alone, thereby increasing the probability that shells received by nonchiefs in ceremonial payments would be returned to their keeping to circulate in the ring. To the extent that a chief had other lower denominations in his possession he would also be able to let debtors pyramid their debts until they were obligated to the extent of a No. 18. At that point the chief would be assured that the debtor would continue to pay him interest, and that if the debtor ever obtained a No. 18 from a sale or a wedding, that shell would come straight back to him also. Limitations on the giving of pig feasts by nonchiefs would also tend to minimize leakage of No. 18 shells (cf 1928:88, cited above) to nonchiefs. The leaks could never be entirely stopped—even the hypothetical model cited above implies that there should be twenty-one chiefs for twenty shells, with the twenty-first receiving the shell in the transaction that starts the circulation. The existence of social mobility testifies to the possibility of new-comers entering the ring of chiefs. Yet the members of the ring, by collusion, could buttress their own positions. They could assume the aura of legitimacy referred to above and control access to power.

Some of the conditions under which collusion is likely can be spec-ified. The shell denomination concerned would have to be in short supply to permit oligopoly control to be obtained. It would have to be a denomination in periodic demand by most individuals in the system (women and pigs are universal desirables among Melanesian males). The possibility of the ring being broken by access of nonchiefs to higher denomination *ndap* would be reduced by a sharp discrepancy between the numbers of the monopolized denomination shell and of the next higher denomination. At the same time, the efficiency of the ring would be increased to the extent that pyramiding of debt could also be used to make nonchiefs owe the appropriate shells. Nonchiefs could also be better persuaded to accept the manipulations of such a ring if, in theory at least, they had the possibility open to them of pyramiding their own loans up to the crucial denomination, and thus of entering the ring themselves. On all these grounds the No. 18 shell would meet the formal criteria for oligopoly control.

The ethnography also indicates the corollaries of such a control: the infrequency of circulation of values higher than No. 18, the payment of debts of No. 18 by the same value plus either work or additional small shells, and the apparent generosity (1928:67) with which chiefs lend out No. 18 shells to promising young men at virtually no interest, presumably as an investment designed to involve the young man as a political supporter as he gains skills in financial manipulation. The chiefs would also expect a different attitude toward shells of the crucial value and above from that expressed toward shells below this value, even though it would be ideologically important for chiefs to insist that the shells all form part of a single system, governed by the same formal cultural rules. Armstrong expresses exactly this situation thus (1928:68):

Nos. 18 to 22 seem to be in a somewhat different position from the lower values . . . . My informants did, however, state that the same principles operate with these: that a No. 17 becomes a No. 18, a No. 18 a No. 19 and so on—in just the same way as with the lower values. Yet, as . . . in the example given . . . a No. 18 can be borrowed for a short time without the debt increasing . . . . Nos. 18 to 22 are peculiar in one other respect. They have a certain sacred character. No. 18, as it passes from person to person, is handled with great apparent reverence, and a

crouching attitude is maintained. . . . Probably Nos. 17 and below have a sacred-
ness and prestige proportional to their position in the series, but I am inclined to
think that there may be a real gap, in this respect, between Nos. 17 and 18.

I would submit that all these ethnographic peculiarities (and their
obscurity) can be predicted as the effects of a game coalition between
people calling themselves chiefs, seeking to maximize rationally their
long-term gains by manipulating the formal rules to suit their particular strategy.

CHANGES IN THE SYSTEM

The analysis of the operation of the Rossel Island system at one
time period with only one set of numerical parameters makes it clear
that changes in those parameters could make for dramatic changes in
the operation of the system without any change taking place in the
formal cultural rules. Population changes (assuming a virtually constant stock of *ndap*) would alter the ratio of shells to adult males and
would alter the denomination at which intervillage borrowing and the
naming of individual shells becomes important. It would alter the rate
of transactions and up to a certain point would increase the dependency of nonchiefs upon chiefs for the use of No. 18. Chiefs would keep
larger followings. But increased velocity of circulation of No. 18
would also increase the likelihood of leakage of shells to nonchiefs,
and at a certain point the closed state of the ring would be expected
to break down. With it would go changes in the uses of and attitudes
toward higher denomination shells.

Changes in the availability of goods and services would also affect
the system. The lower values, up to about value No. 4, would seem to
have been so widely distributed and readily exchanged as to have the
characteristics of multipurpose, divisible coins. With more services and
goods available, the money supply would have to increase propor-
tionately, and in due course a system of simple relationships between
coins would be expected to emerge as the rate of transactions reached
a crucial level. In practical terms, I would predict that No. 4 may have
become equivalent to a shilling, and in time replaced by it, with other
low denominations becoming equivalent to fractions of a shilling, and
perhaps remaining in use as small change.

The possibility of the emergence of oligopolies at levels other than
No. 18 should also be considered. The decrease in the numbers of
shells between denominations No. 14 and No. 15 would make this a

possible locus for an oligopoly to develop, but the universal desirability of European axes (costing No. 11) might indicate a lower value for such control. At this point, however, the nature of the supply of axes—presumably through European monopolistic traders, or through Rossel Islanders earning money by work on plantations or gold mines —would tend to make oligopoly by chiefs unlikely. It might be predicted that, with trade stores and Australian money replacing *ndap* in transactions up to those of denomination No. 11, the circulation of all higher values might begin to resemble that described by Armstrong for values above No. 18. Interest in the form of cash would accompany reciprocal exchanges, loans and repayments, and the complexities of the earlier Rossel system of equivalents would be lost.

FORMAL ANALYSIS VS. SUBSTANTIVE ANALYSIS

It must still be demonstrated that a formal analysis is indeed more powerful than a substantive analysis in explaining more empirical facts from fewer assumptions.

Barić (1964) gives a sympathetic exposition of Armstrong's ethnography but concentrates on the relationship of the system to productive investment, by which she means the accumulation of larger quantities of nets, land, canoes, etc. (1964:48). Her conclusion is that the shell money system was virtually a zero-sum game, as relatively few transactions were aimed at investing, and "despite great activity in the economic sphere, aggregate capital is largely maintained at the same level, although individuals may become wealthy." She virtually ignores Armstrong's abundant evidence that new goods such as saucepans and steel axes had already been included in the system by 1920, and that circulation rates of high denomination *ndap* had changed shortly before 1920. It may be granted that the technological level of Rossel Island meant that relatively little increase was possible in the use of material capital goods to produce additional foodstuffs—the availability of abundant sago and fish would seem to have made additional food production unnecessary—but it would seem that great variations were possible in the volume of services produced. What the shell money system permitted was the accumulation of command over services by chiefs and nonchiefs alike; entrepreneurs, it would seem, were constantly trying to increase the volume of services they commanded, and may well have been progressively increasing the aggregate volume of services available in the society as a whole. The apparent stagnation of Rossel Island in terms of volume of material goods available should, from the dynamic picture suggested by formal analysis, suggest that something (presumably technology) was "positively stopping" (*contra* Barić 1964:49) growth in this particular direction.

Barić (ibid.) does deal with the relationship between shell money and power, but interprets the two as separate.

There were several routes to prestige and power. The sheer accumulation of liquid capital was one way: . . . Reckless expenditure could purchase prestige by financing activities in the form of feasts or the purchase of ceremonial canoes. The ceremonial canoes were the capstone of the edifice of wealth. They were the monopoly of the chiefs, in effect, since those who could get them . . . became chiefs.

Attempts at accumulation of shells were the strategies of the unprogressive middle levels of society. Expenditure that may have seemed reckless to Barić can be explained in terms of the purchase of command over services of particular types. Ceremonial canoes, purchaseable only by No. 20 *ndap*, at a time when circulation of values over No. 18 was minimal, could only be obtained by a limited few—those who could dispose of cannibal victims, big houses, or land—any of which would obtain No. 20 shells for them. Barić, in each case, is forced to distort the ethnography. More generally she forces herself into a static interpretation of Armstrong's data by myopically considering "economics" as dealing only with goods and not with services. The description of feasts, marriage payments, and payments for the services of prostitutes (*ptyilibi*) bulks large in Armstrong's work but is virtually ignored.

Dalton's analysis of the data tries to show that "Rossel Island economy is not integrated by market exchange" and that "if all the *ndap* shell transactions . . . were abolished, subsistence livelihood of Rossel Islanders would remain unimpaired" (1965:55). Theoretically, Dalton (cf. Belshaw 1954, Salisbury 1962a) tries to revive the dead issue of the nature of primitive money in terms of substantivism (Cook 1966). Dalton's analysis must be evaluated in the light of the fact that it almost invariably does not explain the ethnography as Armstrong's informants related it, but denies the accuracy of Armstrong's data.

Thus Dalton says (1965:54): "There are . . . faults in Armstrong's analysis. . . . He . . . regards all transactions as commercial purchases." And (1965:57): "It is about as useful to describe a pig feast on Rossel as buying a pig with a No. 18 *ndap* as [it is to describe a

Western marriage in terms of buying the ring]. To do so one must ignore the folk view of the event." In fact, Armstrong states (1928: 59): "Any commodity or service may be more or less directly priced in terms of [*ndap* shells]." And (1928:88): "A pig feast is known as *bwame bwobe* [pig-buy]. . . . One man, A, [makes] insulting remarks about the pig of another man, B; whereupon B retorts by suggesting that A buy the pig." The "folk view" is clearly one of purchase. Certain fish are subject to buying and selling with No. 11 shells "even from an own brother" (1928:86). Marriage too is clearly viewed as the purchase of services for a No. 18 shell, though not as a purchase of the person of the bride. This emerges clearly from a comparison of marriage with the purchase by a group of men of the services of a *ptybili*, also with a No. 18 shell. The latter transaction involves no additional handing over of a series of lower denomination *ndap* to the clan of the *ptybili*, such as is involved in the marriage ritual, although otherwise the rituals are similar (1928:97). The owners of a *ptybili's* sexual services receive payments from other men who utilize her services temporarily, and each co-owner receives a No. 18 *ndap* from the eventual husband of the group *ptybili* when she settles down with a single individual. By contrast, the ritual for *ptybili* purchase does nothing to allocate rights over the children she produces; these rights are purchased in the marriage ritual by the subsidiary payments to the bride's clan relatives. Armstrong's informants were vague and even contradictory in their statements about the rarity with which *ptybili* produce children, about the advantages any of her children may possess by having several fathers, and about the wide dispersment of relationship terms for *ptybili* children.

Dalton also criticizes Armstrong for treating *ndap* as twenty-two types within a single logical set and for adopting a numbering system that suggests a uniform relation between each category. He concludes: (Dalton 1965:55–56)

"What is clear, however, is that shells below No. 18 are not convertible into shells 18–22 by borrowing and repayment. One cannot start with a No. 1 or 17, and by lending work it up to a No. 18–22. . . . Convertibility via borrowing and repaying . . . most certainly breaks down between Nos. 17 and 18. I suspect between Nos. 10 and 11 as well. . . . It is very clear that the entire series is not linked . . . because the uses to which the shells 18–22 are put are of an entirely different order from the uses of lower shells. . . . Without exception Nos. 18–22 enter noncommercial transactions exclusively.

The ethnography has already been cited which directly contradicts each of these statements. Informants directly state that the relation between No. 17 and No. 18 is the same as that between Nos. 18 and 19, and can in theory be interchangeable in terms of borrowing and repaying. The series is clearly linked, though the small numbers and special uses of all shells from about No. 12 upwards means that there is a steady and progressive change in attitudes of individuals to shells. In the folk view, all transactions involving shells are exchanges of them for goods and services, which denotes commerce. What is true (and Armstrong devotes several pages [1928:81–84] to analyzing the components of collective purchase in a pig feast, and components of kinship) is that the number of additional noncommercial relationships involved is much larger for a high-denomination than for a low-denomination transaction.

Dalton also feels that Armstrong's comments on the sacred nature of high-denomination shells mean that "Nos. 18–22 are obviously treasure items." This, Dalton feels, justifies his contradicting the ethnographic evidence that *ndap* is a unitary set. It is clear that Dalton has never seen the display of ten $100,000 bills in a Las Vegas gambling saloon. Ethnographically they could be described by a paraphrasing of Armstrong (1928:68): "They have a certain sacred character; [such bills are viewed] with great apparent reverence, and a [gasping and pointing] attitude is maintained. . . . [They] are almost always kept enclosed and are not supposed [to be taken out of their case] to see the light of day." In Las Vegas, people make pilgrimages to view the $1,000,000 in bills; the shrine is lavishly decorated, and temple watchmen, armed with guns, see that nonsacred commoners do not come into dangerously close contact with the sacred objects. There is no question but that the ten pieces of paper could, in theory, be converted into an equivalent number of, say, ten-cent cigars. Formal analysis and an understanding of game theory explains why they are not converted.

What the formal analysis enables one to demonstrate is that despite the rigidities imposed on Rossel Island's economy by its small size, its simple technology, and the difficulties of balancing supply and demand for goods and services within a single island, all aspects of life—from the purchase of fish or baskets to the obtaining of unskilled labor for a month, the specialized services of a *ptybili* or legal rights to children—are to some extent regulated within one single system of exchange. The system motivates individuals to supply services to catch

fish or to breed pigs. It rewards those who are adept financial entrepreneurs. It "increases the necessity for doubling and redoubling
social links" (Barić 1964:39) in a sparsely populated land. And it
provides the basis for political loyalty to about twenty chiefs. It is
a flexible system, though formal analysis suggests that this flexibility
is not unlimited without a change in the formal rules. All this is
accomplished by the circulation of less than a thousand chips of shell,
which Armstrong (1928:64) felt in "the native point of view" were
most nearly equated with units of time: "e.g. a wife could be said to
cost a year, a basket of taro a week, and so on." For all that Rossel
Island does not meet the specifications of the "perfect market" of
classical economics, I feel it has been demonstrated that whatever
island-wide integration there was in 1920, was almost entirely an
effect of market exchange.

NOTES

1. This analysis has been progressively refined in the light of questions by students in Pacific ethnography courses since 1957. I wish to acknowledge this help, but
to accept full responsibility for errors remaining.

2. Armstrong's volume is cited hereafter merely as (1928).

3. Dr. A. Rapoport pointed out in discussion that it is only where contingency of
expectations is involved that game theory becomes a more powerful analytical tool
than probability theory or linear programming. Unfortunately the pure theorist,
advancing the mathematical precision of analysis, needs to be able to specify or control the payoff matrix before predicting the results of the game. The task of the
empirical or applied worker is to work back from results to the payoff matrix, and
he is thus merely the user of theoretical findings, not the advancer of theory.

REFERENCES

Armstrong, W. E. 1928. Rossel Island. Cambridge: Cambridge U. Press.
Baric, L. 1964. Some Aspects of Credit, Saving and Investment in a 'Non-Monetary'
    Economy (Rossel Island) in Capital Saving and Credit in Peasant Societies, ed.
    R. Firth and B. S. Yamey. London: Allen & Unwin, pp. 35–52.
Belshaw, C. S. 1954. Changing Melanesia. London: Oxford U. Press.
Cook, S. 1966. The Obsolete Anti-Market Mentality. American Anthropologist
    68:323–45.
Dalton, G. 1965. Primitive Money. American Anthropologist 67:44–65.
Foster, G. M. 1965. Peasant Society and the Image of the Limited Good. American
    Anthropologist 67:293–315.
Salisbury, R. F. 1959. Joking Relations and Ritual Ambiguity. Paper presented at
    American Anthropological Assoc. Meetings, Mexico City, December 1959.

————. 1962a. From Stone to Steel. Cambridge and Melbourne: U. Presses.

————. 1962b. Comment on "The Feet of the Natives Are Large" by J. S. Berliner. Current Anthropology 3:70–71.

————. 1966. Politics and Shell-Money Finance in New Britain *in* Political Anthropology, ed. A. Tuden, V. Turner, and H. Swartz. Chicago: Aldine Press.

————. in press. Anthropological Economics. Englewood Cliffs: Prentice-Hall.

Wallace, A. F. C. 1961. Culture and Personality. New York: Random House.

CHAPTER 5

Bernhardt Lieberman

Combining Individual Preferences into a Social Choice

How persons in interaction combine their individual preference patterns into a social choice is a fundamental question about which there has been much speculation, and an amount of mathematical work; but there have been few, if any, empirical studies dealing directly with the question.[1] The problem is ubiquitous; examples abound. The eleven members of the Security Council of the United Nations must decide to take or not take some action; a president of the United States must be selected from the millions of eligible citizens, but particularly from the dozen or so likely possibilities; a university research institute must plan a research program that will interest its members who have diverse preferences and satisfy its sources of support; consumer goods must be produced and distributed to satisfy the preferences of millions of consumers; Congress must apportion the $50 billion defense budget among the Army, Navy, Air Force, and Marines; and a family must decide whether it is to live in the city or a suburb. All of these diverse decisions have something in common: In some way the preferences of different individuals or groups must be summed up or amalgamated into a social or group choice.

The work reported in this paper was performed under a contract with the United States Office of Education, Department of Health, Education and Welfare, under the provisions of the Cooperative Research Program. Additional support came from the University of Pittsburgh's International Dimension Program supported by the Ford Foundation and the University. I am grateful to Robert Glaser, J. Steele Gow, Jr., James Kehl, and Richard Park for their encouragement and support of this work, and to M. Hinich, L. Brownstein, J. Sawyer, J. Coleman, W.E. Vinacke, and M. Mandelker for ideas and comments.

Portions of this paper were presented orally at the meetings of the Psychonomic Society in Chicago in October 1965; at the meetings of the Eastern Sociological Society in Philadelphia in April 1966; and at the Sixth World Congress of Sociology in Evian, France in September 1966.

Societies, groups, and organizations have produced a variety of decision-making procedures: the majority vote with veto power; the majority vote without veto power; the economic market mechanism; the dictatorial father who decides unilaterally where the family shall live; bargaining and persuasion among the Joint Chiefs of Staff; the advisers to the Secretary of Defense who use techniques of modern mathematical economics; the executive committee or governing board that reaches a consensus and imposes its decisions on a larger group; and the system of primary elections and conventions for the selection of the presidential candidates. Group decisions are made in these and many other ways.[2]

SOME BRIEF HISTORICAL REMARKS

Mathematical work dealing with these election and social choice problems appears to have had its origin in the second half of the eighteenth century in the work of Borda and Condorcet. An anomalous situation, which has been termed variously the paradox of voting or the Condorcet effect, has intrigued thinkers for almost two hundred years. Its fascination stems from the fact that it illustrates that the very structure of a social choice situation can produce a perplexing or disturbing result. Consider the following situation.[3]

Let 1, 2, 3 be three alternatives; let A, B, C be three individuals and let (A, B, C) be the community. Let $1 > 2$ mean 1 is preferred to 2. If for A, $1 > 2, 2 > 3$, and we assume transitivity, then $1 > 3$. Similarly for B, if $2 > 3, 3 > 1$ then $2 > 1$. For C, if $3 > 1, 1 > 2$ then $3 > 2$. Since a majority, A and C, prefer 1 to 2, and a majority, A and B, prefer 2 to 3, we would hope that a majority also prefers 1 to 3. But this is not the case, since B and C prefer 3 to 1.

This perplexing situation becomes more vivid if we consider an analogue of it, the following game, where side payments, payoffs among players, are not allowed. The game is described by the following payoff matrix.

Alternative	Payoff to		
	A	B	C
1	30	10	20
2	20	30	10
3	10	20	30

In this situation, the three players, A, B, and C must select a single alternative from among 1, 2, and 3. If they choose 1, A receives 30 dollars (or jobs if the payoff is patronage in a political situation), B receives 10, and C receives 20. If alternative 2 is chosen, A receives 20, B receives 30, and C receives 10. If they choose 3, A receives 10, B receives 20, and C receives 30. Examining this situation, we can see that A prefers 1, B prefers 2, and C prefers 3. Since side-payments are not allowed, there is nothing in the structure of the situation that will enable the three participants to come to some agreement about the selection of the alternative. If side-payments were permitted, the three could agree on alternative 1, for example, and A could give B a payment of 10; there would then be an equal division of the rewards, one possible and common outcome. The situation is indeed perplexing, and nothing in its structure gives a clue to its solution. As we have defined the situation, even the decision-rule is not specified; we have not said whether a majority vote or a unanimous choice is required to select the alternative.

Another possible way of obtaining a group choice in this situation would be to present two of the three alternatives, have the three players choose the one they prefer, and then have them compare the third alternative with the alternative they preferred from the first pair. However, if this is done, the order of presentation of alternatives will effect the outcome. For example, if 2 and 3 are compared first, 2 will be preferred by a majority. Then, if 2 is compared to 1, 1 will be preferred by the majority and will be the group choice. If, however, the first pair considered is 1 and 3, and then 2 is compared with the survivor, the group choice will be 2. For theorists seeking a rational, universal social choice procedure, the fact that the order of presentation of alternatives effects the outcome is highly unsatisfactory.

Situations such as this and similar aberrant situations helped to stimulate mathematicians to investigate the formal properties of election processes. The general problem the theorists attempted to solve can be stated as, "How can we design an election procedure that will produce a result consistent with the preference patterns of the participants? How can we design an election procedure so that the order of the presentation of alternatives does not spuriously determine the outcome? How can we assure ourselves that the 'wrong' candidate is not selected?" Borda, Condorcet, Laplace, Francis Galton, C. L. Dodgson (Lewis Carroll) and others have considered the problem.[4]

In the late nineteenth century, and in this century, economists set themselves the task of discovering a social welfare function, a general rule or process by which any given set of individual preference patterns could be merged into a social choice. For the purpose of this discussion, the social welfare function can be defined as follows.[5]

> *Social welfare function*—a rule or process which produces a group or social choice from the individual orderings of alternatives or from the preferences of the individuals involved. The rule must produce a satisfactory social choice, in every case, no matter how contradictory the preferences of the individuals involved.

In a work that has since become classic, Arrow (1963) demonstrated that given a number of reasonable conditions about the choice structure, where there are at least two persons involved and three or more alternatives to choose from, it is not possible to construct a general social welfare function. He also demonstrated that where the alternatives are limited to two, no matter how many persons are involved, the majority decision rule is a satisfactory social welfare function. Arrow's work served as a stimulus to a variety of theoretical studies of the normative question.

THE NORMATIVE AND THE DESCRIPTIVE PROBLEMS

The problem of combining individual preferences into a social choice has both normative and descriptive aspects. The normative question is, briefly, how *should* we combine individual preferences to obtain sensible, consistent, or rational results? The descriptive question is, essentially, how *do* individuals, groups, and economists actually amalgamate their preferences?

For two reasons it seems appropriate to raise the descriptive question. First, Arrow has shown that, if we allow only ordinal measurement or ranking, it is not possible to obtain a general social welfare function. But the fact that Arrow has demonstrated the impossibility of the abstract task does not prevent individuals from actually merging their preferences. Each day innumerable decisions of this kind are arrived at. In fact, attempts to circumvent the Arrow paradox raise behavioral or descriptive questions. Luce and Raiffa (1957) discuss a number of ways of overcoming the difficulties presented by Arrow. These include obtaining more data about the values or preferences of the participants. This process involves utilizing behavioral scaling methods, and also gives some information about the strengths of preferences of the participants. Where we can obtain measures of the strengths of preferences by utilizing risky alternatives, lotteries, and well-established behavioral scaling techniques, we can often obtain a satisfactory resolution of difficult social decision questions (Luce and Raiffa 1957:ch. 14).

Consider the following example of two persons, A and B, and two alternatives, 1 and 2. A ranks the alternatives 1, 2; B ranks the alternatives 2, 1. If we assume that neither party has sufficient power to determine the outcome, the preference structures lead to a stalemate, an irreconcilable conflict. However, if we can take into consideration the strengths of preferences of the participants, the following example makes it clear how trivial the case can be. Consider the case of a husband and wife who are considering going to a movie (1) or a concert (2). The husband prefers 2, the wife prefers 1. If the husband's preference of 2 over 1 is only slight, but the wife's preference is very great—she actively dislikes the music being performed on that night—in all likelihood, the conflict will be resolved in favor of going to the movie, and with relatively little effort and ill-feeling.

Even this example reveals that people in actual social decision situations have a variety of techniques for resolving difficult problems of social choice. The resolutions may or may not be optimal or particularly rational, but it is of considerable interest to examine the techniques carefully.

RELATIONSHIP TO PSYCHOLOGY AND ANTHROPOLOGY

For some time now, psychologists have seen the relationship of the issues raised here to their attempts to describe and explain human behavior. Anthropologists, however, have been slow to see the relevance of such problems to their own work, and so it is worthwhile to make that relevance explicit. These problems undoubtedly have bearing on the intellectual activity of anthropologists, both to those doing what may be called traditional anthropology—qualitative, holistic studies of social groups or societies—and to those anthropologists who are doing more behavioral, quantitative studies.

The point has certainly been made before that the traditions and customs of any social group or society serve, among other functions, that of conflict resolution. Most conflicts in a social group contain some element of conflict of interest or, in the terms of this analysis, conflicting preference patterns. The traditions and customs of both Western and non-Western societies prevent conflicts from arising that stem from contradictory preference patterns, and are, therefore, conflict resolution mechanisms. These conflicts may exist in many domains of behavior: the economic domain, the family-personal domain, the domain of permissible sexual behavior, and the domain of political behavior.

Incest taboos may be interpreted as quite successful attempts to prevent family members from expressing their sexual preferences for each other. The assignment of certain economic activities to certain families or subgroups of a particular society serves to prevent other members of the society from expressing their preferences for desirable occupations, with the resultant economic conflict. Established matrilocal or patrilocal residence patterns avoid the conflicts that might arise among newlyweds about where they are to reside, should they have conflicting personal preferences about the matter. Many of our traditions or customs could have arisen out of a need to resolve conflicts that are seen to be either inevitable or very likely.

The research that could be done using the methods of analysis employed here should be of interest to anthropologists. Indeed, they have been doing this kind of research for quite some time, without the benefits that quantitative analysis yields. Some cross-cultural research on methods of conflict resolution has been done by social psychologists working, generally, with literate Western societies. It would be of considerable value to look at the conflict resolution mechanisms of non-Western societies and national groups.[6]

The notion of maximization provides us with an important, provocative problem, one that may stimulate an amount of interesting cross-cultural research. The theory of games and the literature dealing with social choice involve the assumption that individuals behave in such a way as to maximize some value, either monetary payoff or a utility of some kind. The decision-making literature indicates that this assumption is not wholly realistic or descriptive of behavior in our Western culture, but at the same time the evidence is such that we cannot deny that some notion of maximization, or action in one's interest, is characteristic of much human behavior. Thus the degree to to which the maximization notion is an adequate descriptive or explanatory principle is an unanswered question. An even more provocative and stimulating question is the degree to which a maximization notion is descriptive of nonliterate groups. Cross-cultural research using situations such as the Condorcet paradox, two-person games, and three-person games involving coalitions should yield fascinating results.

HOW DECISIONS ARE ACTUALLY MADE

In the discussion above we saw that Arrow demonstrated that given certain reasonable conditions, it is not possible to obtain a general social welfare function; but we also saw an example of a husband and wife who, with little effort, were able to make a satisfactory social choice, although they had contradictory preference patterns, by taking into account each other's strengths of preference.

Difficulties arise when preference patterns are contradictory. Often but not always, persons involved in making a choice have consistent preference patterns that enable them to make a large number of group choices with little difficulty. In addition, persons who cluster together often have similar preference patterns over a wide range of choice domains prior to their interaction in a group. As they function together and interact, their preference patterns become more similar, resulting in a large number of social choices that are made with little difficulty.[7] However, many situations yield a constellation of preference patterns that lead to disagreement about social choice, and it is these perplexing situations that present the intellectual and practical challenges.

The conduct of international affairs provides us with situations in which numerous anomalous and paradoxical preference patterns exist. It is often difficult in international affairs to make side-payments. Husbands and wives, political leaders in a legislature, faculty members in a university department, and the employees of complex organizations often have many ways in which they can bargain, negotiate, and effect side-payments—ways that enable them to effect satisfactory social choices in difficult situations. But in the conduct of international affairs the fundamental interests of the participants are often in intractable conflict, and internal constraints—national politics—may operate on the leaders to prevent them from striking what might be desirable bargains.

If we examine just how group decisions are arrived at, we may note that a variety of behavioral processes or factors influence the outcome. These vary from the power of the various members—for a single member of the group may have sufficient power to determine the group choice—to the strength of preferences of the participants and the personality and intellectual characteristics of those involved. We will discuss the various determining behavioral processes under the following headings.

1. The distribution of power
2. The joint welfare function
3. Bargaining and coalition processes
4. Individual differences and characteristics of the participants
5. Group processes and phenomena
6. Previous experiences and commitments of the group members, and the possibility of future interaction

The Distribution of Power

In many situations the social choice is effected rather simply and directly. A single person has the power to determine the decision, and where the preference patterns of those involved are contradictory or anomalous, he exercises that power. The dictatorial father who decides where the family shall live; the president of a small college who makes an appointment when his deans and faculty cannot agree; the president of a small company who holds 51 percent of the stock of the company and who makes a decision by himself when his employees are in hopeless disagreement—all these are examples of the exercise of dictatorial power.[8]

At the opposite extreme from the situation of dictatorial power is a situation in which power is equally distributed among all participants involved in the decision process. Perhaps the most vivid and detailed example of such a situation is the election described in C. P. Snow's novel, *The Master*. Snow describes in detail the bargaining, personal preferences, unconscious processes, and other considerations that exist when a group of eleven men, all with equal power and the desire to exercise it, produce a social choice.

However, in most decision situations the power is not so simply distributed among the participants in the decision; in the large number of social choice situations power is neither equally divided among all participants nor does a single person hold sufficient power to determine the decision. More often power is diffused among participants, with some having a great deal, others having very little, and some having a moderate amount. Often the exact distribution of power among those involved is not known even to the participants. Each has some approximate estimation of the power distribution, but the distribution of power may be only imprecisely defined, and judgments about relative power may differ.

To obtain an understanding of how social choices are made, it is necessary to clarify the role of power in the decision process. Although there have been many interesting speculative analyses of power in the sociological literature, little of it sheds useful light on the social choice problem.[9] Recently, however, the literature of game theory has produced some insightful notions that bear directly on the processes of social choice. Subsequent sections of this paper will deal with the distribution and role of power among a group of persons who must effect a social choice. Shapley's ideas (Shapley 1953), as well as those of Shapley and Shubik (1952), will be discussed; their notion of power is termed σ-power here. A notion of power, termed δ-power will be introduced which will emphasize the participants' perception of their own power to influence the decision process.

σ - Power

Shapley and Shubik have offered a method for evaluating the distribution of power in social choice situations where a specific decision must be made and the voting power of each participant is known. A committee in which each member has a single vote, the Security Council of the United Nations where the major powers have a veto, and a corporation where the power is distributed according to the ownership of stock are examples of bodies in which such situations occur.

The notion of power, which is termed σ-power here, attempts to solve the problem that is raised by the fact that power is not always distributed exactly as votes are distributed. When one man holds 51 percent of the stock in a corporation, for many purposes he holds complete power, and the decision processes of such a group usually reflect this reality. The persons involved usually defer to the power-holder. They attempt to influence decisions by influencing the majority stockholder. In the situation in which each person has a single vote the σ-power distribution is identical to the distribution of votes. In a group of four persons, where the votes are distributed 10-5-5-1, the person holding the ten has more than 50 percent of the power, though his votes total less than 50 percent of the total.

Shapley and Shubik offer a definition of power in which the power of each member of a decision-making group depends on the chance he has of being crucial to the success of a winning coalition; the chance he has of effecting a winning coalition. Hence, where one man is a winning coalition he has complete power; where each person has a single vote, each has equal σ-power. In situations between these extremes, the power distribution is not so clear, and the calculation of σ-power is more subtle.

The Shapley and Shubik definition of power does not take into consideration the many personal, political, and sociological factors that affect any analysis of power in an actual social choice but, as they point out, their scheme is a very useful first approximation of the actual power distribution in a committee or group situation. They explain the general rationale for their definitions of power as follows:

Consider a group of individuals all voting on some issue. They vote in order and, as soon as a majority has voted for a resolution, it is declared passed. The voting order of the members is chosen randomly and it is possible to compute the frequency with which an individual belongs to the group whose votes are used to effect the decisions; and more importantly, it is possible to compute how often the person's vote is pivotal. The number of times the person is pivotal, yields the index of σ-power. This index yields a measure of the number of times the action of an individual affects the decision, changing the state of affairs of the group. The Shapley and Shubik scheme credits an individual with $1/n$th power where there are n persons, each holding one vote. If votes are weighted unequally, the resulting power distribution is complicated. Generally more votes mean more power, but σ-power does not increase in direct proportion to an increase in votes.

Considering the passage of a bill in our executive-congressional system, the σ-power of the House of Representatives, the Senate, and the President are in the proportion of 5:5:2; and the σ-power indices for a single congressman, single senator, and the President are in the proportion 2:9:350. In the U. N. Security Council, which consists of eleven members, five of whom have vetoes, the σ-power measure gives 98.7 percent to the Big Five and 1.3 percent to the six small powers. Each major nation has a power ratio greater than 90 to 1 over a single smaller nation. A share owner in a corporation, who holds 40 percent of the stock with the remaining 60 percent distributed equally among 600 small share owners has a power index of 66.6 percent. The 400:1 ratio in share holdings yields a power advantage greater than 1,000 to 1.[10]

It is quite clear that this very precise measure of power in a committee system is only an approximation of the realities of the decision process in social choice situations. As a result, it is necessary to introduce another concept, δ-power, which is designed to describe the power distribution the participants in a decision process actually act upon.

δ-Power

In some committees or social decision situations, where the decision-rules and voting weights are explicitly formulated, the σ-power index can serve as an excellent first approximation of the actual distribution of power among the participants. When the appropriate historical, sociological, and psychological analysis is done, it is possible to obtain a realistic picture of the role power plays in effecting the social choice. However, in a large number of social choice situations decision mechanisms are not explicitly defined, and the participants behave on the basis of their own beliefs about, or their own perceptions of, their power. Understanding these phenomena is essentially the understanding of a set of beliefs, a social-psychological process. Any analysis of a complex social choice process, where the power mechanisms are not explicitly defined, requires this analysis of the δ-power distribution—an analysis of the participants' beliefs about their own power to influence the decision.

The σ-power and δ-power analyses are not unrelated, for in the dictatorship situation and in the situation of equal or nearly equal distribution of power, the participants ordinarily have reasonably accurate perceptions of their power. In the former situation the persons involved usually attempt to effect the decision by influencing the powerful person; in the latter situation the persons involved are usually aware that their power is $1/n$th of the total. In the situations between these two extremes, where it takes some effort to compute the σ-power distribution even when we know the Shapley formula, the most confusion occurs, and the participants may be confused or uncertain about their power.

In complex organizations, this complex and indefinite power situation is often present. Two, three, ten, or even more people may share the power to determine a decision. A detailed analysis of the facts of the situation and the perceptions and beliefs of the participants is necessary to untangle the threads of the power relations.

The Joint Welfare Function

In the example of the husband and wife who had contradictory preference patterns, we saw that the conflict was solved simply and directly. This resolution was made possible because the husband perceived that his wife had a strong distaste for alternative 2 and a strong preference for alternative 1, while he had only a slight preference for 2 over 1. Difficult social choices may be resolved by taking into account the strengths of preferences of the participants. A decision process that allows a single group member to veto a proposal makes explicit use of the belief that a single, strong negative preference should be allowed to outweigh all other positive preferences. The veto provisions of the U. N. Security Council voting procedures and the ability to veto entrance into membership into college fraternities and adult social clubs are examples of this process.

When this technique is used and persons involved in the social choice process take into account the strength of preferences of other participants, it becomes clear that some intuitive process involving interpersonal comparisons of utility is involved. We may hypothesize that the decision process is one in which some *Joint Welfare Total* is maximized. Where a difficult social choice decision is made, we hypothesize that intuitive interpersonal comparisons of utilities are made.[11]

If we examine the husband-wife decision to go to the movie in these terms, the following analysis may shed light on the decision. We assign the following utilities to the situation.

Alternative	Payoff to		Joint Payoff
	H	W	Sum
1	8	10	18
2	10	−30	−20

If the couple goes to the movie—alternative 1 is selected—the payoff to the group is 18 whereas if they go to the concert—select alternative 2—the payoff to the group is − 20.

It is possible to develop a more sophisticated line of reasoning using a simple algebraic model suggested by Sawyer.[12] We have hypothesized that a group tends to select the outcome that offers the highest joint welfare total (JWT). The JWT may be computed as follows:

Let individuals be designated A, B, . . ., Z.

The payoffs to the individuals are $P_a, P_b, \ldots, P_z$.

The alternatives to be chosen from are designated $1, 2, \ldots, n$.

The payoff to the set of individuals for the various alternatives are designated $P_{a1}, P_{a2}, \ldots, P_{zn}$.

A payoff to another person may not have the same value to oneself as an equal payment to oneself. This may be expressed in the model by assuming that a payoff to another person is some fraction or multiple of the payoff to oneself. Then the parameters that reduce a payment to another to a payment to oneself may be designated:

$$x_{ab}, x_{ac}, \ldots, x_{ba}, x_{bc}, \ldots, x_{zx}, x_{zy}$$

where x_{ab} is the fraction that transforms a payment to B into a payment to A.

The members of a group that is faced with a decision communicate among themselves, and in this process they are able to communicate to each other—in some intuitive or perhaps explicit way—the utilities of the various alternatives to each other. Once these communications are possessed by the members of the group, some intuitive multi-person, interpersonal comparison of utilities process occurs. Discussions, bargaining, clarifications, and the like occur, and then the group choice is made.

We are now in a position to examine how a group of individuals may determine the JWT of the various alternatives from which they must select a group choice. Consider the example of the payoff matrix presented on page 96. The JWT's may be computed once the parameters are hypothesized.[13] If, for person A, a payoff to another person is worth one half of a payment to himself, then $x_{ab} = x_{ac} = 0.5$; and if for person B, a payoff to another is worth just as much as a payoff to himself, then $x_{ba} = x_{bc} = 1$; and if for C, a payoff to another is worth only one-one hundredth of a payment to himself, then $x_{ca} = x_{cb} = 0.01$. The JWT's can be computed using the following formulas:

$$\text{JWT (Alt. 1)} = P_{a1} + (x_{ab}P_{b1} + x_{ac}P_{c1}) + P_{b1} + (x_{ba}P_{a1} + x_{bc}P_{c1})$$
$$+ P_{c1} + (x_{ca}P_{a1} + x_{cb}P_{b1})$$

$$\text{JWT (Alt. 2)} = P_{a2} + (x_{ab}P_{b2} + x_{ac}P_{c2}) + P_{b2} + (x_{ba}P_{a2} + x_{bc}P_{c2})$$
$$+ P_{c2} + (x_{ca}P_{a2} + x_{cb}P_{b2})$$

$$\text{JWT (Alt. 3)} = P_{a3} + (x_{ab}P_{b3} + x_{ac}P_{c3}) + P_{b3} + (x_{ba}P_{a3} + x_{bc}P_{c3})$$
$$+ P_{c3} + (x_{ca}P_{a3} + x_{cb}P_{b3})$$

Substituting the values of the first payoff matrix and the values of $x_{ab}, x_{ac}, \cdots, x_{cb}$ we can compute the value of JWT (Alt. 1):

$$JWT \text{ (Alt. 1)} = 30 + [0.5(10 + 20)] + 10$$

$$+ [1(30 + 20)] + 20 + [0.01(30 + 10)] = 125.4$$

Similarly:

$$JWT \text{ (Alt. 2)} = 110.5 \quad \text{and} \quad JWT \text{ (Alt. 3)} = 125.3$$

Since the Joint Welfare Totals of Alt. 1 and Alt. 3 are approximately equal and larger than the Total of Alt. 2, we hypothesize that it is unlikely that Alt. 2 will be chosen. The probabilities of choosing Alt. 1 and Alt. 3 are approximately equal. However, the arguments concerning the JWT's are but one factor of the many that determine a social choice. For the simple example of the husband and wife who had to choose between the concert and the movie, the maximization of JWT appears to be an adequate hypothesis. In other more complex decision situations, the many factors dealt with in this paper may modify the decision. For example, where one person has the power to determine the decision, he may select the alternative that maximizes the payoff to himself, though another alternative might have a higher JWT. Some other relevant factors will be discussed below.

Bargaining and Coalition Formation

When persons must combine contradictory preferences into a social choice in situations in which the power distribution does not permit a single individual to determine the outcome, the process is successfully completed usually because the participants are able to bargain, negotiate, form coalitions, compromise, and make side-payments among themselves. The social choice situation in a realistic setting is ordinarily complex enough so that the persons involved may effect a satisfactory social choice by producing an outcome that yields some rewards to each participant who holds some power. This procedure of dividing the rewards of the social choice situation is analogous to the payoff function—and the phenomenon of making side-payments—of game theory. In fact, in the earlier explication of the Condorcet effect, the ordinal statements of the original paradox were transformed into a game-like statement, assuming cardinal measures of the utilities.

Thus, the theory of games of strategy may be seen to be a theory for the production of social choices among individuals with different preference patterns. Payoff functions are the ways of expressing the preference patterns of the persons involved; the person prefers the outcome with the largest payoff to himself, or in the case of the non-zero-sum game, the alternative with the highest Joint Welfare Total.

[Game theory has both descriptive and normative aspects. The entire corpus of solution theory may be considered prescriptions for the production of reasonable social choices. Two-person, zero-sum theory prescribes a reasonable value of a game when the parties involved are in direct conflict. In two-person, non-zero-sum, and n-person theory, solutions—to the extent that they are successful—prescribe the social choices the parties should make when elements of conflict and cooperation are both present.]

In a series of papers, Thomas Schelling has offered some hypotheses concerning bargaining processes and has related them to choices, decisions, and strategies in the conduct of international affairs. Schelling is primarily responsible for an entire reorientation of game theory, from the zero-sum, non-zero-sum orientation to one in which social choices are viewed as being on a continuum, from pure coordination through mixed motive games to pure conflict games. Schelling has offered a variety of provocative hypotheses about the role of communication, bargaining, threats, promises, and a variety of other behavioral phenomena. Schelling's work can also be interpreted as offering hypotheses concerning certain social choice problems (Schelling 1960).

Since most social choices can be effected only if coalitions are formed, processes of coalition formation must be understood if an understanding of social choice mechanisms is to be obtained. Gamson (1964:81–110) recently reviewed experimental studies of coalition formation and found "an encouraging convergence of theoretical explanations of coalition formation." He discusses four "theories" of coalition formation: a minimum resource theory, a minimum power theory, an anticompetitive theory, and an utter confusion theory.

The minimum resource theory "emphasizes the initial resources to effect a decision which the players bring to the situation, rather than their strategic bargaining position." The central hypothesis states that a coalition will form in which the total resources (weights or votes) are as small as possible, while still being sufficient to effect a decision favorable to the coalition that has formed (Gamson 1964:86).

The minimum power theory is a modification of the minimum resource theory. It makes use of the Shapley value and states that all participants will demand a share of the payoff proportional to their pivotal power (σ-power). This pivotal power hypothesis is again a minimum resource hypothesis, but in this case the power of the winning coalition is defined by the Shapley value, σ-power (Gamson 1964:88).

Gamson (1964:90) describes a hypothesis about the formation of coalitions derived from the work of Vinacke and his associates. Players whose behavior supports the anticompetitive hypothesis are focused on maintaining the social relationships in the group. An anticompetitive norm exists against efforts to strike the most advantageous deal possible. Coalitions will form along the lines of least resistance.

The fourth hypothesis is an "utter confusion theory" (Gamson 1964:92):

Many coalition situations are conducted under conditions which are not at all conducive to rational calculation and analysis. It is well known that political conventions, for example, are frequently scenes of bedlam. Thus, according to this theory, coalition formation is best understood as an essentially random choice process. The coalition which forms will be the result of such fortuitous events as a chance encounter or a missed telephone call.

Individual Differences

When individuals actually are attempting to merge their preferences into a social choice, the characteristics of the individuals undoubtedly play some role. It is possible to hypothesize that certain cognitive-intellective factors such as intelligence, bargaining ability, and persuasiveness do have an effect. Some people may be particularly skillful bargainers, or particularly skillful in the task of persuasion, and they may effect a social choice in their favor. Also, certain personality factors may affect outcomes: a more aggressive person may be more effective in causing the outcome to be favorable to himself. Even though at this time it is not possible to specify what particular factors or individual characteristics do affect outcomes, there is every reason to believe, a priori, that individual characteristics do affect outcomes.

The few studies that have been done that have attempted to examine the effect of individual differences on bargaining and negotiation behavior have been rather disappointing.[14] Undoubtedly, individual differences do affect the outcomes of bargaining processes; however, until now it has been difficult to specify precisely what individual characteristics affect outcomes in a particular way. This is probably because our studies of individual differences, though there are many of

them, have not isolated significant factors that affect bargaining behavior. It may also be that the part played by individual differences
may be small and may be masked by the formal, structural properties
of the bargaining situations.[15]

Group Processes

The extensive literature of the field of small groups bears upon the
present analysis, which deals with the summation of individual preferences of members of a small group. Although the literature is unco-
ordinated and contains few, if any, general principles that further our
understanding of the processes of social choice, numerous studies yield
isolated results that are relevant to the present problem. Vinacke and
Arkoff (1957:406–14) and Lieberman (1962:203–20) found that in cases
of three-person interaction two individuals may unite and form a
coalition against a third whom they perceive as stronger in order to
gain rewards from the stronger-appearing person. Schelling, too, has
argued that in a bargaining situation the weaker member may gain concessions from the stronger because the two have coordinate interests
and the stronger must yield concessions to the weaker (Schelling 1960).

Careful review of the small group literature would undoubtedly
reveal other studies that describe phenomena and characteristics of
individuals functioning in a group situation which will shed light on
social choice processes. These many phenomena considered together
may detail a picture that is not particularly elegant or simple, but then
it is likely that an understanding of the processes of social choice,
when we obtain it, will not be simple or elegant either.

Past and Future Commitments

One set of processes that undoubtedly have great influence on the
social choice problem, but have been virtually unstudied, are the processes involving the effect of past commitments and decisions, and
anticipations of the effect of future social choice situations and commitments on the present problem. Difficult social choice situations,
where preference patterns are hopelessly contradictory, may be resolved because of the past experience of the group, or because those
members of the group who have their preferences satisfied can make
commitments about future social choices, making concessions or
promises in advance.[16]

The group in an actual social choice situation is usually one with
a significant past history and with the prospect of a continued lengthy

existence. This feature often enables the participants to make a difficult social choice but is particularly difficult to study experimentally and even empirically. However, a thorough treatment of the question of social choice must deal with such questions.

CONCLUSION

The general problem raised in this paper, that of understanding the processes involved when a group of individuals must amalgamate their preferences to produce a social choice, has been seen to be a very general and complex one. It will be very difficult to study all its aspects in a single empirical or experimental study; actually the problem reduces to a number of subproblems, about which some evidence and knowledge already exists. This evidence comes from studies of bargaining and coalition processes, theoretical discussions of the interpersonal comparison of utilities, and theoretical and empirical studies of the role of power in decision processes.

The particular way this paper analyzes the general problem is, of course, not the only way it can be conceptualized. The rubrics under which the various discussions were organized were used primarily because they were convenient and, to some extent, convincing. Further analyses and study may very well yield another, equally convincing, but somewhat different organization. For example, the entire discussion of the interpersonal comparison of utility might very well have been subsumed under the discussion of individual differences. The parameters hypothesized may account for much of the variance involved in social choice processes, and these parameters may reflect stable characteristics of individuals and differ significantly among individuals.

At any rate, when our understanding of social choice processes is deepened and organized, it is likely that a complex picture of many factors operating, and operating with interactions among them, will emerge. As already stated, it does not matter how some persons value a payoff to others in a group if the others have the power to determine the group decision. To understand such a social choice it is necessary to understand the preference patterns of the powerful members of the group and how the less powerful members influence the decision-makers. Carefully done experimental and empirical studies are necessary to develop an understanding of social choice processes.

NOTES

1. Before preparing the initial draft of this paper, I was not able to find any theoretical discussions of the descriptive questions involved, and only one empirical study. After I had distributed copies of the draft, Professor Harrison White told me of Professor James Coleman's current work on the problem. Coleman's ideas can be found in his "Collective Decisions," *Sociological Inquiry* (Spring 1964), pp. 166–81; "Foundations for a Theory of Collective Decisions," *Amer. Journal of Sociology*, 71 (May 1966), pp. 615–27, "The Possibility of a Social Welfare Function", mimeo., Johns Hopkins University, November 1964. There are some similarities between Professor Coleman's and my own work, though he has taken a somewhat different—more normative—approach. The one empirical study is Clyde Coombs, "Social Choice and Strength of Preference," in R. M. Thrall, C. H. Coombs, and R. L. Davis, eds., *Decision Processes*, New York: Wiley, 1954. This paper offers the thesis that a considerable body of work done in other contexts can be interpreted to be related to the social choice question.

2. Two different problems have been mixed together in this introductory discussion: social choices in large groups such as national elections, and social choices in small groups or committees. The ideas presented in this paper are relevant to decision-making by small groups and committees. Since the literature, until now, has dealt with the normative question, it was really not necessary to make this distinction. However, the empirical processes involved in elections, where n is large, and in decisions by small groups are obviously quite different.

3. For a discussion of the history of the general problem and the Condorcet effect see: Arrow (1963); Luce and Raiffa (1957:ch. 14); Duncan Black, *The Theory of Committees and Elections,* Cambridge: Cambridge U. Press, 1958; and William H. Riker, "Voting and the Summation of Preferences," *Amer. Political Science Rev.*, 55 (December 1961), pp. 900–11.

4. See the references in note 3, especially Black, for discussion of the contribution of each of these men.

5. This definition is not rigorous but will serve for the present discussion. For a rigorous definition see Arrow (1963:23). p. 23.

6. I am aware of two articles in the anthropology literature that make use of the notions discussed here. They are: Frederik Barth, "Segmentary Opposition and the Theory of Games: A Study of Pathan Organization," *J. of the Royal Anthropological Inst.*, 89:5–21; and William Davenport, "Jamaican Fishing, A Game Theory Analysis," in *Papers on Caribbean Anthropology* (Yale U. Publications in Anthropology Nos. 57–64) 59, pp. 3–4.

7. It seems worthwhile to make this obvious point because the social choice literature seems to concern itself only with preference patterns leading to conflict. Of course, these are the provocative situations.

8. The terms dictatorship and dictatorial power are used here, as they are in the social choice literature, with no opprobrium or other value judgement attached.

9. For other discussions of power see: Robert Bierstedt, "An Analysis of Social Power," *Amer. Sociological Rev.*, 15 (December 1950), pp. 730–36; Amitai Etzioni, *Modern Organizations*, Englewood Cliffs: Prentice-Hall, 1964; Herbert Goldhamer and Edward Shils, "Types of Power and Status," *Amer. Sociological Rev.*, 45 (September 1939), pp. 171–82; John R. P. French, Jr., "A Formal Theory of Social Power," *Psychological Rev.*, 63 (May 1956), pp. 181–94; Harold D. Lasswell and Abraham Kaplan, *Power and Society*, New Haven: Yale U. Press, 1950; John C. Harsanyi, "Measurement of Social Power in n-Person Reciprocal Power Situations,"

Behavioral Science 7 (January 1962), pp. 81–91. The empirical work most directly related to the ideas expressed here has been done by Edgar Vinacke and his students and colleagues. A number of studies have been done dealing with power and coalition formation in three-person groups. References can be found in George Psathas and Sheldon Stryker, "Bargaining Behavior and Orientations in Coalition Formation," *Sociometry*, 28 (June 1965), pp. 124–44.

10. This discussion follows the Shapley and Shubik presentation very closely. For further discussion of these ideas see Shapley and Shubik (1952:787–91).

11. A word seems to be in order about the frank use here of interpersonal comparisons of cardinal utilities. It is generally agreed that we have no satisfactory formal treatment of cardinal utilities that will enable us to make rigorous statements about interpersonal comparisons of the utilities. However, this paper contends that it is profitable to hypothesize that individuals do make intuitive, interpersonal comparisons of the various alternatives facing them, and that these comparisons serve as one determinant of many social choices. Specifically the hypothesis offered is that a joint welfare total is maximized. It is also possible, I believe, that this hypothesis can, with a bit of effort, be confirmed or refuted by experimental and empirical work. Discussion of the problem can be found in Luce and Raiffa (1957:33, 131, 345); John C. Harsanyi, "Cardinal Welfare, Individualistic Ethics and Interpersonal Comparisons of Utility," *Jl. Political Economy*, 63 (1955), pp. 309–21; Clifford Hildreth, "Alternative Conditions for Social Orderings," *Econometrica*, 21 (1953), pp. 81–94; and John C. Harsanyi, "Cardinal Utility in Welfare Economics and in the Theory of Risk-Taking" *Jl. Political Economy* 61 (1953), pp. 434–35.

Discussions of the problem of interpersonal comparisons of utility are complex and contradictory. To compound the confusion, a group of statisticians identified as "Bayesian Statisticians" have recently advanced arguments that imply—if they do not explicitly state—that individuals are able or can be taught to make interpersonal comparisons of cardinal utilities. The root of the difficulty lies in the fact that our rigorous knowledge of the measurement of behavioral phenomena is inadequate and fragmentary. For a description of the Bayesian position, see Robert Schlaifer, *Probability and Statistics for Business Decisions,* New York: McGraw-Hill, 1959. For a discussion of the current state of measurement theory, see Patrick Suppes and Joseph L. Zinnes, "Basic Measurement Theory," in R. Duncan Luce, Robert Bush, and Eugene Galanter, eds., *Handbook of Mathematical Psychology,* V. I, New York: Wiley, 1963, pp. 1–76.

It is also possible, I believe, to demonstrate rigorously the possibility of making sensible interpersonal comparisons of utility. For the present, we assume that where payoffs are made using money, utility and money are equal.

12. I am indebted to Professor Jack Sawyer of the University of Chicago for suggesting this approach. He developed an Altruism Scale which is a measure "for assessing directly the value one places upon the welfare of another in relation to his own." Sawyer's method involved two people, Person and Other. The current treatment is a generalization of Sawyer's method. See: Jack Sawyer, "The Altruism Scale: A Measure of Cooperative, Individualistic, and Competitive Inter-personal Orientation," *Amer. Jl. of Sociology*, 71 (January 1966), pp. 407–16.

13. In actual analyses of specific social choices these parameters can be obtained using any one of many available scaling procedures. Sawyer has used ranking and direct scale estimation procedures. See Sawyer, pp. 3–9.

14. For a review of this literature see Philip S. Gallo, Jr. and Charles G. McClintock, "Cooperative and Competitive Behavior in Mixed-Motive Games," *Jl. of Conflict Resolution*, 9 (March 1965), pp. 68–78. Also, Fouraker and Siegel hypoth-

esize that three bargaining types exist: The simple maximizer (M), the rivalist (R), and the cooperator (C). The maximizer is concerned solely with his own profit; the rivalist may reduce his opponent's profit in his desire to surpass his rival; the cooperator derives some satisfaction from the prosperity of his opponent. See Lawrence Fouraker and Sidney Siegel, *Bargaining Behavior*, New York: McGraw-Hill, 1963.

15. Technical information and special competence can be considered individual characteristics that may be influential in some committee decisions. Often the person having such competence may have very little power, yet he may be most influential in effecting a decision.

16. Professor Coleman has treated this problem at greater length in his work cited above. In addition, he has discussed certain "alternatives to consent," such as crime and revolutionary activity. One could also consider withdrawal from the group and the use of violence as social choice mechanisms. However, these processes, though they often do produce a social choice, are beyond the scope of the present discussion.

REFERENCES

Arrow, Kenneth J. 1963. Social Choice and Individual Values. 2d ed. New York: Wiley.

Gamson, William. 1964. Experimental Studies of Coalition Formation *in* Advances in Experimental Social Psychology, I, ed. Leonard Berkowitz. New York: Academic Press.

Lieberman, Bernhardt. 1962. Experimental Studies of Conflict in Two-Person and Three-Person Games *in* Mathematical Methods in Small Group Processes, ed. Joan Criswell, Herbert Solomon, and Patrick Suppes. Stanford: Stanford U. Press.

Luce, R. D. and H. Raiffa. 1957. Games and Decisions. New York: Wiley.

Schelling, T. C. 1960. The Strategy of Conflict. Cambridge: Harvard U. Press.

Shapley, L. S. 1953. A Value for *n*-Person Games *in* Contributions to the Theory of Games, II, ed. H. W. Kuhn and A. W. Tucker. Princeton: Princeton U. Press.

Shapley, L. S. and Martin Shubik. 1952. A Method for Evaluating the Distribution of Power in a Committee System. American Political Science Rev. 48:787–92.

Vinacke, W. Edgar and Abe Arkoff. 1957. An Experimental Study of Coalitions in the Triad. American Sociological Rev. 22:406–14.

CHAPTER 6

Robert Kozelka

A Bayesian Approach
to Jamaican Fishing

IN Davenport's classic article (1960), he uses game theory to analyze strategies in a Jamaican fishing village. Allowing some leeway for the estimated numerical data, his results are in good accord with an overall minimax strategy by the fishermen. That is, he finds that to make the minimum gain as large as possible a certain mixed strategy is appropriate and that, in fact, the percentage of fishing captains following each of the pure strategies in the mixed strategy is as close as possible to this optimal strategy, given the discreteness involved.

The purpose of this paper is to examine further into the idea of optimal strategies, using, in particular, decision-theoretic notions rather than game-theoretic ones. The results cannot be any closer to observation than Davenport's (in fact, they are quite different), but the assumptions back of the ideas to be presented seem more realistic. In any case, the various decision-theory concepts may be more useful to the anthropologist than the basic notions of game theory.

A central assumption of two-person zero-sum game theory is that the second (minimizing) player is both rational and operating in such a way as to diametrically oppose the interests of the first player. The definition of rationality is clearly set forth in von Neumann and Morgenstern (1955:28): A *rational* man operates so as to maximize expected utility, or, in the game theory situation, to maximize minimum expected utility.

A great deal has been written about games against nature; see, for example, Savage (1954) and Blackwell and Girshick (1954). It is very doubtful whether nature consciously maximizes her expected

I wish to express my appreciation to the Summer Seminar in Quantitative Anthropology for the suggestion that the analysis presented here might be of interest.

utility, even assuming nature has a utility function. If we assume that the first player's utility reflects that of the second (i.e., that nature's utility for being fished can be measured by expected income in pounds), it is still generally agreed that any assumption regarding nature's malevolence is untenable. One should not, therefore, play a game against "inanimate nature" as one would play against a "rational" player. How, then, should one play?

Davenport writes, "Let it be quite clear that the writer in no way professes to understand the mathematics of proof of the theory of games as set forth by its authors." Similarly the present author forgoes any quarrel with Davenport's figures. The point of this article is: Given the estimates of average yield per fishing month, is there a "better" way to choose an optimal strategy? Although ordinary statistical decision theory deals with *losses* from certain strategies, the formulation here is in terms of *gains*; one may convert to the standard statistical format by replacing each gain g_i (average yield), by the quantity maxgain $-g_i$. This in no way changes the appropriate strategies under various rules.

Davenport also writes, "There is absolutely no way for the fishermen to predict when the current will come or go, nor can they tell from shore if the current is running or not." If this is the case, one can think of current as appearing randomly with probability (to use his figure) 0.25. It is time to introduce some terminology. We assume there are two "states of nature": $\theta' = $ current, $\theta'' = $ no current. The fishermen have three "actions": I = fish inside, I–O = fish in-out, O = fish outside. With the states of nature are associated "a priori probabilities": $w' = \Pr(\theta') = \frac{1}{4}$, $w'' = \Pr(\theta'') = \frac{3}{4}$. Using Davenport's figures, one also has a "gain table" or set of expected (monthly) payoffs as follows:

	I	I-O	O
θ'	17.3	5.2	−4.4
θ''	11.5	17.0	20.6

The reader will recognize the latter simply as Davenport's game matrix.

Now given no information about the actual state of nature except the a priori probabilities, the fishermen can calculate their expected gain, E, from each action using these a priori probabilities. We find

$$E[I] = \tfrac{1}{4}(17.3) + \tfrac{3}{4}(11.5) = 12.95$$
$$E[I–O] = 14.05$$
$$E[O] = 14.35.$$

Thus if the fisherman are "rational," in the sense of acting to maximize expected gain, they should take the one action they never take: Put all of their pots outside. If, in fact, "both figures for the outside strategy may be too low" (Davenport's observation), the expected gain would be even larger for action O.[1]

It is not difficult to see that if rational behavior is maximizing expected utility, then having only a priori probabilities and a gain table will always make the optimal strategy a single action, unless two or more actions lead to the same expected gain. One should note, furthermore, that the expected gain under this optimal strategy is higher (14.35) than that (13.3) achieved by the optimal mixed strategy derived from game-theoretic considerations.

Why this discrepancy in results? The answer is in the second assumption—the malevolence of nature. If the fishermen always take action O against a malevolent player (nature), that player will always play action C (current running) and the fishermen will lose 4.4. But suppose nature is not malevolent but only indifferent. Suppose further that nature "tips her hand" in the sense that there is a relation between current running and observed sea conditions. (We now go beyond Davenport's data in order to illustrate some further decision-theoretic concepts.) If θ' and θ'' continue to represent the states of nature, let Z' and Z'' represent the *observations* "sea conditions suggest current running" and "sea conditions suggest current not running," respectively. Further, suppose that what conditions suggest and the actual occurrence or nonoccurrence of current are compatible only ⅓ of the time. That is

$$\Pr(Z' \mid \theta') = \Pr(Z'' \mid \theta'') = \tfrac{1}{3}, \qquad \Pr(Z'' \mid \theta') = \Pr(Z' \mid \theta'') = \tfrac{2}{3}$$

(The numbers are for illustration only, to keep the computation simple.) On the basis of the sea conditions we can define nine "pure strategies," which are pairs of actions specifying what to do depending on whether Z' or Z'' is observed. They can be conveniently tabulated as in Table 1.

TABLE 1. PURE STRATEGIES

Strategy No.	Actions	G' = Exp. Gain $\mid \Theta'$	G'' = Exp. Gain $\mid \Theta''$
S_1	I, I	17.3	11.5
S_2	I, I–O	$9.2\overline{3}$	$13.\overline{3}$
S_3	I, O	$2.8\overline{3}$	$14.5\overline{3}$
S_4	I–O, I	$13.2\overline{6}$	$15.1\overline{6}$
S_5	I–O, I–O	5.2	17.0
S_6	I–O, O	-1.2	18.2
S_7	O, I	$10.0\overline{6}$	$17.5\overline{6}$
S_8	O, I–O	2.0	19.4
S_9	O, O	-4.4	20.6

In the strategy pairs, the first action entry refers to the action taken if Z' is observed and the second action entry refers to that taken if Z'' is observed. The expected gain is computed by multiplying the
. probability of taking the specific action by the gain of that action, given the appropriate state of nature, and then summing over the two actions. For example, given strategy S_3 and state of nature θ', one observes Z' —and hence takes action I —with probability ⅓ and gains 17.3, whereas if one observes Z'' he takes action O — with probability ⅔—and gains -4.4. The expected gain is thus

$$⅓(17.3) + ⅔(-4.4) = 2.8333 \ldots = 2.8\overline{3}$$

The computation for S_3 and θ'' is $⅓(11.5) + ⅔(20.6) = 14.5\overline{3}$. The other values are computed similarly.

It is clear by comparing the entries that the results of some strategies render those strategies undesirable. If the expected gains for a given strategy, S_j, are smaller *for each state of nature* than those for strategy S_i, we say S_i *dominates* S_j or that S_j is *not admissible*. From Table 1, S_2 and S_3 are dominated by S_4, S_5 is dominated by S_7, and S_6 by S_7 and S_8. Hence the *admissible* pure strategies are S_1, S_4, S_7, S_8, S_9. Of these, S_4 has its smaller gain larger than the smaller gain of any of the others, so it is the *maximin pure strategy*. (If we were dealing with losses, the corresponding idea would be to minimize the maximum loss, hence a *minimax strategy*.) Note that we have not defined the maximin strategy to be optimal, nor have we required a malevolent opponent. Several different definitions of optimality have been suggested, of which maximin is only one; (see, for example, Milnor 1954). In particular, maximin does not take account of the a priori probabilities w' and w''.

For only two possible states of nature, it is instructive and convenient to think of the expected gains as points in two-dimensional space. These are plotted in Fig. 1. Geometrically, a mixed strategy must

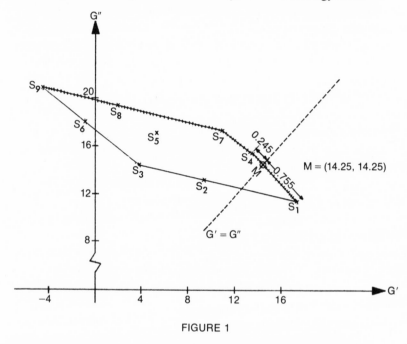

FIGURE 1

produce a point on the line segment joining its pure-strategy components, so the set of *all* expected gain points forms a "polyhedral convex set"; this set is the region bounded by the line segments in the figure. The cross-hatched line segments indicate the admissible mixed (and pure) strategies. It is clear from the figure that a strategy is dominated if it lies below and to the left of another strategy, and that a pure strategy may be dominated by a mixed strategy without being dominated by any other pure strategy. (For an extensive explanation of the geometry of the two-state problem, see Chernoff and Moses [1959].) Furthermore, the maximin strategy can now be found as the intersection of the line $G' = G''$ with the set of admissible strategies, and the proportions of the resulting line segment give the proper mixture of these strategies. For these data, the intersection is at the point

(14.25, 14.25) and the corresponding mixed strategy is at $(0.245S_1,$ $0.755S_4)$. This is indicated in the figure by M. A suitable adjustment handles the case where the line $G' = G''$ does not intersect the convex set of expected gain points.

We emphasize three points of the above argument: (1) Nowhere have we defined the maximin strategy to be "optimal." (2) While the concept of a mixed (randomized) strategy may have some validity for activities against rational opponents, as in determining hunting grounds by casting bones, the executive found by his board of directors to be making decisions by use of a random number table may soon be looking for another job. (3) The a priori probabilities of the states of nature have not been used.

Returning to von Neumann's definition of rationality, we define an optimal strategy as one which maximizes "expected" gain. Actually, since the expected gain table was constructed, as the name implied, from expected values, some other expectation must be involved. In fact, we will consider the expectation by the a priori probabilities of the entries in the expected gain table. Thus we are really trying to maximize expected expected gain—call this *Bayesian expected gain*, following the statistical terminology. For strategies S_1 and S_9 (and S_5, which is dominated), the Bayesian expected gains are simply the values computed at the beginning of this paper, since the actions involved are independent of the observations Z' and Z''. The Bayesian expected gains for all admissible pure strategies are as follows:

Strategy	S_1	S_4	S_7	S_8	S_9
Bayesian expected gain	12.95	14.69	15.70	15.05	14.35

These are computed, naturally, by taking the weighted average of the expected gains G' and G'' by the a priori probabilities w' and w'' respectively. Now since the expectation of a weighted sum is that sum of the component expectations, the Bayesian expected gain of a mixed strategy must lie between the Bayesian expected gains of the components. Thus the maximum Bayesian expected gain (called the Bayes expected gain corresponding to w' and w'') must occur at a pure strategy point (called the *Bayes strategy* corresponding to w' and w''). In the example, the Bayes expected gain is 15.70, occurring for the Bayes strategy S_7.

Again the geometry is instructive. The Bayesian expected gain, for a given strategy S_i, is $w'G' + w''G''$. For given w' and w'', $w'G' + w''G'' = k$ defines a family of parallel straight lines. These lines have nonpositive slope (since both w' and w'' are between 0 and 1), and k increases as the family is traversed upward and to the right. Hence to maximize the Bayesian expected gain by some strategy in the convex set is to find the line $w'G' + w''G'' = k_{max}$ which is farthest to the "northeast" and intersects the convex set. This is indicated in Fig. 2. The value of k_{max} is, of course, 15.70, occurring at the strategy point S_7 on the line $\frac{1}{4}\ G' + \frac{3}{4}\ G'' = 15.70$. We remark that

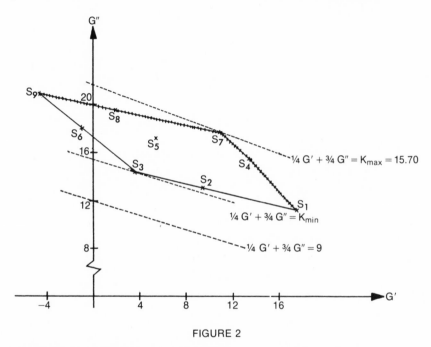

FIGURE 2

the maximizing straight line must intersect the strategy set in at least one pure strategy point, which means that if one makes decisions on the basis of Bayes strategies one need never consider mixed strategies. Whether or not such a result is desirable or realistic depends on one's definition of optimality.

SUMMARY

The purpose of this paper has been to investigate possible definitions of optimality in situations where the underlying assumptions of game theory seem to be inappropriate. Statisticians have long considered the idea of hostile nature, required for game theoretic optimality, to be meaningless or unnecessary. Without some further probabilistic assumptions, this does away with the concept of a minimax strategy in problems like those considered by Davenport in his paper on a Jamaican fishing village. Such problems, known to the statistical trade as "no-data" problems, are usually solved by directly maximizing expected gain (minimizing expected loss). However, the minimax optimal strategy reappears when decisions take into account expected gains (losses) based on nondeterministic observations which are related to nature's "strategies" (states). However, such optimality leaves out of account any a priori information available. Taking expectations over these a priori probabilities incorporates *all* of the various kinds of rational information. This, together with the usual optimality definition, results in one (or more) optimal pure strategies called Bayes strategies with corresponding maximized expected gain.

These ideas have been illustrated geometrically in the two-dimensional problem of Davenport. The results generalize in a straightforward fashion to problems of higher dimension. For these generalizations and for the relationship between Bayesian considerations and classical statistical test procedures the reader is invited to consult either Chernoff and Moses (1959) or Blackwell and Girshick (1954), depending on the level of his mathematical sophistication.

NOTES

1. It is not clear whether by "too low" Davenport means that the values 20.6 and − 4.4 should both be replaced by numbers *greater than those numbers* or *by numbers farther away from zero*. In the former case, the expected gain from strategy O would be even larger; in the latter, strategy O might no longer be optimal if − 4.4 is replaced by a *loss* which is *larger negatively*.

REFERENCES

Blackwell, D., and M. A. Girschick. 1954. Theory of Games and Statistical Decisions. New York: Wiley.

Chernoff, H. and L. E. Moses. 1959. Elementary Decision Theory, New York: Wiley.

Davenport, W. 1960. Jamaican Fishing: A Game Theory Analysis *in* Papers on Caribbean Anthropology: Yale U. Publications in Anthropology No. 59, pp. 3–11.

Luce, R. D., and H. Raiffa. 1957. Games and Decisions. New York: Wiley.

Milnor, J. 1954. Games Against Nature *in* Decision Processes, ed. R. M. Thrall et al., pp. 49–59. New York: Wiley.

Savage, L. J. 1954. The Foundations of Statistics. New York: Wiley.

von Neumann, J., and O. Morgenstern. 1955. Theory of Games and Economic Behavior, 3rd. ed. Princeton: Princeton U. Press.

PART **II**

EXPERIMENTAL
GAMES

CHAPTER 7

Anatol Rapoport

Games as Tools of Psychological Research

A psychologist's interest in games may stem from two different sources. First, he may view a game as a model of a situation abstracted from life, a replica cut down in size to be examined experimentally in the laboratory. Typical examples are business and military games, used both in teaching and research. Research in this sense is often understood as a search for answers to practical questions, questions of the form "What would happen if . . .?" Games of this sort (usually called simulations) have also been used to test psychological hypotheses: for example, whether the use of threats is or is not advantageous in certain types of bargaining situations, or whether persons with certain personality characteristics are more or less likely to take aggressive action and concomitant risks.

Clearly, the value of the answers to questions of this sort—their relevance to real life—depends crucially on the degree to which the simulation has captured the essentials of the real situation. Verisimilitude becomes an important factor in the design of such experiments. If abstraction and simplification are undertaken to increase control, and so presumably to facilitate analysis of the observations, an increase of "realism" must be paid for in greater difficulty of control and greater complexity of analysis. Where to draw the line so as to get the most from this tradeoff is always an important methodological question.

The psychologist may also become interested in games from another point of view. A record of a formal game of strategy is essentially a sequence of decisions made with a view of achieving certain ends. The psychologist may be interested in the thought processes which underlie such decisions. The logical analysis of games of strategy, however, was undertaken not by psychologists but by mathematicians. In their formulation, a game is a mathematical problem to be solved. A solution is defined in terms of certain strategies prescribed to respective players—or, where applicable, in terms of certain coalition formations and appropriate divisions of joint winnings—in such a way that the outcome of the game satisfies some intuitive notions of rationality. This means roughly that the outcome of the game is for each of the players the best that he could achieve, given the rules of the game and the constraints resulting from the strivings of all the other players to achieve their goals.

In seeking solutions of games, the mathematician is guided by certain mathematical criteria, which supposedly reflect the rationality of the players. It turns out that while, in some types of games, solutions that satisfy the proposed mathematical criteria also satisfy the intuitive notions of rationality. In other types of games this is not the case. These discrepancies put the concept of rationality itself under a cloud of ambiguity. It becomes clear that the deeper analysis of the very meaning of rationality would have to be undertaken if the term is to represent a useful point of reference either in the theory of decision or in psychology.

In what follows, we hope to show how this analysis leads into most interesting psychological problems. These problems arise not from the content of the situations (formal games have no content in the sense of relatedness to specific life situations) but rather from their logical structure. There is a hierarchy of levels of decision problems, and the concept of rational decision becomes progressively more dependent on specific psychological or even ethical hypotheses as we pass to more complex levels of decision problems. Game experiments, viewed as research tools from this basically theoretical point of view, may be considered as a method of generating, clarifying, and developing the ramifications of these hypotheses.

TYPES OF DECISION PROBLEMS AND GAMES

The simplest decision problem is one where the decision-maker (whom we shall call the player) has complete control of the outcomes. That is, the correspondence between his actions and the outcomes is one-to-one. If this correspondence is known, and if the player has a preference rank order for the outcomes, the rational decision is defined obviously as the choice of action which leads to the most preferred outcome.

In real life, decisions are often difficult because the correspondence between actions and outcomes is not known. However, important as it is for the subject to have factual knowledge about the situation in which he finds himself, the search for this knowledge, or a theory of how it is obtained, are not in the province of decision theory. Decision theory is concerned with the problem of arriving at a decision after all the available relevant facts are known. That such problems are far from trivial can be seen in those situations where the outcomes are not in one-to-one correspondence with the subject's choices; that is, where the subject does not control the situation alone. When the control of outcomes is divided among two or more players, we are dealing with decision problems which arise in games.

As an example, consider the following decision problem. The player is faced with the choice of saying Yes or No. He is told that if he says Yes, he may either lose $1 or win $5 depending on whether someone (or something) else chooses Yes or No respectively. Should the player say No, he will either lose $2 or win $10, again depending on whether someone's (or something's) decision will be Yes or No respectively. Moreover, the player is assured that the other decision is to be made independently (that is, in ignorance) of his own decision. The decision situation is pictured in Matrix 1 (Fig. 1). How shall a rational player decide?

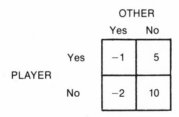

FIGURE 1. Matrix 1: Scheme of a decision problem in which the player has only partial control of the outcomes. An outcome is represented as a payoff to the Player which is determined by a pair of simultaneous choices, namely the Player's, who chooses a horizontal row, and the Other's, who chooses a vertical column.

In contrast to the previous decision problem, here the correspondence between choices and outcomes is not one-to-one. The one-to-one correspondence is between joint choices and outcomes, and the joint choices cannot be determined without further information about how the other's choices are made.

In short, in order to make a rationalizable, though not necessarily rational, decision, the subject must assume some rule which governs the decisions of the Other. He may, for example, assume that the Other is simply a random device, which chooses Yes and No with certain prescribed probabilities. If so, the subject can choose so as to maximize the mathematical expectation of the utility which he associates with money gains. His choice will then depend on the utilities he assigns to the money gains and the probabilities assigned to the Other's choices. If the Other is assumed to choose Yes and No with probabilities (0.5, 0.5), and if utility is proportional to money, then clearly No is the choice that maximizes expected utility gain. But if the Other chooses Yes with probability 0.9, then clearly Yes is the proper choice.

The foregoing reasoning applies if the Other's choices are indeed governed by a random device. However, the Other may be a player like the subject, and may have interests of his own regarding the outcomes. In particular, the Other's interests may be diametrically opposed to the player's; e.g., what the Player gains may be the Other's losses, and vice versa. In this case, in the game represented by Matrix 1, the rational player who assumes that the Other also is rational ought not ascribe probabilities to the Other's choices. He ought to assume that the Other will certainly choose Yes, since the Other wins money with Yes, regardless of how the Player chooses, and loses money with No, also regardless of how the Player chooses.

Assuming, then, that the Other will certainly choose Yes, the Player should clearly choose Yes, because he is sure to lose, and this choice minimizes his loss.

The above example illustrates a situation is which it is easy to decide what to do, once one knows the rules according to which another decision-maker (whose choices, jointly with one's own, determine the outcomes) makes his decisions. Not all decision situations are of this sort. Consider a slight change in Matrix 1, resulting in Matrix 2 (Fig. 2).

| | | OPPONENT | |
		Yes	No
PLAYER	Yes	−1	−5
	No	−2	+10

FIGURE 2. Matrix 2

Here the Player faces an Opponent whose payoffs are the negatives of his own. If the Player chooses Yes, he loses $1 or $5, depending on whether the Opponent chooses Yes or No. If the Player chooses No, he loses $2 or wins $10, again depending on the Opponent's Yes or No. Neither the Player's choice nor the Opponent's is now obvious, for it is to the Opponent's advantage to choose No if the Player chooses Yes, and vice versa. The Player could guess the Opponent's choice, if he made his own choice known to him; but it is not to the Player's advantage to make his choice known to the Opponent. It would serve the Player well to cause the Opponent to believe that he (the Player) will choose Yes, so as to induce the Opponent to choose No (in the hope of winning $5) and then win $10 by choosing No. But how is it possible to make the Opponent believe one's intention when the Opponent knows that one's interests are opposed to his? Perhaps one should tell the Opponent the truth in the hope that the Opponent will think one is lying and so deceive him. But if the Opponent is rational, he will have taken this possibility into account.

A way out suggests itself, namely the use of bluffing. Bluffing is essentially the principle of keeping the Other guessing regarding one's intentions. In poker, for example, a skillful player will on occasions make large bets when he holds a weak hand and small bets when he holds a strong hand, in order to prevent the other players from inferring the strength of his hand from the size of his bet. The relevant question in bluffing is how often one should lie and how often tell the truth to strike the optimum balance. Game theory provides a method of calculating these frequencies. For example, in the game represented by Matrix 2, the Player should choose Yes ¾ of the time (naturally randomizing his choices) and No ¼ of the time. If he does this he will guarantee himself an average (or expected) payoff of -1.25; i.e., he will be sure of losing not more than that much per play on the average. This may seem unfortunate from the Row chooser's point of view, but he cannot do better against an equally rational player (the column chooser) who, by choosing Yes $15/16$ of the time and No $1/16$ of the time, can guarantee himself a payoff of 1.25 per play.

We have now examined four types of decision problems. In each case, the task of making a rational decision amounted to that of finding an appropriate decision-rule and of applying it. The distinction among these problem types is essentially a distinction among the corresponding decision-rules. In the simplest case, where outcomes are completely determined by choices, the decision-rule was the simplest: choose so as to let the most preferred outcome obtain. The rule amounts to an awareness of cause and effect, clearly a component of rationality. Note that this rule does not apply in the second (lottery) example. There is no choice that leads with certainty to the most preferred outcome. To solve this problem, a new decision-rule must be introduced. It involves a new pair of concepts: a numerical utility (more precise than a simple preference order), and a probability of an outcome. The decision-rule is to maximize expected utility, and its application requires a calculation. This rule, however, does not apply to the third example, where a rational opponent is assumed. Here a new principle emerges, namely that of the maximin, the maximization of the minimum payoff associated with each choice. In the last example, this principle alone does not suffice. It must be combined with the expected gain principle, which leads to the concept of mixed strategy; i.e., letting a random device choose one's own strategies in order to deny information to the opponent.

Different as the solutions are, they have one thing in common. Once one has understood the decision principle, there is little doubt left that it is a rational one and that in using it one does the best one can under the circumstances. As we take the next step in what could be called a hierarchy of decision problems, an altogether different picture emerges: The concept of rationality itself becomes ambiguous, as illustrated by the well-known examples of dilemma games.

The dilemma games belong to the class of non-zero-sum games, or mixed motive games, namely those in which the interests of the players clash only partly. The most famous of the dilemma games, the so-called Prisoner's Dilemma, is illustrated in Matrix 3 (Fig. 3).

Here the interests of the two players coincide to the extent that each prefers the outcome CC (lower right) to DD (upper left). However, a simple argument shows that it is in the interest of each player to choose D, for he does better with D regardless of the other's choice.

Closely related to Prisoner's Dilemma is the Game of Chicken, shown in Matrix 4 (Fig. 4).

As in Prisoner's Dilemma, CC is preferred by both players to DD. However, in contrast to Prisoner's Dilemma, D is here not unconditionally preferred by each player. Rather, D is preferred if the Other should choose C, but C is preferred if the Other should choose D. If the Player comes to the conclusion that it is prudent to choose C in

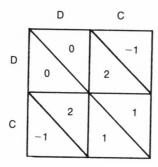

FIGURE 3. Matrix 3: The Prisoner's Dilemma Game. In a non-zero-sum game the payoffs to both subjects must be entered into the outcome cells. The lower left entry in each cell is the payoff to the row chooser, upper right to the column chooser.

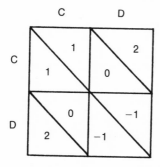

FIGURE 4. Matrix 4: An example of the Game of Chicken.

order to avoid the large loss at DD, he may well ascribe this prudence also to the Other. But if he does, then he feels safe in choosing D, until he realizes that the Other may have come to the same conclusion.

Thus the game of Chicken, like Prisoner's Dilemma, also contains a paradox, but of a different sort. If the two players know each other to be prudent, then each may feel that he himself will be acting rationally if he chooses D. But the choice of D is not prudent. Thus prudence and rationality are split. It seems rational to be bold on the assumption that the other is prudent, but it is rational to be prudent if the other is bold. If, in the Game of Chicken, one assigns to the other the same characteristic as to oneself, the result is not satisfactory, though it is in Prisoner's Dilemma, because if both are bold, disaster obtains; if both are prudent, one has missed the chance to get the greatest gain by being bold. Mixing strategies does not help; it can be shown that no mixture gives both as much as CC, which we have already seen is not satisfactory. In the language of game theory, CC is not an equilibrium.

To illustrate the differences among various related games, the following additional types are represented in Matrices 5–8 (Fig. 5).

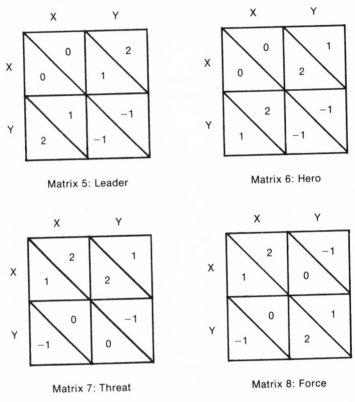

Matrix 5: Leader

Matrix 6: Hero

Matrix 7: Threat

Matrix 8: Force

FIGURE 5. Four additional examples of dilemma games. As in Chicken and in Prisoner's Dilemma, the natural outcome has been placed in the upper left cell.

In order to fix ideas, we have chosen as a reference point the natural outcome, which in the examples selected obtains if each player plays prudently and avoids the choice where he might get the worst (negative) payoff. This outcome has been placed in the upper left corner of each matrix. Next, we shall consider the game from the point of view of the row chooser, whom we shall now call Row (the other being called Column).

We shall examine each game in the light of how Row feels about the natural outcome. Note that Row can effect a shift from this outcome, but only downward to YX, while Column can effect a shift only to the right, namely to XY. The kinds of shift each can effect from any of the outcomes can be seen immediately if one remembers that Row can move only up or down, while Column can move only right or left.

Suppose the natural outcome obtains in the Leader Game (Matrix 5). Row might consider shifting to YX, if he were sure that Column would stick to his X. Then a shift would be advantageous not only to him but to Column as well, clearly a rational act. On the other hand, Column may be contemplating a similar move. If both shift, both lose. Should Row, then, stay put? But if Column also comes to that decision, neither gets what he might have got if only one shifted. Who should shift? (Communication is forbidden.) Each wants to be the one to shift, because the shifter gets the bigger gain. The shifter then assumes the role of a Leader, that is, one who by acting benefits both himself and others, but himself more than others. However, there cannot be two leaders. One or the other must yield the leadership.

The situation in the Hero Game is similar, except that here the shifter rewards the Other more than himself. That is, by shifting he becomes a "hero." Here each wants the other to be the hero. But if neither takes the initiative, neither gets what he might. As in the preceding case, there cannot be two heroes.

Note that a similar analysis shows Prisoner's Dilemma to be a Martyr Game, a martyr being one who rewards others at cost to himself. In contrast to the Leader Game and the Hero Game, there is room for two martyrs. In fact, if both decide to become martyrs, both gain. For analogous reasons, Chicken could be called an Exploiter Game, an exploiter being one who benefits himself while harming others. There is no room for two exploiters.

In the Threat Game, neither player is motivated to shift away from the natural outcome. However, Row is less satisfied with the natural outcome than Column. If, for the moment, we allow communication between players, Row can now threaten Column, coupling his threat with an appeal to fairness: "You ought to give me a chance to get 2 once in a while, which you can do by shifting to XY. If you refuse, I will shift to YX, and we shall both be the losers." Note that it is more advantageous for Column to give in and shift to XY once in a while (he can always shift back to XX) than to suffer the consequences of

Row's shift. Note also that Row's shift is effective only if it is not, carried out, in the sense that once YX occurs, it is not in Column's direct interest to shift to YY. Column may, to be sure, be sufficiently farsighted to shift to YY, so as to give Row the opportunity to shift to XY where he will be happy. However, Column might have shifted to XY directly and so have avoided the bad outcomes YX and YY. It is in this sense that Row's threat is effective.

In the Force Game, Row is again the dissatisfied player. Now he has no threat against Column, for Column would rather let Row shift to YX than shift himself to XY. However, by actually shifting to YX, Row can force Column to shift to YY (since Column prefers YY to YX.) In YY the roles of Row and Column are interchanged. Column can now enforce a return to XX via a shift to YX.

Thus, in an iterated Force Game, a pair of players might oscillate between XX and YY, each time passing through the "bad" outcome YX. As a result, Row will get on the average $\frac{1}{4}$ $(-1 + 2 + -1 + 1) = \frac{1}{4}$ per play, and Column will get $\frac{1}{4}$ $(0 + 1 + 0 + 2) = \frac{3}{4}$ per play each time they go through the cycle. Had they stayed at either XX or YY, one of them would get a whole unit per play and the other two units. However, which player would get more cannot be decided simply by assuming that each player is rational and knows that the other is rational. Indeed, all of the non-zero-sum games discussed here serve as examples of decision situations where the concept of rational decision cannot be clearly defined without further assumptions. For this reason they can be appropriately called dilemma games.

As a final example of this sort, consider a game in which three players are to divide $3 among them by majority vote. An equal division immediately suggests itself as a rational solution. However, it also seems rational for two of the players to refuse to vote for equal division, since they constitute a majority and so can get the $3 for themselves. But then the question arises how they are to divide the $3 between them. Again an equal division suggests itself. However, each player could do better by enlisting the help of the third (frozen out) player to whom he can offer a bribe in any amount smaller than $1.50. But then he himself becomes vulnerable to a coalition formed between his newly acquired partner and his erstwhile partner, since both of them can gain by combining against *him*. Again the concept of rationality becomes ambiguous.

It is just this ambiguousness of rationality in the contexts of mixed-motive games and of coalition games which brings to the forefront psychological components of the thought process other than those related to rational calculations of self interest. We have seen that a player in a mixed-motive game or in a coalition game is subjected to cross pressures from which he cannot escape by a straight-forward rational calculation. He may be faced with questions such as:

Should I respond to his bid to cooperate, or should I exploit his vulnerability?
Should I make myself vulnerable by offering to cooperate?
Does he mean to do what he threatens?
Can I get away with a threat, or will he call my bluff?
If I force him to shift, will he do the same to me next time, with the result that we both will be worse off than if I had let things stand, even though he gets more than I? What price justice?
How much should I offer him to enter a coalition with me? If I enter a coalition with him, will he be tempted to desert the coalition if he gets a better offer?

The behavior of subjects playing games of this sort suggest propensities to answer these questions one way or another, indeed by actions rather than words. These propensities clearly depend on thought processes and on certain features of the objective situation, e.g., the payoffs involved. Therefore, the use of such games offers an opportunity to tap the thought processes and perhaps to make inferences about the underlying psychological factors.

The principal advantage of the game method in psychological research lies in the circumstance that, while the thought processes so tapped are quite rich in psychological content (i.e., are not merely algorithms like the thought processes of artificial intelligence devices), the experimental tool itself is an extremely simple one. The data in a series of experiments with games of the sort described are protocols of clearly defined choices, with which the psychologist has become familiar in conditioning and rote-learning experiments. The statistical characteristics of such protocols, or populations of protocols, can be examined with the help of standard statistical techniques. Observed regularities can be described in an organized fashion by mathematical models. The parameters of these models can serve as a link between formal rigorous theory—the deductions leading from the models to the observed regularities—and significant psychological content, since these parameters can often be quite naturally interpreted in terms of rich psychological concepts: trust and suspicion, responsiveness and vengefulness, caution and daring, dominance and submission, adherence to principle and opportunism. We shall discuss the establishment of these connections below. First let us indicate some broad classes of experiments that can be carried out. We shall concentrate only on the two-person, two-choice, non-zero-sum games, the so-called 2 × 2 mixed-motive games. The reader may well imagine the extension of the method to other types of games.

TYPES OF EXPERIMENTS WITH 2 × 2 GAMES

Important distinctions exist between (1) iterated plays and single (one-shot) plays; (2) experiments with two bona fide subjects and those with one subject and a stooge; and (3) negotiated games and non-negotiated games.

Iterated, Non-negotiated Games with Two Bona Fide Subjects

In non-negotiated games, the players are prevented from communicating with each other. Implicit communication, however, can take place via the players' choices, which are announced by the experimenter following each play. Thus the protocols can be considered as records of interaction between paired players.

The objects of interest are the statistics in a population of protocols. The most obvious statistics are the frequencies of the four types of paired choices. These have different behavioral or psychological meanings in the different games. For example, in Prisoner's Dilemma (Matrix 3), the outcome CC suggests that the players are cooperating. The outcome DD obtains if each plays safe. The unilateral outcomes represent attempts at cooperation by one player, which are exploited by the other.

In the Game of Chicken (Matrix 4) it is, on the contrary, the CC outcome which suggests that each player is playing safe. The unilaterals CD and DC suggest dominance or intimidation of one player by the other, while DD results from a stubborn refusal of either player to give in to intimidation, or from an attempt by each to intimidate the other. In other games the corresponding interpretations readily suggest themselves.

The frequencies of the outcomes can be expected to be related to the particular payoff matrix of a given game type. For example, the "amount of cooperation" in Prisoner's Dilemma (as reflected in the C frequencies) can be expected to be an increasing function of the two payoffs associated with the C choice and a decreasing function of the two payoffs associated with the D choice. Experimental data tend to confirm the above hypothesis. In particular, it appears that both the temptation of getting the biggest payoff and the fear of being the sucker operate against the choice of C in Prisoner's Dilemma. The question naturally arises as to which motivation, greed or fear, is stronger. The question might be answered by varying the payoffs so as to calibrate the one against the other to obtain equal average C frequencies. (Note that the actual magnitudes of the four payoffs in any of the games can be varied independently, subject only to the constraint of preserving their orders of magnitude.) However, this method presupposes a great sensitivity to variations in payoffs, whereas, in fact, the changes in choice frequencies as functions of the payoffs are masked by rather large statistical fluctuations. These fluctuations could be reduced by using very large numbers of players to determine the average frequencies associated with each payoff structure. Another method is to break up the Prisoner's Dilemma game into two games, where only greed operates in one and only fear in the other. This approach requires the use of a stooge and as discussed in a subsequent section.

Other interesting statistics are the frequencies with which a player shifts his strategy, given each of the four outcomes of a game. For example, in Prisoner's Dilemma, either player's shift away from CC constitutes a breach of tacitly established cooperation. If the outcome was CD, then Row's shift (to DD) represents a refusal to be exploited, or retaliation; while Column's shift (to CC) represents a positive response to Row's bid for cooperation. If the outcome was DD, a shift by either player suggests the initiation of cooperation at the risk of becoming a martyr.

In the Threat Game (Matrix 7) the shifts have different meanings. Row's shift from the natural outcome suggests a revolt against the inequality of the payoffs in that outcome. A shift by Column, however, suggests appeasement (to forestall Row's revolt). Again Row's shift from YX to XX could be interpreted as a purely rational act, since both players gain from it. In a way, however, this shift suggests a retreat by Row from an attempt to force the outcome XY via Column's shift to YY, followed by XY. Column's shift from YX to YY seems on the face of it to be irrational, since it makes both players worse off; but it can also be interpreted as a signal of concession to Row, following Row's revolt; for the next rational shift by Row to XY achieves the aim of the revolt. Finally, Column's shift from XY to XX serves Column's immediate interest; but Column may be deterred from shifting for fear of another revolt by Row. Cooperation in the Threat game might be defined as an alternation between XX and XY. Note that only Column controls this alternation, so that he can give Row an average payoff (blackmail) anywhere between 1 and 2 units, depending on the relative frequency of XX and XY. An interesting question is, how much will Column give Row to keep him from revolting?

A still more refined analysis singles out the distributions of random variables generated by the protocols, viewed as realizations of a stochastic process. In Prisoner's Dilemma, for example, the lengths of runs of the various outcomes are random variables whose distributions can be studied empirically. Of particular interest are the runs of unilateral outcomes CD and DC, for the length of such a run indicates the persistence of a player in an attempt to induce cooperation by setting an example. Correspondingly, unilateral runs in Chicken reflect the dominance of one player over the other. Long runs have been called lock-ins. An interesting question is whether a lock-in is self-reinforcing or self-inhibiting. In the former case, the longer a lock-in lasts, the more likely it is to last still longer; in the latter case, the longer it lasts, the more likely it is to be terminated. This question can be answered by a reconstruction of the stochastic process assumed to underlie the generation of the protocols. The answer has an obvious bearing on the psychological dynamics of the lock-ins, whether they are representative of continued cooperation, dominance-submission, noncooperation, resistance to intimidation, or any other interpretation suggested by the context of the game.

The time courses of the statistics reflect the learning aspects of the process. For example, the average C frequency in a population of protocols or Prisoner's Dilemma typically declines in the early phase of an experimental run (of some 300 plays), and increases in the late phase. On the other hand, the variance of this variable typically increases throughout the run. The indication is that players are progressively recruited into CC and DD lock-ins, the increase of the mean of C being due to the eventual predominance of the former over the latter. The impression is that the players learn first to distrust one another and only later to trust one another.

Single-Shot Plays

Interesting and important as the study of interactions and of the learning process is in an iterated game, it is natural to want to eliminate these effects in order to study the decisions in their pure form; that is, in the decisions that can be related to the payoffs of the game without the complicating factors of interaction and learning. For this purpose, we must see how the subjects choose when they know that they will play the game only once. It is especially important to obtain such information in the case of Prisoner's Dilemma. In iterated plays of this game it is conceivable that a great deal of cooperation results simply from mutual deterrence. Once a lock-in on CC occurs, it is likely to continue if each player refrains from defecting to D for fear of eliciting immediate retaliation by the other. To what extent such deterrence-induced cooperation is stable becomes an interesting question in its own right. Equally interesting, however, is the question of the extent to which subjects will cooperate in the absence of deterrence.

The single play experiment offers an opportunity to explore this question. The choice of C in Prisoner's Dilemma cannot be rationalized in a single play, for D is more advantageous regardless of how the other plays, and the fear of retaliation is irrelevant. Hence, if we observe C choices in single plays of Prisoner's Dilemma, they should be ascribed either to error or to reasoning based on considerations other than a simple comparison of payoffs. One kind of reasoning which might induce C is that based on the Kantian categorical imperative: Act in a way that would benefit you if others acted in the same way. In the context of Prisoner's Dilemma, this principle clearly induces the C choice.

In single-play experiments, frequency can no longer refer to the frequency of choices by a single player. In such cases, we define frequency as the ensemble mean, i.e., the fraction of a population of players making the choice in question. It is, of course, possible to have a player participate in single play situations on several occasions, if we make sure that the occasions are sufficiently separated so that experience can be disregarded.

The design of experiments with single plays presents a number of difficulties. It is uneconomical to engage a pair of subjects for an experiment that takes only a few seconds. The design can be made more efficient by having the subjects play a large number of plays of the same game and of different games in a single session, not informing them of the outcomes until the entire session is finished. In this way, interaction and learning are eliminated, and every play can be considered as a single play. However, if all of the games are of the same type (say, Chicken) the player may make a blanket decision, for example, to be bold and so to play D, which he will then apply to every play. Since he gets no feedback, he has no reason to change this decision. If the purpose of the experiment was to see how the propensities to play D are affected by the particular payoff matrix, e.g., how severely unsuccessful brinkmanship is punished, this purpose will be defeated, because the games will not be differentiated with respect to the observed D frequencies. It is advisable, therefore, to mix several game types in a session involving plays without feedback, since the mixture may inhibit blanket decisions.

Note that in plays without feedback it is unnecessary to match subjects, since interactions do not occur. Subjects can be run in groups of arbitrary size and matched arbitrarily at the end of the session just to determine the payoffs. It is also advisable to control for the position of each game in the series by randomizing the serial order.

The Use of a Stooge

If one of the players is a stooge, i.e., uses a prescribed strategy in an iterated game, then the strategy used by the stooge can be taken as an independent variable. The use of a stooge is, of course, warranted only in iterated plays. The strategies can be quantified along several different scales. In a completely randomized strategy, the parameter can be simply the frequency of one choice or the other. Thus in Prisoner's Dilemma or in Chicken, it is interesting to examine the statistics of the protocols of the real players as functions of the C frequencies prescribed for the stooge. In particular, it is of interest to examine the protocols of players playing against the completely cooperative, or against the completely uncooperative, stooge.

If, instead of prescribing choice frequencies, one prescribes the shift frequencies, then the stooge is playing conditional strategies. In particular, if the stooge playing the role of Column, in Prisoner's Dilemma, never shifts from CC or DD, and always shifts from CD or DC, he is playing a tit-for-tat strategy; that is, he matches the real player's preceding choice. Intermediate shift probabilities can, of course, also be prescribed. Other types of strategies are those involving varying numbers of unconditional initial choices, to give the impression of being cooperative and uncooperative followed by some standard strategy. The independent variable in this case is the length and the kind of the initial unconditional strategy.

Note that the threat Game is not symmetric with regard to the players. Therefore, in this game the role of the stooge as Row is different from that as Column. As Row, the stooge may be assigned the frequency of shifting from XX to YX (revolt) and from YX to XX (acquiescence). As Column, he can be assigned a frequency of shifting from YX to YY (yielding to revolt), from XX to XY (forestalling the revolt), and from YX to XX (reestablishing his advantage).

The stooge is needed also in the process of separating greed from fear as motivations in Prisoner's Dilemma. Consider the games represented in Matrices 9 and 10 (Fig. 6).

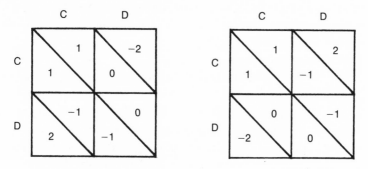

FIGURE 6. Matrix 9: Greed (left); Matrix 10: Fear (right).

In the Greed Game, Row does not fear Column's defection from CC, since Column has nothing to gain from it. But he himself is tempted to defect, since he stands to gain. In the Fear Game, Row is not tempted to defect, but he sees that Column is so tempted, so that Row may defect in self-defense out of fear of getting − 1. Note that if the fear is unjustified, Row does even worse if he defects (cf. accidentally triggered preventive war, Othello's tragedy, etc.). Now what is a Greed Game for Row turns out to be a Fear Game for Column, and vice versa. Therefore, if two bona fide subjects play this game, interactions between greed and fear will take place, and the separate effects of each will be masked. A stooge, on the other hand, can play a prescribed constant strategy which makes possible the comparison of the real subject's behavior in both games under a standardized condition.

Negotiated Games

In negotiated games, the players are permitted to confer with each other and to settle the outcomes by agreeing either on one of the given outcomes or on a specified mixture of outcomes. There exists a body of theory of arbitration and bargaining in which such agreements are prescribed on the basis of some reasonable assumptions about the nature of bargaining between rational players, and perhaps some principles of equity. There are several such theories. In some games their prescriptions coincide, but in other games they differ. The differences stem from varying assumptions concerning the way the magnitudes of the payoffs are to be standardized so as to allow an equitable interpretation of the gains or losses of the players; or with regard to the so-called status quo point (the outcome resulting from breaking off negotiations), with which the final settlement is to be compared.

These differences of outlook are not essential in the context or clearly symmetric games like Prisoner's Dilemma and Chicken, i.e., games which look exactly alike from the point of view of each player. They may, however, lead to different prescribed solutions in asymmetric games. For this reason, the asymmetric negotiated games present greater theoretical interest than symmetric games. A natural question arises as to the relative predicting power of the different theories of bargaining with regard to the observed negotiated outcomes of these games. For example, Nash's bargaining theory prescribes XX as the negotiated outcome of the Threat Game, while Shapley's theory prescribes XY. This is the result because the reference point in Shapley's theory is the security level of the players: what each player could get if he played the game against an opponent with diametrically opposed interests. In the Threat Game, Row's security level is 1, while Column's is 0. Consequently Row has the advantage. In Nash's theory, on the other hand, the threat potentials of the players are compared. Thus, the only threat open to Row is Y. Column's response to this threat is X. The resulting status quo point puts Row at a disadvantage relative to Column. As for Column, his threat is X. Row's best response to this threat is X, which already guarantees to Column the largest payoff. To view Nash's solution from still another point of view, imagine what happens if each player bids for his largest payoff, i.e., both players stand pat with X where their respective largest payoffs are. The outcome is XX, which is again Nash's solution. A claim of rationality can be made for it, because both of the players cannot do better in another outcome. Note that in Prisoner's Dilemma and in Chicken, if both players bid for the largest payoff, the resulting outcome, DD, is not rational in the sense of a negotiated game, because both players can do better with CC and so rational negotiations should have achieved this outcome.

Not only the outcomes of negotiated games but also the bargaining process itself can be viewed as a source of data. If hard data are desired, the bargaining process must be formalized in terms of a prescribed repertoire of offers and counter-offers, which can be recorded. The records then constitute a population of protocols to be analyzed statistically in the same way as the choice protocols in non-negotiated games. Clearly, when we pass to negotiated games, we depart from the simplest possible game situations embodied in the non-negotiated game. In doing so, we perhaps approach greater verisimilitude with respect to real-life situations, but we pay for it in increasing complexity of data and hence with greater difficulty of analysis.

THE VARIABLES IN GAME EXPERIMENTS

Game experiments, like any other controlled experiments, are designed to reveal relations between independent and dependent variables. There are obvious advantages in expressing these relations quantitatively—in particular, the opportunity to construct mathematical theories which summarize the observed regularities in the protocols. We have already mentioned several naturally quantifiable variables: the distributions of the random variables singled out in the process, and the statistics of these distributions. These are the experimentally observed (hence the dependent) variables of the process. Their psychological relevance has already been discussed. The independent variables are those which are imposed by the process itself (e.g., the number of plays elapsed in an iterated game), and those that can be experimentally manipulated, (e.g., the payoffs, the strategies prescribed to a stooge, etc.).

For the psychologist, the independent variables of crucial importance are the individual subject himself and his state of mind. Thus psychologists, to the extent that they have become interested in game experiments, have tended to view the game as a projective test and the following situation has developed in the past eight years or so. Of the simple mixed-motive games, the most extensively, if not exclusively studied has been Prisoner's Dilemma. This is understandable in view of the publicity this game has received, and in view of the difficult choice the non-negotiated game offers between conflict and cooperation—a choice that seems to capture the very dialectic of social and even of international life.

Most research on Prisoner's Dilemma revolves around cell designs, in which different kinds of people, or different conditions, or both, occupy the several cells, while data processing amounts to a comparison between the respective C frequencies (the index of cooperation), or corresponding analyses of variance.

In view of the established procedures in experimental psychology, this development was perhaps inevitable. In my opinion, however, the use of a game as a single index instrument stems from a misconception about where the power of this instrument lies. It certainly does not lie in the precision with which a single index reflects either the personality or the state of mind of an individual subject. In a single play, a given choice in a 2×2 game may or may not be elicited by countless stimuli, external and internal, many of them possibly irrelevant to the experimental situation. Thus it seems more appropriate to view a choice (say, C in Prisoner's Dilemma) as a probability. So conceived, C is a probability subject to both systematic and random fluctuations. The difficulty is compounded by the circumstance that measures taken to reduce random fluctuations in the performance of a single subject or pair (such as taking longer sequences of plays as samples) tend to increase the systematic fluctuations, and vice versa. The only way to reduce sample variance, and so improve the estimates of such a statistic, is to use large homogeneous populations of subjects in the generation of protocols. What constitutes a homogeneous population is difficult to determine. Intuitively, however, one would guess that obvious differences between population samples (sex, age, large cultural distance, etc.) offer better opportunities for using the subject as an independent variable than more subtle individual differences, assessible by tests, whose validity presents a separate problem.

At any rate, the necessity of estimating statistics in large subject population samples precludes the use of factorial designs with many cells. The estimate of statistics from individual protocols is practically out of the question, because it is almost certain that the underlying stochastic process is not even approximately ergodic (i.e., one in which time samples yield the same statistics as ensemble samples); and so,

any reliable estimates require sequences of plays much longer than
are practicable in a laboratory.

Because of these difficulties, it is unrealistic to try to enrich the
experimental game approach by introducing broad variations in the
independent variables by elaborate factorial designs. The obverse of
this common error is the failure to utilize the richness already embodied in the method, that is, the intricate network of dependent variables. To put it in another way, experimental games tend to be used
currently so as to read off at most one or two behavioral indices
under a great variety of imposed conditions, usually suggested by
cues taken from real life, or from already existing psychological
theories. Since different investigators are interested in different
aspects, the results tend to become haphazard accumulations of unrelated masses of data, doubtful in generality and validity because
of the small numbers of subjects in each condition. In my opinion,
it would be advisable to reverse this procedure, that is, to concentrate
on a few standard formats of experiments and to exploit the wealth of
information inherent even in the simplest class of games. In the first
instance, one should examine the whole gamut of dependent variables
residing in the statistics of the protocols. These variables are tightly
interlaced by mathematical interdependence. Answers to questions regarding them can be much more easily organized into a coherent
theory than results derived from more or less improvised manipulations of externally imposed conditions. If one is intent on enriching
the method by enlarging the range of the independent variables, one
would do better to concentrate on varying the payoff structures of the
games. If one takes only the rank order of the magnitudes into account, there are seventy-eight nonequivalent 2×2 games. Of these
twenty-one are trivial (no-conflict games), three are of relatively slight
psychological interest (pure conflict games), and the remaining ones
are all mixed-motive games, which fall into ten discernible types, each
illustrating one or more intriguing psychological aspects of mixed-
motive conflict. (An enumeration of all 3×3 games is out of the
question since their number exceeds $(9\,!)^2/72 \approx 1.8 \times 10^9$, or almost
2 billion.)

Here, then are questions naturally suggested by the method. Experimental psychologists would do well to let themselves be guided at
first by these questions, so as to acquire a full understanding of what
is inherently involved, both logically and psychologically, in the great

variety of situations revealed by objectively analyzable strategic structures of the games. Only in the light of this understanding can the questions of special interest to the psychologist be formulated precisely, and the relevance of the method to long-standing psychological questions be assessed with confidence. Then the method can be developed in the direction of greater generality and applicability along the lines that show the greatest promise.

REFERENCES

Braithwaite, R. B. 1955. Theory of Games as a Tool for the Moral Philosopher. Cambridge: Cambridge U. Press.

Deutsch, M. 1958. Trust and Suspicion. J. of Conflict Resolution 2:267–79.

Luce, R. D. and H. Raiffa. 1957. Games and Decisions. New York: Wiley.

Rapoport, A. 1965. Game Theory and Human Conflict in The Nature of Human Conflict, ed. E. B. McNeil. Englewood Cliffs: Prentice-Hall. Pt. 3, Ch. 10, 195–226.

———. 1966. Two-Person Game Theory: The Essential Ideas. Ann Arbor: U. of Michigan Press.

Rapoport, A. and A. M. Chammah. 1965. Prisoner's Dilemma: A Study in Conflict and Cooperation. Ann Arbor: U. of Michigan Press.

Rapoport A. and M. Guyer. 1966. A Taxonomy of Games. General Systems XI.

Rapoport, A. and C. J. Orwant. 1962. "Experimental Games: A Review," Behavioral Science 7:1–37.

CHAPTER 8
Anatol Rapoport
Albert M. Chammah

The Game of Chicken

THE Game of Chicken simulates the basic features of brinksmanship and appeasement. In its simplest form, it can be represented as a 2×2 game (two players, each having a choice between two strategies, C and D). The payoff matrix is shown in Fig. 1. The payoffs satisfy the inequalities

$$T > R > S > P \qquad 2R > S + T$$

	C_2	D_2
C_1	R, R	S, T
D_1	T, S	P, P

FIGURE 1. Payoff matrix for the Game of Chicken.

The designation of the strategies and of the payoffs is adapted from the corresponding designations in Prisoner's Dilemma (cf. Rapoport and Chammah 1965), to which Chicken is closely related. In Prisoner's Dilemma, C designates the cooperative strategy, so called because the choice of C by both players amounts to a tacit cooperation, which results in the maximal joint payoff; D designates the defecting strategy. The payoff R is reward for cooperation; T stands for the temptation associated with largest individual payoff; S stands for the payoff to the unilateral cooperator (the "sucker" or the "saint"); P stands for the punishment for double defection. These designations are applicable with some modification also in the game of Chicken.

The essential difference between the two games is that whereas in Chicken S > P, in Prisoner's Dilemma P > S. Consequently, while in Prisoner's Dilemma, strategy D dominates strategy C for both players and so leads to the dilemma (because the outcome DD is worse for

The research work on which this paper is based was supported by Public Health Service Grant NIH-MH-4238–06.

both players than CC), in Chicken neither player has a dominating strategy. Indeed, the best response to the choice of C by the other player is to choose D (preemption), while the best response to D is C (appeasement). Nevertheless, Chicken presents a dilemma of its own. If player 1 assumes that player 2 is "chicken," i.e., will play C as the obviously prudent choice (note that C is a maximin strategy), player 1 may feel safe in playing the "daring" strategy D. But if he assumes that the other has come to the same conclusion, he cannot play D.

The usual argument for brinksmanship is that if one can convince the other player that one is unalterably committed to D, for example, by letting him know that one has deliberately destroyed one's own freedom of choice (burned one's bridges), then one can safely play D against a rational opponent. Thus, Herman Kahn (1965) suggests that in playing Chicken on the road, one might deliberately and conspicuously remove the steering wheel and throw it away. This gives the opposing driver no choice but to swerve from the collision course (i.e., choose the appeasing "chicken" strategy C). Aside from the fact that the formal noncooperative game does not provide for opportunities of communication, the unalterable commitment to the daring strategy D has certain practical drawbacks, as, for example, in the case where the player to be intimidated reasons exactly as the intimidator. Imagine the chagrin of a preemptor as he sees that the driver of the oncoming car has removed *his* steering wheel at precisely the same moment.

Returning to the formal difference in the strategic structures of Prisoner's Dilemma and of Chicken, we observe that the payoff matrix of Prisoner's Dilemma has a single equilibrium, namely the outcome DD. An equilibrium is an outcome such that if a player departs from it by choosing another strategy, he does not improve his payoff and, in general, impairs it. In Prisoner's Dilemma, DD is such an outcome. Chicken, on the other hand, has two such equilibria, namely $C_1 D_2$ and $D_1 C_2$ as seen in Fig. 1.

If, as some maintain, the solution of a noncooperative game must be an equilibrium, then the solution of Prisoner's Dilemma must be DD, the only equilibrium. Chicken, according to this view, has at least two "solutions," $C_1 D_2$ and $D_1 C_2$. If, however, we demand further that a solution of a symmetric game must not favor either player (since in formal game theory the players are assumed to be psychologically identical) neither of the above solutions of Chicken is satisfactory, because each of them favors one or the other player.

Besides the two equilibria mentioned, Chicken has still another equilibrium. This third equilibrium favors neither player. Let each player choose strategy C with probability

$$p(C) = \frac{S - P}{(T - R) + (S - P)} \tag{2}$$

Because of Inequalities (1), it can be easily seen that $0 < p(C) < 1$, as, of course, should be the case with a probability. Then it can be shown that as long as one of the players plays the mixed strategy given by Equation (2), the payoff of the other does not depend on the strategy chosen. Hence a way of preventing the other from trying to get more via preempting D (or, indeed, via any mixture of C and D) is to play this mixed strategy, whereby the other's motivation to defect is removed. If both players use it, neither has any motivation to depart from it.

If the two players play the mixed strategy given by (2), each obtains an expected gain of

$$G = \frac{ST - RP}{(T - R) + (S - P)} \tag{3}$$

If we multiply the right side of (3) by $[(T - R) + (S - P)]$ and take into account the inequalities in (1), we observe that $G < R$, i.e., both players get less by choosing the equilibrium mixed strategy than they would have gotten by choosing the minimax strategy, C.

Therefore, Chicken is a dilemma game like Prisoner's Dilemma. One plays the equilibrium strategy in self defense, as it were. Each is acting reasonably in removing the other's temptation to preempt, since preemption by both spells disaster for both. Yet the payoff to both players choosing the equilibrium strategy is less than it would be if each resisted the temptation to preempt and trusted the other to do the same. This would lead to the choice of the maximin strategy C by both players, which in this case (unlike Prisoner's Dilemma) is not only a choice which results in the maximum joint payoff, but also a prudent choice (being a maximin strategy).

In contrast with the equilibrium strategy in Prisoner's Dilemma, which is always the pure strategy D, regardless of the payoff matrix, the symmetric mixed equilibrium strategy of Chicken does depend on the payoffs. Therefore, if one should take seriously a normative theory based on the prescription of a symmetric equilibrium, one would hypothesize that the relative frequency of C choices in a large number of plays would correspond to the probabilities in the strategy mixture given by Equation (2).

In actuality, the normative prescriptions of game theory are seldom realized in laboratory experiments. It is not even possible to make accurate estimates as to what degree the experimental results depart from those expected on game-theoretical grounds, since one cannot assume that the actual payoffs, say in money, correspond to the players' utilities. Game-theoretical analysis is of value only to the extent that it reveals the strategic structure of the game. Once the strategic structure is revealed, it can be used as a source of ideas in constructing a psychological theory of the game, as, we hope, will become clear in the analysis of our experimental results.

METHOD

For the most part, we shall be describing the statistics of a volume of data obtained from lengthy runs of iterated plays. The method is the same as that used in our studies on Prisoner's Dilemma (Rapoport and Chammah 1965). The emphasis will be not on attempts to determine the psychological parameters of individual subjects (as is often the case in learning experiments) but rather on the gross statistical features of the accumulated protocols in relation to the situational variables, e.g., the payoffs of the several games and the time (i.e., the number of plays) elapsed. We shall, however, as in the case of Prisoner's Dilemma, compare the performances of two populations, male and female. We shall also compare the gross features of the performance in Chicken with that of Prisoner's Dilemma.

In assessing differences and trends, we shall not, except occasionally, evaluate the statistical significance of the observed differences, Since our purpose for the present is not the confirmation or the refutation of specific hypotheses but rather the generation of hypotheses. Such hypotheses will be suggested by the observed differences or trends. If some of the hypotheses so suggested seem sufficiently interesting, it is our hope that subsequent work will be aimed at putting these hypotheses to severe tests. We believe that all the results which reveal the psychological features of the game situation can be valid only in the gross statistical sense, and not with respect to any individual, much less with respect to a particular play or a short sequence of plays.

Statistical results approach certainty only when they are obtained from very large masses of data.

In the experiments to be described, we used games of the Chicken type with five different payoff matrices, shown in Fig. 2.

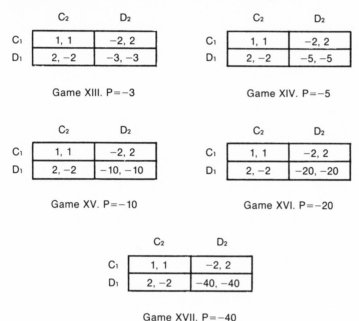

Game XIII. P=−3

Game XIV. P=−5

Game XV. P=−10

Game XVI. P=−20

Game XVII. P=−40

FIGURE 2. Payoff matrices for Games XIII to XVII.

Note that R, T, and S are held constant throughout, while P decreases montonically (is negative and increases in magnitude) from Game XIII to Game XVII. The designations of the games follow the chronological notation of a larger experimental series. We shall also refer to each game by the magnitude of its P payoff. For example, C(10) will mean the frequency of C choices observed in Game XV.

Our subjects were fifty pairs of University of Michigan male students and fifty pairs of University of Michigan female students, ten pairs being assigned to each game shown in Fig. 2. The two players of each pair were seated side by side facing the experimenter and separated from each other by a partition. After the rules of the game (the results of each pair of choices) had been explained and the subjects' questions answered, the subjects played one of the five games 300 times in succession. The successive choices were indicated silently to the experimenter by pointing to one of two cards, representing C and D choices respectively. No communication between the players was allowed. Following each play, the experimenter announced the outcome, which was entered on score sheets both by the subjects and the experimenter. After every twenty-five plays, each subject computed his net gain or loss for that block. At the end of the session the gains or losses were converted into money at 1 mil per point and added to or subtracted from the subjects' pay for participating in the experiment.

STATIC RESULTS

The Frequencies of C Choices and of the Four Outcomes

Table 1 shows the frequencies of the C choices in percent of total number of plays in each of the given games in each population, and the frequencies prescribed by the equilibrium solution, given by Equation (2).

TABLE 1. FREQUENCIES OF C CHOICES IN PERCENTAGE OF PLAYS

Game	Theoretical (Equilibrium)	Observed Male	Observed Female
XIII (P = −3)	50%	64%	64%
XIV (P = −5)	75	73	69
XV (P = −10)	89	63	54
XVI (P = −20)	95	77	56
XVII (P = −40)	97	81	76

It is interesting to compare these results with analogous ones obtained in Prisoner's Dilemma games. Recall that the equilibrium solution of Prisoner's Dilemma prescribes D unconditionally. Indeed, even if the game is played many times in succession, the outcome being announced each time, it can be shown that the unconditional choice of D is the only equilibrium strategy in the super-game induced by the finitely iterated game, if the number of plays is known to each player. In practice, unconditional choice of D is practically never observed in long runs of Prisoner's Dilemma, at least in the laboratory studies. Hence, in this case, the average player cooperates with greater frequency than is prescribed by the equilibrium solution. In Chicken, on the other hand, the tendency seems to be in the opposite direction. The average subject cooperates with a frequency smaller than is prescribed by the equilibrium solution. The only exception is Game xiii, which, of all the five games, is closest to Prisoner's Dilemma. (If R. T, and S are held constant and P increases, Chicken turns into Prisoner's Dilemma when P becomes larger than S.)

We conclude, therefore, that the difference in the strategic structure between Prisoner's Dilemma and Chicken is attenuated in the experimental setting. Judging by the frequencies of C choices, this difference is not as great as one would expect it to be on game-theoretical grounds.

Next we examine the observed C frequencies in relation to P. According to the equilibrium solution, these frequencies should increase as P decreases. Common sense suggests the same trend, since other things being equal, the tendency to choose C should increase as the outcome DD is punished more severely. This tendency is observed in Prisoner's Dilemma (cf. Rapoport and Chammah 1965:39). However, the observed trend in Chicken is not perfect. There is a reversal from $C(5)$ to $C(10)$, which may be due simply to a statistical fluctuation but conceivably to other reasons. The possibility that the reversal is real rather than a reflection of a sampling error is corroborated by the same reversal observed in both populations.

As the punishment for DD becomes more severe with decreasing P, there may be two pressures operating on the subjects. One is an increasing pressure to play C, since D entails a risk of a larger loss if DD should obtain. However, there may also be an increased pressure to play D, perhaps based on the belief that as the punishment for double defection becomes more severe, each player expects that the other will be reluctant to take the punishment associated with retaliation. On the other hand, when the punishment becomes excessive, the temptation to preempt may be attenuated by the prospect of the great risk. It is thus conceivable that some moderate value of P, neither too small to make retaliation seem certain, nor too large to make preemption too risky, induces the maximum temptation to preempt. The statistical significance of the observed inequality $C(10) < C(5)$ is almost at the 0.01 level (median χ^2 two-tail test). The statistical significance of the observed inequality $C(10) < C(20)$ is at about the same level.

Let us now refine our data, separating the four outcomes resulting from paired choices, namely the double cooperative (CC), the double defecting (DD), and the unilateral (CD + DC). Note that in the case of a homogeneous population there is no point comparing the frequencies of CD and DC, since the labeling of the players is arbitrary.

The frequencies of the four outcomes in percent are shown in Table 2.

TABLE 2. FREQUENCIES OF OUTCOMES RESULTING FROM PAIRED CHOICES

Game	Men			Women		
	CC	CD + DC	DD	CC	CD +DC	DD
XIII (P = −3)	48	32	20	46	34	19
XIV (P = −5)	60	26	14	54	29	17
XV (P = −10)	48	29	23	36	37	27
XVI (P = −20)	61	31	07	37	39	25
XVII (P = −40)	68	25	07	57	38	05

We note that the reversal of the trend reflected in the equalities $C(5) > C(10) < C(20)$ is accounted for both by smaller frequencies of the CC outcomes and by larger frequencies of DD outcomes in Game xv. In the remaining games, CC increases and DD decreases montonically with increasing numerical magnitude of P. The unilaterals (CD + DC) show no discernible trend.

The Conditional Frequencies

There is yet another way of looking at the data—with a greater resolving power, as it were. Consider the probability that player $i(i = 1, 2)$ will choose C following the outcome (CC), i.e., the conditional probability

$$x_i = p\ (C_i \mid C_iC_j) \tag{4}$$

and similarly,

$$y_i = p\ (C_i \mid C_iD_j) \tag{5}$$
$$z_i = p\ (C_i \mid D_iC_j) \tag{6}$$
$$w_i = p\ (C_i \mid D_iD_j) \qquad (i = 1, 2) \tag{7}$$

Psychologically, x_i can be interpreted as the propensity to continue cooperating after a collusion has been established; y_i is the propensity to give in to the other's preemption of D; z_i is the propensity to respond to the other's bid to cooperate; w_i is either the propensity to give in under the pressure of punishment or a bid to cooperate. These conditional probabilities have a similar but not identical interpretation in the context of Prisoner's Dilemma.

Table 3 shows the mean values of x, y, z, and w, (obtained from corresponding frequencies) averaged over all the subjects playing each game and also the grand means, averaged over the games. The table

TABLE 3. AVERAGE MEAN VALUES OF X, Y, Z, AND W

Game	Men				Women			
	x	y	z	w	x	y	z	w
XIII (P = −3)	.77	.45	.48	.40	.82	.51	.49	.39
XIV (P = −5)	.90	.53	.42	.36	.88	.44	.40	.36
XV (P = −10)	.78	.50	.62	.42	.79	.48	.36	.39
XVI (P = −20)	.85	.60	.69	.53	.72	.55	.48	.49
XVII (P = −40)	.90	.57	.64	.50	.82	.66	.52	.52
Mean	.84	.53	.57	.44	.81	.53	.45	.43

gives us some indications about how the differences in the C frequencies in the different games may come about. We note, for example, that the dip in Game XIV is due almost entirely to the correspondingly smaller values of x in both men and women. This corroborates to some extent our conjecture that a moderate value of P is more conducive to attempts to preempt (i.e., to defect from CC) than either large or small values.

Next we note that the chief difference in the mean propensities of men and women is in the magnitude of z. (By the median χ^2 test, this difference is significant at about the 0.08 level.) We could therefore make the following conjecture: The smaller frequency of C choices in women playing the game of Chicken stems principally from their smaller propensity to respond cooperatively to the cooperative choices of the partner. A similar result was obtained from our studies on Prisoner's Dilemma.

Skewness

Another interesting variable is skewness. Consider a block of fifty plays. Suppose one or the other player preempts successfully—repeatedly plays D, forcing the other player to play C in order to avoid the worst payoff at DD. Then, assuming player 2 to be the preemptor in this block, there will be a predominance of CD outcomes in the block. If player 1 is the preemptor, there will be a predominance of DC outcomes. It follows, since the CC's and DD's contribute equally to C_1 and C_2, the predominance of one over the other will be reflected in the excess of CD's over DC's, or vice versa.

In order to normalize this index, we introduce

$$Q = \frac{10 \, |C_1 - C_2|}{\sqrt{(C) \cdot (D)}} \qquad (8)$$

where C_1, C_2, $C = C_1 + C_2$, and $D = 100 - C_1 - C_2$ are the numbers of the corresponding choices in the block. Actually Q is the number of standard deviations by which the observed value of $C_1 - C_2$ departs from the expected value (which is 0) under the null hypothesis that in the parent population of which the block is a sample, $C_1 = C_2 = C/2$ and that the distribution of the random variable C_i is binomial.

Note that the value of Q is indeterminate if all the outcomes in a block are either CC or DD. We could in such instances set $Q = 0$, since neither player has a predominance of C's or D's over the other. However, such blocks may also be due to the lock-in effect, as can be readily surmised from the fact that the frequency of occurrence of such blocks is much greater than can be accounted for statistically, assuming the choices of the two subjects to be independent.

Therefore we shall calculate our average Q's in two ways: (1) by including the pure CC or DD blocks, for which we set $Q = 0$, and (2) by excluding such runs. Obviously the Q's will be larger in the second case. We shall call this modified index Q^*.

Table 4 shows the values of Q and Q^* averaged for each of the five games.

TABLE 4. AVERAGE VALUES OF Q AND Q* FOR FIVE GAMES

Game	Q Men	Q Women	Q* Men	Q* Women
XIII (P = −3)	1.1	1.5	1.4	1.8
XIV (P = −5)	0.8	0.8	1.1	1.1
XV (P = −10)	1.1	1.0	1.2	1.1
XVI (P = −20)	1.1	1.2	1.6	1.4
XVII (P = −40)	1.4	2.5	1.9	3.1
Mean	1.1	1.4	1.4	1.7

Note that the theoretical expected value of Q is approximately 0.8—that is, the mean of the absolute value of a normally distributed variable, whose mean is zero and whose standard deviation is one. We surmise that preemption, or the concomittant appeasement, is reflected in the excess of Q and of Q^* over the expected value. This excess is somewhat attenuated in Q compared with Q^* by the lock-in effect, which tends to diminish skewness.

We note also that except for the reversal $Q(5) < Q(3)$, skewness tends to increase with the magnitude of P, which makes intuitive sense, because retaliation becomes more difficult as $|P|$ increases in absolute value. Note especially the high values of Q and Q^* in Game XVII observed in women. One is tempted to conjecture that women tend especially to preempt, or to yield to preemption, when the risk associated with retaliation becomes very high. Whether the initial reversal is real is an interesting question. Note that it occurs both in men and in women. If it is real, then the effect may be related to the one discussed above with regard to a similar reversal in C.

The "Appeasement Failure" Index

The final variable we shall examine is the "appeasement failure" index defined as

$$M = \frac{(1-y)(1-z)}{yz} \tag{9}$$

The significance of this ratio is the following. Consider a unilateral run of any length. In this situation one player, whom we shall call the preemptor, keeps on playing D, while the other, whom we shall call the appeaser, plays C. Presumably the latter has given in to the former's bid for the T payoff. He does not venture to retaliate with D for fear of receiving the worst payoff, P. We now ask what is likely to happen when the run ends, i.e., when one or the other player or both change their strategy. One of three events can happen: (1) The appeaser finally rebels by switching to D (even though he punishes himself by doing this), while the preemptor continues with D; (2) the preemptor repents by changing to C, while the other player continues with C; (3) the changes take place simultaneously so that the players switch roles. Ignoring (3) for the time being, the last mentioned outcome, let us consider the ratio of frequencies of (1) and (2), namely, how much more frequently does a unilateral run end in DD than in CC? Formally this ratio is represented by (9). We modify the definition somewhat by considering only unilateral runs of length two or longer.

The correspondingly modified ratios *M* for each game in the male and female populations are shown in Table 5. We note that *M* roughly decreases as the magnitude of P increases. That is to say, as the punishment becomes more severe, the preemptor is more likely to become converted sooner than the appeaser quits appeasing. This effect may be due either to the appeaser's increasing reluctance to retaliate or to the preemptor's greater readiness to respond to the other's cooperation in view of the greater punishment associated with the expected retaliation.

TABLE 5. APPEASEMENT FAILURE INDEX (M) FOR MEN AND WOMEN

Game	Men	Women
P = −3	.85	2.15
P = −5	1.46	1.87
P = −10	1.24	1.74
P = −20	.45	1.47
P = −40	.52	.28
Mean	.90	1.50
Weighted mean[a]	.84	1.15

[a]The weighted mean is obtained from the ratio of the total number of unilateral runs in all five games ending in DD to the total number of such runs ending in CC.

We now inquire what happens after the players have switched roles. Our data indicate that, following a switch, the DD outcome is on the average (using weighted means) 1.5 more frequent than CC in the male population and 3.7 times more frequent in the female population. If unweighted means are used, the corresponding ratios are 2.6 and 4.0. Evidently the disappointment of the relenting preemptor in finding himself suddenly in the appeaser's role is stronger than the appeaser's desire to establish cooperation.

THE TIME COURSES OF THE VARIABLES

So far we have examined the data from a static point of view, comparing the central tendencies across games and populations. Let us now examine the data from the dynamic point of view, with respect to the trends, if any, in the several parameters in the course of the iterated plays. For this purpose, we combine the data obtained from the five games. For purposes of comparison we keep separate the data obtained from the male and female populations.

The Initial Trend

The variable to be examined first is the running mean frequency of C, averaged over overlapping fifteen successive plays, i.e., 1–15, 2–16, 3–17, etc. We wish to see whether the initial learning leads to an increase or a decrease of cooperative choices. The comparison between the male and female population is shown in Fig. 3.

We see that there is a distinct difference between the initial time courses: The men's time course remains almost constant, while that of the women shows a distinct decline. Note, however, that men and women start with almost the same C frequencies. This result, incidentally, was remarkably consistent throughout the experiments on Prisoner's Dilemma. Whatever sex differences were observed were revealed only in the course of long iterated runs.

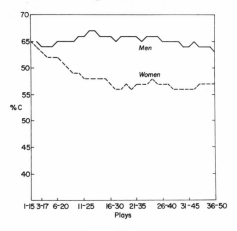

FIGURE 3

The Gross Trends in C, CC, CD + DC, and DD

We shall next take a grosser view of the overall time courses of our variables. Our time unit will now be the 50–play block.

From Fig. 4 we see that on the whole, the frequency of C choices increases. That is, both populations considered as a whole seem predominantly learning to cooperate in the iterated game of Chicken, so that the initial downward trend is reversed at some point.

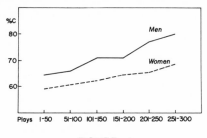

FIGURE 4

Figure 5 shows the average time courses of CC, CD + DC, and DD. We see that on the whole the frequency of CC increases at the expense of CD + DC, while DD remains constant or, perhaps, is slowly decreasing. The trends, where they occur, are somewhat more pronounced in the male population than in the female.

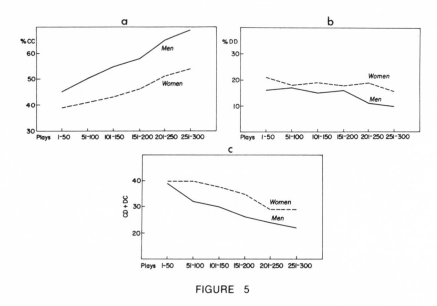

FIGURE 5

The Trends in x, y, z, w

Figure 6 shows the average time courses of the conditioned probabilities, *x, y, z,* and *w*. We see that, to the extent that any trends are discernible, they are upward in *x* and perhaps in *z*, and very slightly downward in *w*. No trend is discernible in *y*. If these trends are real,

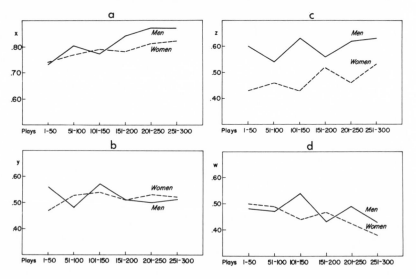

FIGURE 6

they indicate that on the whole both populations are learning to continue cooperating when they are in CC (learning *not* to preempt), and also learning to continue defecting when in DD (learning not to give in in the deadlock). They also seem to be learning to respond with cooperation to the other's cooperative choice. The rate of learning of the conditional choices (if learning occurs at all) is considerably smaller than that of the simple choices (cf. Fig. 5 and 6).

We see from Fig. 7, which shows the time courses of Q and Q^*, that there is no discernible learning effect in Q except possibly toward the end, in women. We note also that both Q and Q^* are larger in women throughout. Apparently the preemption-appeasement episodes are more frequent in the female population.

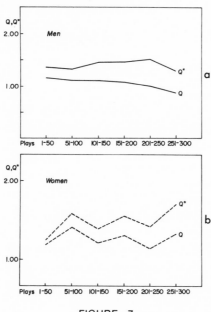

FIGURE 7

COMPARISON OF CHICKEN WITH PRISONER'S DILEMMA

We have already pointed out that while the pressure to choose D in Prisoner's Dilemma is unconditional, operating regardless of whether the other player is assumed to have chosen C or D, it is not unconditional in Chicken. It can be rationalized only if the other player is assumed to have chosen. One could therefore conjecture that on the whole, Chicken will exhibit more C choices than Prisoner's Dilemma.

However, there are other factors to consider. It is conceivable that just because retaliation is more costly than acquiescence in Chicken, there is additional motivation to choose D. The point is that, while in Prisoner's Dilemma there is little prospect of getting away with a long stretch of rewarded D's since the other player actually stands to gain by retaliating, there is such a prospect in Chicken since the other player stands to lose by retaliating. On the face of it, therefore, one cannot say a priori which game will exhibit the larger C. Let us look for the answer in data. For comparison we have chosen two games of the Prisoner's Dilemma type. The payoff matrices are shown in Fig. 8.

	C_2	D_2
C_1	1, 1	−2, 2
D_1	2, −2	−1, −1

	C_2	D_2
C_1	5, 5	−10, 10
D_1	10, −10	−1, −1

FIGURE   8. Payoff matrices: Game IV (left); Game XI (right).

Games IV and XI (and again our notation follows that of an established series) are closest to the games of Chicken with which they are compared. In Game IV, R, T, and S are identical numerically to the corresponding payoffs in Games XIII—XVII. In Game XI, R, T and S are all multiplied by a factor of five, so that their ratios are equal to the corresponding ratios in Game IV. Previous analysis of the data obtained from Games IV and XI (twenty male pairs and twenty female pairs playing Prisoner's Dilemma) showed that these two games are indeed very similar to each other. We shall therefore combine the data from these two games.

Figure 9 shows the comparison of C, CC, CD + DC, and DD frequencies. We see that there is more over-all cooperation in Chicken than in Prisoner's Dilemma with numerically identical or proportional R, T, and S. We conjecture, therefore, that the pressure to defect, based on the possibility of being able to get away with, is not as strong as the direct pressure to defect based on the dominance of D. From Fig. 9a, 9b, and 9c we see that the increase in the C frequency observed in Chicken compared with Prisoner's Dilemma is due primarily to the increase in the frequencies of the unilateral outcomes (CD and DC) at the expense of DD. The increase of CC frequencies (Fig. 9b) is comparatively slight in women and negligible in men. We can therefore conjecture that Chicken shows more cooperation than Prisoner's Dilemma primarily because of the severity of the punishment

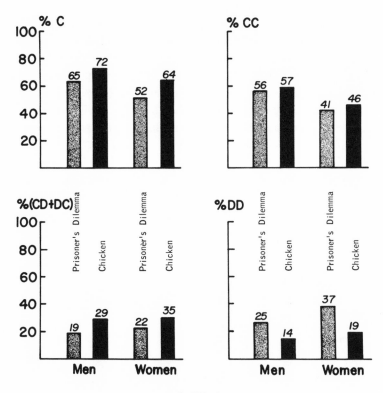

FIGURE 9

for double defection. There is no evidence in the data shown in Fig. 9 either for or against the conjecture that the temptation to preempt is strengthened by the prospect of getting away with it. However, evidence for just this conjecture does appear when we compare the two games with respect to the conditional frequencies, x, y, z, and w. This comparison is shown in Fig. 10.

The implication of the comparison is clear. The mean values of x in Chicken are actually *smaller* than those in Prisoner's Dilemma. Note that the gain ratio (T/R), is the same in all our games. If we consider instead the gain difference, i.e., $T - R$, we see that in Game xi this difference ($T - R = 5$) is actually greater than in all the Chicken games ($T - R = 1$). Thus we might expect that in terms of the temptation to increase one's payoff by defecting to D from CC, the effect should be equal or greater in the composite Prisoner's Dilemma game. We observe the opposite. Thus our conjecture is that the prospect of getting away with it does play a part in Chicken (which it does not in

Prisoner's Dilemma) in contributing to the D frequencies. Clearly this tendency is more offset by other tendencies, as can be seen in the comparisons between the other conditional frequencies. Specifically, all three of the remaining conditional frequencies, y, z, and w, are larger in Chicken than in Prisoner's Dilemma. The greatest difference is in the values of w. The reason seems clear: There is a strong pressure to escape from the larger punishment associated with DD in Chicken.

The differences in y can be attributed to the appeasement pressure in Chicken, namely a reluctance to retaliate, that is, to switch to D from unilateral C. Again this is understandable in view of the greater punishment for DD.

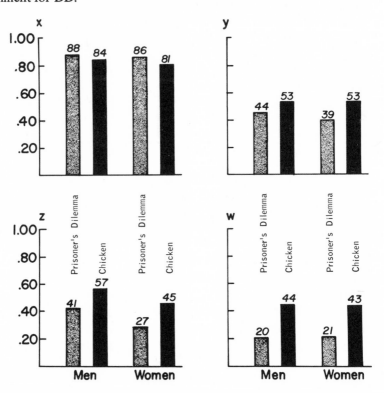

FIGURE 10

Most interesting is the difference in z. Why should the preemptor in Chicken repent more frequently than in Prisoner's Dilemma? It cannot be because he is more sure that retaliation will eventually occur. In fact retaliation is actually less certain in Chicken, as can be surmised from the larger magnitude of P and seen directly in the larger value of y. It must therefore be the magnitude of the prospective punishment associated with retaliation, which induces the preemptor to retreat from D to C more frequently in Chicken than in Prisoner's Dilemma. In other words, within the range of the payoffs examined, the magnitude of the punishment for DD is a more effective deterrent than the certainty of the punishment.

At this point one might be tempted to speculate on the relevance of this result to some current theories of deterrence. Penologists some- times argue that certainty of conviction is a more powerful deterrent of crime than the severity of punishment. Something of this sort may also be at the basis of the various theories of measured response, which have supplanted the short-lived doctrine of massive retaliation in the thinking of American strategists. Our results with Chicken seem to show the opposite: More severe punishment seems to be a more effective deterrent than more certain punishment. It goes without say- ing that a generalization from a laboratory game played for pennies to real life problems, some of global magnitude, is foolhardy, and we are comtemplating nothing of the sort. Our only purpose in drawing the analogy is to point out that even in the simplest conceivable situa- tion, like the 2×2 laboratory game, fine distinctions must be made before one ventures to state general principles such as "Certainty of punishment is a more effective deterrent than magnitude of punish- ment," or vice versa. (Nothing in our arguments implies any con- clusion concerning the deterrence potential of progressively more severe punishments when the degree of certainty, in real life remains constant.) Aside from the problem of finding a common measuring stick ("a tradeoff") between severity of punishment and certainty of punishment, the very notion of deterrence needs to be specified more precisely. In our games, for example, the magnitudes of both x and z are measures of deterrence. The former is a measure of the extent to which a player is behaving, presumably for fear of retaliation; the latter is a measure of the extent to which a player stops misbehaving for fear of retaliation. (On the other hand, $|w|$ is not a measure of deterrence, because this parameter refers to a state in which the player is already being punished. As for y, it is a measure of the player's propensity to continue to be exploited.)

We see that the sort of deterrence which keeps a player behaving is more effective in Prisoner's Dilemma than in Chicken. Here the certainty of retaliation seems to be the stronger factor. On the other hand, the kind of deterrence which induces a player to stop misbehaving (to quit D, although rewarded, for fear of retaliation) is more effective in Chicken than in Prisoner's Dilemma. Here severity seems to be the stronger factor. We will note, in passing, that the punishment is always actually experienced in our games, unlike some of the punishments which are hypothesized in theories of nuclear deterrence, for example.

Figure 11 shows the comparison of M in the two composite games.

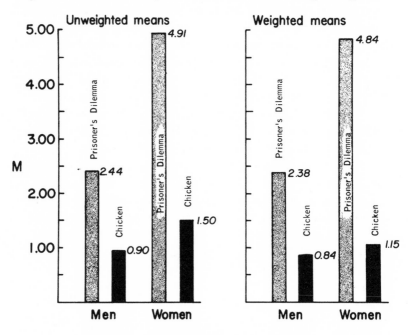

FIGURE 11

It should be noted that the psychological interpretation of M in Prisoner's Dilemma has a meaning different from the corresponding meaning in Chicken. A unilateral run in Chicken is analogous to appeasement, inasmuch as it represents giving in to the preemptor. In Prisoner's Dilemma, on the other hand, a unilateral run does not represent giving in. It has more of the flavor of a pacifist response. The unilateral cooperator could get more by defecting, even if the other player continues to defect. Thus the unilateral runs in Prisoner's

Dilemma are more akin to martyrdom or at least to teaching by example. Thus in the context of Prisoner's Dilemma, M stands for the failure of martyrdom index, while in Chicken it stands for the failure of appeasement index.

From Fig. 11, we see that appeasement in Chicken is more likely to succeed than martyrdom in Prisoner's Dilemma. We see also that both appeasement and martyrdom are more likely to succeed when men play men than when women play women.

Comparison of skewness is shown in Table 6. Column 2

TABLE 6. COMPARISONS OF SKEWNESS

Fraction of Blocks	Normal Distribution	Prisoner's Dilemma	Chicken
Indeterminate		.23	.20
$< 1\sigma$	.68	.63	.60
$< 2\sigma$	.95	.83	.79
$< 3\sigma$	.99	.93	.87
$< 4\sigma$	1.00	.99	.92
$< 5\sigma$		1.00	.96
$< 6\sigma$			.97
$< 7\sigma$			.98
$< 8\sigma$			.98
$< 9\sigma$			.99
$< 10\sigma$			.99
$< 11\sigma$			1.00

shows the expected fractions of blocks in which $| C_1 - C_2 |$ falls within the given number of standard deviations (Column 1) from the expected value (zero) of ($C_1 - C_2$). Column 3 shows the observed fractions in Prisoner's Dilemma (data of men and women combined). Column 4 shows the observed fractions in Chicken. We see that the distribution of Prisoner's Dilemma blocks is only slightly more heavily weighted at the extremes than the normal distribution. This bias is more pronounced in Chicken. The blocks with large deviations give evidence of the preemption-appeasement effect. An analogous effect in Prisoner's Dilemma, which would be interpreted as martyrdom-exploitation, is not nearly as pronounced.

It remains to compare the time courses of the variables in the two composite games. From these we may get an impression of what is being learned in each of the games. For this purpose we lump the data obtained from male and female populations. In the interest of increasing the number of subjects, we shall also include data obtained from mixed pairs playing Games IV and XI (i.e., men playing against women). Thus our Prisoner's Dilemma population will now comprise sixty pairs. (Previous analysis of the data obtained from mixed pairs indicates that on all of the variables examined here their performance falls squarely between the performances of male pairs and that of female pairs.)

The initial trends are compared in Fig. 12. Note that the downward trend is much more pronounced in Prisoner's Dilemma than in Chicken. The slight downward trend observed in Chicken is due entirely to the female population, here combined with the male population (cf. Fig. 3).

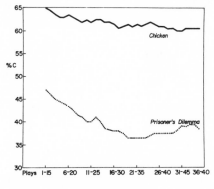

FIGURE 12

The time courses of C, CD, (CD + DC), and DD are shown in Fig. 13. Here we have clear evidence of learning. Briefly, the C frequencies increase, largely through the increase of cooperation (CC) and at the expense of DD and of the unilateral outcomes. The rate of learning seems to be greater in Prisoner's Dilemma than in Chicken. Note, however, that in Chicken, the CC frequencies are higher than in Prisoner's Dilemma and the DD frequencies are already lower in the first fifty plays. Consequently there is less room for improvement in Chicken. On the other hand, the unilaterals tend to decline more rapidly in Prisoner's Dilemma, at least at the start. This is to be expected, since in Prisoner's Dilemma there is a gain, not a cost, associated in switching to D when one has received the sucker's payoff.

The comparison of the time courses of x, y, z, and w is shown in Fig. 14. The clearest evidence of learning is with regard to x. The rate of learning is less rapid in Chicken than in Prisoner's Dilemma, which

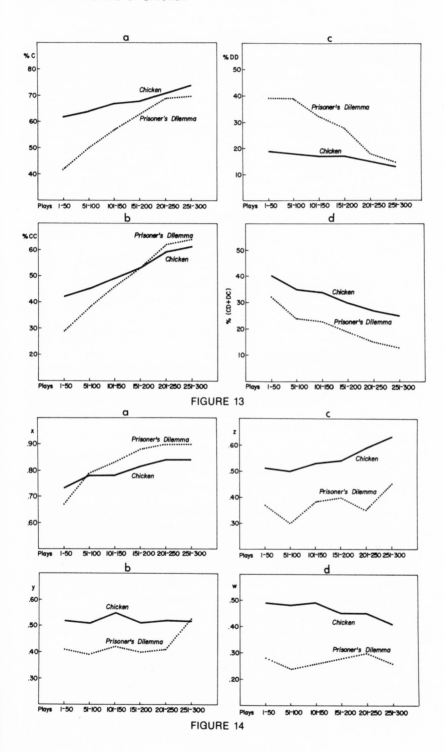

FIGURE 13

FIGURE 14

accounts for the larger values of x observed in the latter game. Note that initially Chicken shows a larger x (i.e., fewer defections from CC). We note also that the most pronounced differences between the two games, i.e., the values of y, z, and w, hold throughout the entire time course.

The time courses of Q and Q^* are compared in Fig. 15.

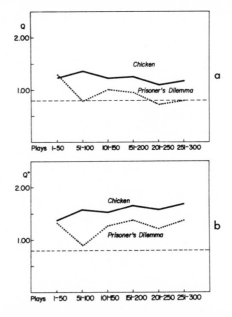

FIGURE 15. The dotted line represents the expected value of Q (and of Q^*) under the null hypothesis that the difference $(C_1 - C_2)$ is subject only to independently statistical fluctuations of C_1 and C_2 around a common mean value.

Note that from the second block on, the value of Q in Prisoner's Dilemma (Fig. 15a) practically coincides with the expected value (0.8) under the null hypothesis. However, when the lock-in effect is factored out, some skewness remains (Fig. 15b). This is perhaps due to the difference in the inherent cooperative propensities between pairs of players randomly selected from a population, in which these propensities are distributed. (Our null hypothesis was, in effect, an assumption that the propensities of each individual fluctuated statistically around the same mean value.) In Chicken, Q is considerably above expectation and so is Q^*, *a fortiori*. These values are also consistently above the corresponding values in Prisoner's Dilemma. This corroborates further our conjecture that the preemption-appeasement effect is operating in Chicken, which is the fundamental difference between Chicken and Prisoner's Dilemma.

REFERENCES

Kahn, Herman. 1965. On Escalation: Metaphors and Scenarios. New York: Praeger.

Rapoport, A. and A. M. Channah. 1965. Prisoner's Dilemma: A Study in Conflict and Cooperation. Ann Arbor: U. of Michigan Press.

PART

APPLICATIONS
OF RELATED APPROACHES

CHAPTER **9**
Hans Hoffmann

A Linear
Programming Approach
to Cultural Intensity

ALMOST thirty years ago, Alfred Kroeber
(1939:223) discussed the significance of cultural intensity in anthropological theory:

> In general, a culture climax or culmination may be regarded as the point from which
> the greatest radiation of culture material has taken place in the area. But it is always
> necessary to remember that as a culture becomes richer, it also tends to become
> more highly organized, and in proportion as its organization grows, so does its ca-
> pacity to assimilate and place new material, whether this be produced within or im-
> ported from without. In the long run, accordingly, high-intensity cultures are the
> most absorptive as well as the most productive. It is by the interaction of both pro-
> cesses that culture culminations seem to be built up. Consequently, an unusually
> successful degree of absorption tends to lead to further "inventive" productiveness
> and outward influencing, and so on, until the process fails somewhere and a condi-
> tion of stability is reached or a decline set in; or a newer center begins to dominate
> the old.

A systematic investigation of such cultural processes requires that
intuitive concepts like "richness" and "organization" be translated into
unambiguous forms. On the level of poetry, a "culture becoming richer"
may evoke very specific images. Unhappily these may not be the same
among different poets. Kroeber, of course, was well aware of this
point and suggested (1939:224) that "if it ever proves possible to find
some objective measure of cultural intensity . . . the history of nonhis-
toric peoples and culture could be better projected than now when
feeling or intuition is our chief guidance."

Clearly the concept of measure is prior to any empirical investiga-

Field work among the Shipibo during 1963 was supported by National Institute
of Mental Health Grant MH 07827–01 and by the Research Foundation of the
State University of New York. The writer is indebted to Sharon Brewer for her
quantitative analysis of the Shipibo field notes, as well as for a number of
fundamental criticisms during the evolution of this paper.

179

tions including those of anthropology. Since mathematics is the conceptual scheme within which empirical investigations are most fruitfully articulated, a mathematical definition of measure (Lightstone 1956:76) seems in order:

Let S be a collection of subsets of a given set such that $(A \cup B)\epsilon S$ whenever $A\epsilon S$ and $B\epsilon S$. We shall say that μ is a *measure on* S if and only if μ is a mapping of S into the non-negative real numbers such that $\mu (A \cup B) = \mu (A) + \mu (B)$ whenever $A\epsilon S$, $B\epsilon S$, and $A \cap B = 0$. NOTE: Any mapping which possesses the stated property is said to be *additive*.

Mathematics can articulate scientific investigations if the empirical data can be interpreted as sets, and empirical processes as operations on these sets. For example, suppose that S consists of sets of people; let $A\epsilon S$, and suppose that $\mu (A)$ is the total income of all members of A. Then μ is an additive mapping of S into the non-negative real numbers; hence μ is a measure on S.

An objective measure of cultural intensity may be developed from a mathematical treatment of anthropological data. It will be sought among the various operations that can be performed on sets of such data. There are at least two strategies for developing a mathematical treatment of empirical data. One involves the piling of empirical data together in the hope that its mathematical structure will eventually suggest itself. This, as pointed out by Atkinson, Bower, and Crothers (1965:20), was essentially Clark Hull's approach:

In his major work, *Principles of Behavior* [Hull 1943], he stated a set of postulates dealing with a number of variables that had been identified in earlier experiments. The postulates were stated both verbally and in the form of mathematical equations. In many cases, the postulate was simply a generalization of an empirical result. How-.ever, the hope was that the aggregation of postulates would jointly imply much more than the specific experimental facts from which they were separately inferred; this was indeed the case.

A second strategy, the approach used here, involves the scanning of abstract mathematical structures in the hope that ethnographic data can be mapped into some of them. A measure of the intensity of cultural organization can then be interpreted within aspects of this structure.

We shall begin with cybernetics, an abstract model dealing with all forms of behavior insofar as they are regular, or determinate, or reproducible. Cybernetics provides a fundamental vocabulary for articulating a culture theory as well as the intellectual posture that shapes its development. As Ashby (1956:3) puts it:

The older point of view saw, say, an ovum grow into a rabbit and asked "why does it do this?—why does it not just stay an ovum?" The attempt to answer this question led to the study of energetics and to the discovery of many reasons why the ovum should change—it can oxidize its fat, and fat provides free energy; it has phosphorylating enzymes, and can pass its metabolites around a Krebs' cycle; and so on. In these studies the concept of energy was fundamental.

Quite different, though equally valid, is the point of view of cybernetics. It takes for granted that the ovum has abundant free energy, and that it is so delicately poised metabolically as to be, in a sense, explosive. Growth of some form there will be; cybernetics asks "why should the changes be to the rabbit-form, and not a dog-form, a fish-form, or even a teratoma-form?" Cybernetics envisages a set of possibilities much wider than the actual, and then asks why the particular case should conform to its usual particular restriction.

At this point the terminology of cybernetics will be superimposed on Kroeber's informal language. We interpret the culture of a tribe or village as a *system*, which is left as an undefined term for the moment. A *state* of a system is a well-defined condition or property that can be recognized if it recurs. The variable "number of culture traits in a tribe" describes one such property. "Number of hours spent fishing by certain villagers during a week" is another. This variable can range from zero to a large number. Each of these values taken by the variable is a possible state of that culture, although it can only be in one of them at one time. In other words, the set of possible states is divided into two subsets: states that have been observed and states that have not been observed. The union of these subsets is called the *phase space* of that system.

Kroeber's phrase *organization of a culture* may be interpreted as a statement about the allocation of a tribe's resources, whether they be wealth, time, emotions, or whatever. Some tribes spend a lot of time hunting, but little on agriculture. A statement about such relative time expenditures abstracts at least a portion of the organization of that tribe's culture. A list of time allocations describes one state of that culture system. Such a list is a compound entity, having a definite number of entries or components. It can be represented as a vector—i.e., an ordered set of numbers that can be manipulated as a single entity. Hence the state of a culture, although made up of many different parts (time allocations of different activities), can be represented as a single vector.

Vectors are manipulated here in their guise of algebraic quantities. An intuitive understanding of these manipulations is essential, however, and it is gained more readily from a geometric point of view. The language of geometry is simpler and more immediately informative than the language of algebra. To say that, in three dimensions, "a plane cuts a sphere in a circle" requires a tangle of three algebraic formulas. When we proceed from three to more dimensions we run up against a conceptual barrier that is somewhat easier to pierce algebraically. Still, even though it is doubtful that we can ever picture the figures of a hyperspace, we can reason about them geometrically. Some of the results arrived at in this manner are, indeed, exceedingly difficult to establish by algebraic methods (Kendall 1961:4).

Returning to anthropology, consider a tribe whose economy consists of hunting and fishing. We set up a two-dimensional phase space and plot hours of hunting along the x-axis and hours of fishing along the y-axis. Each point of this plane represents a possible organization (or state) of that economy. Each point is a geometric representation of a two-component vector. Only one of them, however, can correspond to the observed organization at any time.

The two-dimensional phase space can be moved parallel to itself along a straight line (the time axis) perpendicular to the original space. The first observation was made at zero hours. Some time later, say after 100 hours, interest in fishing has expanded at the expense of hunting. The point corresponding to this organization is further away from the y-axis, and closer to the x-axis than the first point. Moreover, the second is 100 units above the first along the time dimension. A line connecting these two points in what is now a three-dimensional space is the trajectory or world line of that culture's economic organization. Since we now work in three dimensions, the vectors will have three components—hours hunting, hours fishing, and hours from initial observation. The world line connecting the two points is itself a vector with these components: hours hunting$_{100}$ − hours hunting$_0$; hours fishing$_{100}$ − hours fishing$_0$; hours from initial observation.

We have noted that mathematics can articulate scientific investigations if the empirical data can be interpreted as sets, and empirical processes as operations on these sets. However, the inverse problem must also be considered before a mathematical system can be applied validly to the data. Granted that vectors are sets, is there an empirical interpretation for certain operations on these sets? Specifically, does the adding of two vectors of cultural complexity make any sense empirically? We will take the somewhat arbitrary view that if the new set generated by the adding of the vectors can exist in the empirical world, the operation of addition is valid in that scientific discourse, even if no empirical interpretation of the operation itself is immediately apparent. In this case, vector addition defines a new point that is clearly in the space, even though we make no anthropological use of this particular operation.

Mathematically, the set of vectors of cultural complexity can be interpreted as a mathematical system called a *vector space*. These vectors are closed under the operation of addition as long as the population of the village is not arbitrarily restricted. In other words, vector addition implies that a component such as "number of hours spent hunting by a group of villagers per week" must be allowed to expand indefinitely, even though the number of hours in a week is limited to a fixed value. Vector addition is clearly commutative, with zero vector serving as an identity element. A difficulty arises with inverses, which require vectors with negative components. There is no physical activity that takes place in minus two hours. However, if we interpret negative components as reflecting degrees of psychological antipathy to the activity in question, we have an awkward but perhaps acceptable resolution of the difficulty. Vectors of cultural organization can now be interpreted as an Abelian group.

Scalar multiplication presents no difficulties; it is distributive and associative. The scalar "one" is the identity element for multiplication. Thus, in the language of algebra, the set of vectors that measure cultural organization constitutes a vector space. In the language of cybernetics, the elements of this vector space are points of a phase space.

Phase spaces can be used as mere storage devices for empirical data. By exploiting certain mathematical properties, not of the data but of the spaces themselves, however, we can do a great deal more. An example may clarify this. Hull (1943) was interested in describing the trajectory of observed states of a biological organism experiencing learning. His function $sHr = M(1 - e^{-iN})$ is a transformation which takes that biological system through this sequence of states. It predicts which state will be observed at a given point in time. Hull was not, however, concerned with the subset of nonobserved states, and he did not exploit mathematical relationships between elements of the subset "observed" and the subset "nonobserved" states.

A different approach is used in this paper. Mathematical relationships between these two subsets play a central role in dealing with the intensity of cultural organization, as that variable is defined here. In other words we will develop the purely mathematical properties of a phase space, and then exploit them to attain purely anthropological objectives. This mode of attack is distantly analogous to the exploitation of the field concept in physics. A somewhat closer analogy involves the concepts of strategy spaces and outcome spaces in game theory (Blackwell and Girshick 1954:4).

Vector spaces are rather general mathematical structures that take many forms. It is convenient to distinguish them in terms of their *metrics*. These are various abstractions of the "distance between two points," although the interpretation of this phrase can take rather exotic forms. Basically, however, metrics are a collection of functions that map a pair of vectors into the non-negative real numbers. From a more abstract, topological point of view, vector spaces are a special case of metric spaces. These may be described as a nonempty set S (of vectors, in this case) together with a function that assigns to any pair of elements X and Y a real number $d(X, Y)$ provided that this function satisfies three conditions: (1) The distance between two vectors X and Y is zero only if they coincide; (2) the distance between X and Y is the same as the distance between Y and X; and (3) for any three vectors, the distance between any pair of them is less than or equal to the sum of the distances between the other two pairs. Many functions have these properties, including the Euclidean metric $d(X, Y) = \left(\sum_{i=1}^{n} (x_i - y_i)^2 \right)^{\frac{1}{2}}$. A vector space in which this particular distance function is postulated is called a finite dimensional Euclidean metric space. In postulating this metric we have committed ourselves to a flat rather than curved space, a choice congruent with the mathematical limitations of the linear programming approach.

We may summarize by noting that the union of the subsets of observed and nonobserved states of cultural organization constitutes a phase space. Algebraically, the elements of this phase space constitute a vector space. Topologically, it is a metric space, i.e., an ordered pair (S,d) in which S is a nonempty set and d is a metric on S. For each element X of S, one can define a function $d_X: S \rightarrow R^1$ by the formula $d_X(Y) = d(X,Y)$; d_X might appropriately be called "the distance (of Y) from X" (Bushaw 1963:65). In this paper, Y will be taken as an element from the subset of observed states, while X can be taken from either the subset of observed states or from the subset of nonobserved states. The element X will be defined as representing the maximum possible intensity of cultural organization, and the element Y representing actual observed states of the culture. A distance between Y and X will be defined as a measure of the intensity of cultural organization.

Kroeber (1939:222) interpreted the intensity of cultural organization in essentially combinatorial terms: "A more intense as compared to a less intense culture normally contains not only more material . . . as well as more precisely and articulately established interrelations between the materials."

Is there any way to decide which among several combinations of cultural materials and activities are more precisely articulated than others? Can vectors of cultural organization be divided so that those in any one subset are at an equivalent level of articulation? Then if an order relation can be defined on this collection of subsets, we have constructed an objective measure of cultural intensity.

The culture of a tribe is a system of activities—social, ceremonial, economic. As it moves through time, people, goods, and energy are mapped from various parts of this system onto others. A kinship system is a collection of functions that map people from one subset of status positions onto others in the course of their lives. These functions define an endomorphism of a kinship system as the culture moves through time. An economic system is a collection of functions that map people onto several subsets of subsistence activities during the course of a week. Vectors of cultural (economic) organization describe the amount of time spent in each subset per week.

Economic activities produce a variety of nutrients such as proteins and carbohydrates, essential for living. For example, in the Shipibo village of San Francisco de Yarinacocha (Hoffmann 1964:259–76) on the upper Amazon, the writer observed three types of economic activities in July 1963—fishing, farming, and commercial activities. Data on the economic organization of one family of two adult males, two adult females, and three children was collected. Fishing produced fifty pounds of fish which in turn contained 4900 grams of proteins and 0 grams of carbohydrates. Agricultural activity produced 24 pounds of plantains, yucca and fruit which contained 138 grams of protein and 3264 grams of carbohydrates. Commercial activity eventually generated 16 pounds of miscellaneous foods which were estimated to contain 92 grams of proteins and 2176 grams of carbohydrates. This Shipibo family seemed to flourish with a weekly stock of 5130 grams of protein and 5440 grams of carbohydrates, regardless of the source. These data may be summarized in the equations:

$$\tfrac{4900}{50}x_1 + \tfrac{138}{24}x_2 + \tfrac{92}{16}x_3 \le 5130$$

$$\tfrac{0}{50}x_1 + \tfrac{3264}{24}x_2 + \tfrac{2176}{16}x_3 \le 5440$$

This collection of nutrients was acquired through 25 hours of fishing on the part of the family, 19 hours of farming, and 43 hours of commercial activity; i.e., the observed vector of cultural organization was (25, 19, 43). An hour of fishing produced 50/25 pounds of fish, an hour of farming 24/19 pounds of produce, an hour of commercial activity 16/43 pounds of miscellaneous food. Thus (50/25, 24/19, 26/43) is a payoff vector.

Was this the most efficient mix of activities or would a different vector of cultural organization have generated the same amount of proteins and carbohydrates with less effort? We now define a precisely articulated combination of economic activities as one which minimizes the amount of time needed to provide nutrients for one's family. This definition reflects, somewhat tangentially, the spirit of Leslie A. White, who feels that cultural development is determined by the efficiency with which technological means are put to work. In other words we must minimize a cost function:

$$c_1 x_1 + c_2 x_2 + c_3 x_3$$

where the c's are the number of hours needed to obtain a pound of fish, to produce commercial food, and to compare it with the observed cost function (which is the product of the vector of cultural organization and the payoff vector). This vector product is a single number describing the total payoff from that particular organization of economic activities. Then, on the assumption of constant payoffs, one can associate a total payoff with each element in the space of vectors of cultural organization. From the point of view of physics, we have defined a *field*, i.e., a physical quantity (total payoff) which takes on different values at different points in space. More precisely, it is a *scalar field* because it is characterized at each point by a single number.

Payoffs of economic activities are likely to change in the real world; hence the definition of cultural intensity developed here is clearly only a first approximation. However, an analysis of this definition is likely to speed the development of a more realistic approximation. Nonconstant payoffs in a quasi-anthropological setting are discussed by Gould (1965). If each element of the field consists of a row vector which is the product of a row vector of cultural organization and a payoff *matrix* (instead of a column vector), a second approximation can perhaps be constructed, in terms of a *vector field*.

Thus far we have not circumscribed the metric space/vector space/ scalar field in any way, so that its mathematical structure will stand out most clearly. Once this structure has been inserted into the real world of anthropological data, however, its elements have to be partitioned into subsets of feasible and nonfeasible elements. Feasible elements can occur in the world, but nonfeasible elements are mathematical entities that are excluded from the world. A vector of economic organization whose total payoff is less than that needed to support a family is an example of a nonfeasible element. Clearly "exclusion" refers here not to a logical process but to an empirical condition. Inadequate payoff implies an unstable village; outmigration or infanticide may occur. The intensity of such a cultural organization is below a threshold of adequacy; its intensity has degenerated. Feasible vectors thus characterize a stable or growing village culture, nonfeasible vectors an unstable or disintegrating one.

   This empirical relationship between elements of two subsets is called a *constraint*. Ashby (1963:127) defines a constraint as a relation between two sets when the variety that exists under one condition is less than the variety that exists under another. The variety of vectors of cultural organization is not limited. However the variety of feasible vectors is quite limited. Constraints effect this partitioning—i.e., the constraint of adequate payoff selects from the vectors a feasible subset. In a two-dimensional vector space a constraint is represented mathematically as a line or 1-flat that divides it into half-planes. One includes the feasible elements, the other the nonfeasible ones. In three dimensions a constraint is a plane or 2-flat dividing it into half spaces. In n dimensions a constraint is represented as an $(n-1)$-dimensional hyperplane or $(n-1)$-flat which determines a half space bounded by that hyperplane.

   Economic activity cannot occur in a negative number of hours. Hence, three basic constraints immediately present themselves: x_1 (hours spent fishing per week by all relevant family members), x_2 (hours spent farming), and x_3 (hours spent in commercial activities). All three constraints have to be non-negative, that is, $x_1 \geqslant 0$, $x_2 \geqslant 0$, $x_3 \geqslant 0$. Further, since there are only 402 waking hours in the week of a family of 4.5 adults, the time spent on all economic activity is constrained by this figure. That is, $x_1 + x_2 + x_3 \leqslant 402$. Cultural reality is somewhat more complex, however. In Shipibo culture only the men fish. A family with two adult males thus cannot spend more than 222 hours per week fishing. During five of these hours the waves on Lake Yarinacocha are too high for the Shipibo dugout canoes, which further reduces this time to 217 hours; i.e., $x_1 \leqslant 217$. This constraint is biological (sleeping), cultural (males only), and natural (wave action). Both males and females participate in farming and in commercial activity, however, so that $x_2 \leqslant 402$ and $x_3 \leqslant 402$ if neither land nor commercial demand is constrained. Land seems to be fairly plentiful around Yarinacocha, but commercial demand is definitely constrained. Hence the last inequality is superceded by $x_3 \leqslant 54$. Finally we add two previously developed constraints involving the minimum amount of protein and carbohydrates needed per family. Collecting all these together and changing direction of some of the inequalities by multiplying through by -1 results in the following array:

$$-x_1 \leq 0$$

$$-x_2 \leq 0$$

$$-x_3 \leq 0$$

$$x_1 \leq 217$$

$$x_2 \leq 402$$

$$x_3 \leq 54$$

$$x_1 + x_2 + x_3 \leq 402$$

$$98x_1 + 5.75x_2 + 5.75x_3 \leq 5130$$

$$136x_2 + 136x_3 \leq 5440$$

Under certain mathematical conditions a collection of constraints may intersect and carve a region out of this vector space. Such a region is called a *polyhedral convex set*. In two dimensions this is a polygon, in three a polyhedron, in more than three dimensions a polytope, i.e., a figure bounded by a set of $(n-1)$-flats. It can be demonstrated mathematically that convex sets enclose all feasible elements. Depending on the mathematical properties of the collection of constraints, these sets may be bounded or unbounded. In this paper we shall deal with bounded convex sets only.

We now repeat an earlier question in more specific terms. Is there any way to decide which of these feasible elements is more precisely articulated or more intensively articulated than the others? Which element represents the maximum possible intensity of cultural organization? Which of the feasible vectors of cultural organization (i.e., points within the polytope defined by the empirical constraints) minimizes the amount of time needed to provide enough food per family?

Comparable questions have arisen from military programming and planning problems, and in 1947 a solution method, called linear programming, was developed and applied by G. B. Dantzig and his associates in the U.S. Air Force. It can be demonstrated mathematically that the feasible element sought is one of the vertices of the polytope or convex set. Further, the simplex computational procedure devised by Dantzig isolates these vertices and determines which one minimizes the time needed to feed a family.

We have called attention to an existence theorem. A maximally integrated vector of cultural organization exists, given a vector space, a set of constraints, and a payoff function. Further, it can be isolated with purely mechanical and finite computational procedures. Thus a measure of cultural intensity in the form μ (Int. Y) $= d(X,Y)$ seems attainable, where X is the maximally integrated vector, and Y any observed organization of culture. It remains to discuss the distance function itself.

A vector space of culture organization has the mathematical structure of a scalar field—i.e., a field characterized at each point by single number. The structure of this field may be rendered visible by drawing contours or surfaces through all points for which the field has the same value. These surfaces are a family of parallel lines, planes, or hyperplanes, depending on the dimensions of the space. Since the total payoff for all elements of each hyperplane is the same, they may be interpreted as subsets of vectors of cultural organization at an equivalent level of articulation. A function measuring the distance between these hyperplanes defines one order relation on this collection of subsets. However, we are searching for a somewhat less general distance function here, one that measures the distance between a single element (the maximally integrated vector X) and the hyperplane containing the observed vector of cultural organization, Y. This function has been derived by Charnes and Cooper (1961:164–66):

$$d(X, Y) = \left(P - \sum_{i=1}^{n} x_i y_i\right)\left(\sum_{i=1}^{n} y_i^2\right)^{-\frac{1}{2}}$$

where P is the total payoff of the observed vector whose components are $(y_1, y_2, \cdots, y_n)$, and $(x_1, x_2, \cdots, x_n)$ is the calculated vector of maximum integration. This distance function maps the pair of vectors into the non-negative real numbers and thus serves as an objective measure of cultural intensity.

REFERENCES

Ashby, W. Ross. 1963. An Introduction to Cybernetics. New York: Wiley.

Atkinson, Richard C., Bower, Gordon H., Crothers, Edward J. 1965. An Introduction to Mathematical Learning Theory. New York: Wiley.

Blackwell, David, Girschick, M. A. 1954. Theory of Games and Statistical Decisions. New York: Wiley.

Bushaw, D. 1963. Elements of General Topology. New York: Wiley.

Charnes, A., Cooper, W. W. 1961. Management Models and Industrial Applications of Linear Programming. New York: Wiley.

Gould, Peter R. 1965. Wheat on Kilimanjaro: The Perception of Choice within Game and Learning Theory Frameworks in Yearbook of the Society for General Systems Research, V. X.

Hoffmann, Hans. 1964. Money, Ecology, and Acculturation Among the Shipibo of Peru in Explorations in Cultural Anthropology. New York: McGraw-Hill.

Hull, Clark. 1943. Principles of Behavior: An Introduction to Behavior Theory. New York: Appleton-Century-Crofts.

Kendall, M. G. 1961. A Course in the Geometry of n Dimensions. New York: Hafner.

Kroeber, A. L. 1939. Cultural and Natural Areas of Native North America. Berkeley: U. of California Press.

Lightstone, A. H. 1965. Symbolic Logic and the Real Number System. New York: Harper & Row.

CHAPTER **10**

Ira R. Buchler
R. Michael McKinlay

Decision Processes
in Culture:
A Linear
Programming Analysis

Iɴ Mesoamerican studies, "ladder system" refers to two types of political hierarchy. The first type involves an alternation between civil and religious offices (Camara 1952; Nash 1958; Carrasco 1961). In a model career pattern, a man initially assumes a religious cargo, then a civil cargo, and so on. These offices entail a rather substantial outlay of commodities, time, and energy; expenditures that increase in scale as a man ascends the hierarchy. An ideal type of Mesoamerican civil-religious hierarchy is represented in Fig. 1.

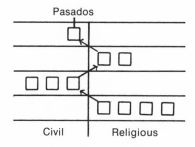

FIGURE 1. Ideal type of Meso-American civil-religious hierarchy. Adapted from Cancian 1964:338.

The writing of this paper was supported by a grant from the Group Psychology Branch, Office of Naval Research. Various expenses involved in its preparation were defrayed by a grant from the Institute of Latin American Studies, University of Texas. I.R.B. would like to express his gratitude to the Research Institute of the Graduate School, University of Texas, for support of this study during May-September 1965, and to the Institute of Latin American Studies, University of Texas for support of a brief visit to Atempan during January-February 1966.

In the second type, civil positions do not count for advancement in the system of religious cargos. Cargos are essentially religious positions, or "offices devoted to the performance of ritual connected with the Catholic church" (Cancian 1965:22). The religious hierarchy of Atempan, Sierra de Puebla, Mexico, is of this type, and may be represented as shown in Fig. 2.

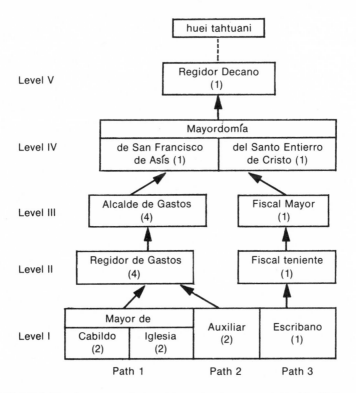

FIGURE 2. The Atempan religious hierarchy. ("ceremonial ladder.") From Buchler (1967).

The arrows in the figure indicate the three paths in the Atempan system, leading to *Regidor Decano*.

Path 1
1.1 *Mayor de Cabildo* or *Iglesia*
1.2 *Regidor de Gastos*

1.3 *Alcalde de Gastos*
  4 *Mayordomía de San Francisco*
    de Asís or *del Santo*
    Entierro de Cristo
  5 *Regidor Decano*

Path 2
2.1 *Escribano*
2.2 *Fiscal teniente*
2.3 *Fiscal mayor*
  4 *Mayordomía de San Francisco*
    de Asís or *del Santo*
    Entierro de Cristo
  5 *Regidor Decano*

Path 3
3.1 *Auxiliar*
1.2 *Regidor de Gastos*
1.3 *Alcalde de Gastos*
  4 *Mayordomía de San Francisco de Asís*
    or *del Santo Entierro de Cristo*
  5 *Regidor Decano*

The relationship of cargo systems to class differentiation has been the topic of a good deal of discussion. Theoretical positions on this topic may be summarized:

(i) *Wolf* (1962:216) suggests that cargo systems liquidate surpluses, level differences of wealth, and consequently inhibit "the growth of class distinctions based on wealth."

(ii) *Carrasco* (1961:484, 489, 491) suggests the following equations: (1) large towns = cargo system with few high-level positions = (or reflects) class differentiation; (2) small towns = achievement ladders = (or reflects) classless communities. No demographic breaking point is specified.

(iii) *Cancian* (1965:107) suggests that "participation in the cargo system reflects an individual's economic rank and determines, in large measure, his social rank."

How individuals ascend ladder systems, and why some cargo careers are terminated on the initial or second level of the system are questions that have, in general, received somewhat less analytic consideration than the general functions of ladders in village social organization. Principles of mobility rather than general functions are the central concern of this paper.

Rather than focusing on the manipulation of economic and political allies, productivity, economic rank, and similar variables, we are concerned with the decision processes underlying ceremonial ladders, that is, the decision processes of the *huei tahtuani, pasados*, or any other group of men who must decide who shall and who shall not advance to positions of high prestige and moral rank. Our rationale for this emphasis may be clarified somewhat by an example from a more familiar cultural context: the academic marketplace. Here, an individual may concentrate his efforts on publication and service to the profession, thereby enhancing his professional reputation. He may devote most of his time to local politics, teaching, and service to the university, or he may employ a mixture of these strategies. It is, however, the evaluation of these strategies by individuals in a position to implement or impede individual mobility, rather than the employment of a particular strategy type (or mixed strategy), that is a significant determinant of career patterns.

This perspective poses the following problems: What are the significant (i.e. criterial) evaluative criteria that are processed in arriving at culturally appropriate mobility decisions? How are alternative strategies evaluated by decision-makers, e.g., the *huei tahtuani*? In evaluating mixed strategies, what are the numerical weights attached to individual strategies? Are numerical thresholds employed in the evaluation of strategies? For example, we would be interested in determining whether there is a significant difference in terms of future mobility within the ceremonial system between an individual who spends the equivalent of 4,000 pesos on a second-level cargo and an individual who spends 3,000 or 5,000. Our interest in numerical thresholds is derived from case histories such as those shown in Table 1 (Buchler 1967).

PAYOFF FUNCTIONS

An approach of this sort directs our attention to other decision problems that cannot be considered in detail in this paper, for example,

TABLE 1. SELECTED CARGO CARRIERS

Year and Cargo	Expenditure per Cargo (pesos)	Number of Cargos	Total expenditure (pesos)	Average expenditure per Cargo (pesos)
Career I				
Escribano (1943)	1,500			
Fiscal teniente (1952)	6,000			
Fiscal mayor (1956)	7–8,000	4(5)	22,500	5,620
Mayordomo de San Francisco de Asis (1960)	8,000			
Elected Regidor Decano (1965–66)	?			
Career II				
Escribano (1947)	1,200	2	4,300	2,150
Fiscal teniente (1956)	3,100			
Career III				
Mayor de Iglesia (1940)	1,500			
Fiscal Mayor (1943)	8,000			
Fiscal mayor[a] (1950)	8,000	4(5)	20,500	5,125
Mayordomo del Santo Entierro de Cristo (1952)	3,000			
Regidor Decano (1964–65)	?			
Career IV				
Escribano (1956)	3,000			
Fiscal teniente (1962)	8,000	2(3)	11,000	5,500
Fiscal mayor (1965)	?			

Career V				
Mayor de Iglesia (1942)	1,500	2	3,500	1,750
Regidor de Gastos (1953)	2,000			

SOURCE: Buchler (1967).
ᵃ Skipped second level in 1943 because of the unavailability of candidates and was therefore required to accept a third-level charge on two occasions (1943, 1950).

TABLE 2. PAYOFF TO POLICE

	Battle	Skirmish	Row Minima
Enter jungle	−5	−7	−7
Protect supplies	+8	+1	+1 (maximin)
Column maxima	+8	+1 (minimax)	

temporal changes in payoff functions. In game theory, according to Shubik (1964:13), one denotes

the set of all possible strategies that can be used by a specific player, whose name is i, by the symbol S_i. This is the set of every possible plan of action that the ith player can have, taking into account his resources, the resources of his competitors, and the rules of the game. Suppose that this player selects a specific strategy, which we will call s_i, out of the set of all his available strategies. Suppose that there are n players. The outcome of the game will depend on the strategy that each of them selects. For every outcome of the game, each player will have a valuation. We call the table which gives the valuation of a player for all outcomes of the game his *payoff function*. We denote the payoff function of the ith player by $P_i(s_1, s_2, s_3, \ldots s_n)$.

The ceremonial ladder of Atempan may be described as a series of games of normalized form (Shubik 1964:14–20); in extensive form, it may be illustrated by means of a game tree. In the normalized form a game is presented as though it consisted of a single move made simultaneously by each player. "The *normalized* form in a very compact manner summarizes all details concerning strategies and payoffs and presents them in a simple array" (Shubik 1964:19). For example, consider Tables 2 and 3 from Shubik 1964:16–17. According to Shubik (1964:17–18):

It is easy to see that both sides will adopt their second strategy. The police will guard supplies and the guerillas will avoid open battle. When we look at the maximum entry in the column of row minima in [Table 2], we observe that it has a value of 1. Furthermore, when we look at the minimum entry in the row of column maxima, we observe that it has the same value. When this holds true, a game is said to possess a *saddlepoint*. It has been suggested by von Neumann and Morgenstern that *the rational* way to play in this type of game is for each player to adopt a strategy which guarantees that each will obtain the *maximin* payoffs or the best of the worst possible outcomes.

TABLE 3. PAYOFF TO GUERILLAS

	Battle	Skirmish	Row Maxima
Enter jungle	5	7	7
Protect supplies	−8	−1	−1 (minimax)
Column maxima	−8	−1 (maximin)	

In the extensive form the vertices in the game tree represent choice points; the branches represent alternatives (Shubik 1964:20). For example, consider Fig. 3:

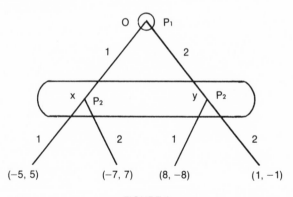

FIGURE 3

In somewhat less formal terminology we would like to pose, at least rhetorically, the following problem: How might an individual's utility function change as a result of his experience on the initial levels of the ceremonial ladder, or any other type of political hierarchy? The following possibilities may be suggested:

1. Prior to assuming a first level cargo, an individual may assign a

relatively high evaluation to the outcome "ascend to moral rank of *Regidor Decano* at any cost." High financial outlays in first and second level cargos may result in a reassessment of the original evaluation of this outcome. Consequently, the outcome "ascend to moral rank of *Regidor Decano* at any cost" may be assigned a low evaluation, and a second level terminal cargo may be assigned a relatively high evaluation.

2. Conversely, an individual may be forced to assume a first level cargo, assign a high evaluation to terminating his cargo career on the first or second level, and then reevaluate the various possible outcomes, assigning a high evaluation to "ascend to moral rank of *Regidor Decano* at any cost."

How utility functions change as a consequence of experience in a political hierarchy is a topic that we can only mention in passing. But we feel that the problem is of sufficient general interest to merit more systematic and formal attention than it has received thus far.

LINEAR PROGRAMMING

Naylor and Byrne (1963:18–19) define the basic problem of linear programming as one of optimizing (minimizing or maximizing) an objective function of the form

$$Z = \sum_{j=1}^{n} C_j X_j \qquad (j = 1, 2, \cdots, n)$$

subject to restraints of the form

$$\sum_{j=1}^{n} a_{ij} X_j \left[\begin{array}{c} \leq \\ = \\ \geq \end{array}\right] b_i \qquad (i = 1, 2, \cdots, m)$$

and

$$x_i \geq 0 \qquad (j = 1, 2, \cdots, n)$$

where

$x_j =$ the quantity of the *j*th variable of interest to the decision-maker, where there are *n* variables being considered: x_j is either an integer 1, if and only if individual *j* obtains a cargo, and $x = 0$ if individual *j* does not.

$c_j =$ the per unit contribution to the objective function (profit or cost) of the *j*th variable, where there are *n* variables: the qualification of individual j in terms of 100's of pesos (average expenditure).

$z =$ the objective function to be maximized or minimized.

$a_i =$ the exchange coefficient of the jth variable in the ith restraint where there are m restraints and n variables: the exchange coefficient for the variable j is equal to 1.

$b_j b_i = .$ the ijth requirement where there are m requirements in all.
For a given j, $b_j = 1$ and the sum along column j.
For a given i, $b_i = 1$ and the sum along row $i \leqslant 1$.

APPLICATIONS

The application of linear programming methods to the cargo system of Atempan may help to uncover the criteria and their relative weights used in the selection of persons for the cargos of this religious hierarchy. If the criteria are adequately quantified, it may ultimately be useful in prediction. The model should therefore be of some relevance to the study of similar processes in political anthropology.

The model to be used is that of the optimal assignment problem used by Gale (1960: 133 ff.). In Gale's terminology the problem may be stated as one of the management of a factory in assigning m individuals I_1, . . . , I_m, to n jobs, J_1, . . . , J_n. We let q_{ij} be the rating or qualifications (stated numerically) of I_i for job J_j. We now assume that the management desires to assign the individuals to the jobs in such a way as to maximize effectiveness as measured by the above ratings.

We now let $X = (x_{11}, x_{12}, . . . , x_{1n}, x_{21}, . . . x_{mn})$, where each x_{ij} is 1 if I_i is assigned to J_i and is 0 if I_i is not assigned to J_i.

If we assume (1) that no individual may hold more than one job and (2) that no job is held by more than one individual, these two facts may be expressed mathematically by the following constraints:

(1) $$\sum_{i=1}^{m} X_{ij} \leq 1 \qquad j = 1, \cdots, n$$

(2) $$\sum_{j=1}^{n} X_{ij} \leq 1 \qquad i = 1, \cdots, m$$

The problem of assigning the individuals now becomes one of maximizing the function

$$f(X) = \sum_{i=1}^{m} \sum_{j=1}^{n} q_{ij}, x_{ij}$$

subject to the constraints (1) and (2) on X.

It is immediately obvious that all individuals will be assigned jobs only if $m \leq n$, that is, the number of individuals is less than or equal to the number of cargos. Within the cargo system it is generally the case that $n \leq m$. Thus, it follows that not every individual will receive a cargo.

When this method is applied to the cargo system of Atempan, the role of the management as selectors is played by the *huei tahtuani*. Each year they select those persons who are to fill the cargos for the ensuing year. The hierarchy consists of five levels. A person is not considered for a cargo on level k ($k = 1, \ldots, 5$ from the lowest to the highest of the hierarchy) unless he has previously held a cargo on level $k - 1$, except under the most extraordinary circumstances. The selection of individuals for any particular level of the hierarchy, therefore, may be considered independent from the selections made for other levels. So the problem of optimal job assignment is now one of five optimal job assignment problems—one for each level of the hierarchy. This is indeed fortunate, for to consider the entire system as one instead of five increases considerably the required computation.

We may now state the optimal problems in the following general terms: on level k of the hierarchy there are n cargos, $J_1, \ldots, J_n$, each of which is to be filled by one individual from those m persons who have previously held cargos on level $k - 1$. The qualifications or rating of individual I_i for cargo J_j is designated by a non-negative integer, q_{ij} (we shall discuss the determination of q_{ij} later). As previously, we let $x_{ij} = 1$, if I_i is selected for J_j; otherwise, $x_{ij} = 0$.

We shall further assume that each cargo will be filled. As stated previously, there are usually more applicants than cargos. Thus, constraints (1) and (2) may be written as:

$$\sum_{i=1}^{m} X_{ij} = 1 \qquad j = 1, \cdots, n \qquad (1.1)$$

$$\sum_{j=1}^{n} X_{ij} \leq 1 \qquad i = 1, \cdots, m \qquad (2.1)$$

Since we have established values for $Q = (q_{ij})$, the solution becomes a mechanical one (and extremely tedious), and the critical problem is to assign numerical values to each of the q_{ij}. In order to do this, we must seek the criteria which the *huei tahtuani* use in making their selections. Then we must decide the relative weights of the criteria and thus combine them into one number for each *(i, j)*.

The problem may be further simplified by assuming that an individual I_i has the same qualifications for each cargo for which he is being considered. Thus we would now have:

$$q_i = q_{i1} = q_{i2} = \cdots = q_{i3} \tag{3}$$

For example, this means that we consider the *Mayordomía de San Francisco de Asís* and the *Mayordomía del Santo Entierro de Cristo* to have the same weights on the various criteria. On level III, we now would consider those candidates for the *Alcalde* positions separately from those for Fiscal mayor. That is, we partition the set $\{J_1, J_2, J_3, J_4, J_5\}$ into $\{J_1, J_2, J_3, J_4/J_5\}$ or $\{J_1, J_2, J_3, J_4\}$ and $\{J_5\}$, where J_1 is the first *Alcalde* and J_5 is Fiscal mayor position. So, for any individual I_i we have $q_i = q_{i1} = q_{i2} = q_{i3} = q_{i4}$.

If we consider the difference of the assignment of I_i to J_j or J_k as unimportant, then there are

$$\frac{m!}{n! \, (m - n)!} \tag{4}$$

possible assignments, where

$$m! = m(m - 1) \cdots 2.1 \tag{5}$$

This is an extensive combinatorial-type problem.

The criteria which, from the ethnography, appear to be most important are:
1. Previous cargo held by I_i.
2. Average expenditure in previous cargos held by I_i.
3. The time which has lapsed since I_i last held a cargo.
4. The age of I_i.

These criteria are the most general. Others have to be considered for specific cargos—for example, a necessary qualification for the cargo of *Escribano* is that one must be able to write. The four general criteria are described in greater detail below:

1. 1. For any individual to be considered for a cargo on level k he must (in nearly all circumstances) have held one on level $k - 1$. If this is not the case, we let $q_i = 0$. Also, if I_i has not held the cargo of *Escribano,* then he is not eligible for the cargo of Fiscal *teniente.* Other specific criteria will be introduced as needed.

2. 1. The average expenditure of I_i will be stated in pesos. If the expenditure at level II is less than 6,000, then $q_i = 0$.

3. 1. If the time lapsed since I_i held his last cargo is greater than five years, then $q_i = 0$. The optimal time appears to be from 2 to 4 years, and in this range we shall assume its value to be constant.

4. 1. The age of the individuals for each level are:

Level	I:	30 years or younger
Level	II:	30 to 35 years
Level	III:	35 to 40 years
Level	IV:	40 to 45 years
Level	V:	46 to 50 years

If the age falls outside of these ranges for the particular level then $q_i = 0$.

Now let us apply the above method to a hypothetical example to see how it would be possible to determine each of the q_i.

The highest level ($k = 5$) has only one cargo to fill: *Regidor Decano*. We shall begin with this case. Let us say that there are ten individuals who have held either the *Mayordomía de San Francisco de Asís* or the *Mayordomía del Santo Entierro de Cristo* (see Table 4).

TABLE 4. MAYORDOMÍA WITH 3,000 TO 6,000 PESOS AVERAGE EXPENDITURE

	Average Expenditures (100's of Pesos)	Time Elapsed (years)	Age	q_i
I_1	56	1 (*)	45 (0)	0
I_2	54	4 (10)	49 (0)	64
I_3	41	3 (10)	46 (0)	51
I_4	37	2 (5)	44 (*)	0
I_5	45	4 (10)	48 (0)	55
I_6	50	1 (*)	47 (0)	0
I_7	47	5 (0)	51 (*)	0
I_8	51	5 (0)	52 (*)	0
I_9	34	3 (10)	47 (0)	44
I_{10}	58	2 (5)	50 (0)	63

*See text.

The initial value taken for the q_i is taken to be the average expenditure during the previous cargos in terms of 100's of pesos. An integer is then assigned to the data in the next two columns and added to the value of the expenditure to give q_i. If an * is inserted instead of an integer, then q_i of the same row will be equal to 0.

In this particular example the choices made were arbitrary for the integers assigned. Given a set of data from the outcome of the selections one could proceed to find the proper constants by working from

the results of the actual selection of cargo holders. It may happen
that one's criteria are inadequate, in which case selection based on
additional criteria may be occurring. For example, it seems likely that,
all else being equal, a candidate from a section with more members on
the *huei tahtuani* would be selected.

If the set Q of the q_i have been determined for each level of the
hierarchy, we may now proceed to solve the integral linear programming problem. Since $f(X)$ is not a continuous function the standard
methods of solving continuous linear programming problems are not
applicable. Fortunately, we are dealing with a finite number of feasible
solutions, which is not generally the case for linear programming
problems of continuous functions. In fact, once we have established
the criteria for selection and their relative weights from data on selections made over a period of years, the solution is readily computed
by using a method similar to the above.

One way of establishing criteria would be to assign random weights
within a limited range of values and to compare the resulting selections
with selections actually made until one arrives at weights which result
in high predictability.

AN ALGORITHM FOR MESOAMERICAN CARGO SYSTEMS

In this section we present the main program (Fig. 4) to calculate
weights for the above criteria in a linear programming model (see
Hymes 1965; and Lamb and Romney 1965). The main program is
divided into subroutines (subroutine: call/weight; call/assign;
call/match) and flow charts (Figs. 5–8). The flow chart for the subroutine match illustrates the important distinction between (IGOT(I) and-
IGETZ(J)) in subroutine call/match, that is, between individuals
who are ethnographically assigned various cargos and individuals who
are assigned cargos by the program. If, in the flow chart for the subroutine, IGOT(I) and IGETZ(J) are not matched, then the program will
reassign relative weights to the specified criteria.

PROGRAM TO CALCULATE WEIGHTS FOR THE CRITERIA IN A LINEAR PROGRAMMING MODEL

DIMENSION KUAL (30), IGETZ (20), IGOT (20),
ITIME (30), IAGE (30), ISPENT (30)
COMMON KUAL, IGETZ, ITIME, IAGE, ISPENT, IGOT,
M, ITIMX, ITIMN, IAGEMX, IAGEM, N, KWATE

```
 1   FORMAT (1514)
     READ 1, M, ITIMX, ITIMN, N, IAGEMX, IAGEMN,
        KWATE
     READ 1, (IGOT (I), I = 1, N)
     READ 1, (ITIME(I), IAGE(I), ISPENT(I), I = 1, M)
15   CALL SUBROUTINE WEIGHT
     CALL SUBROUTINE ASSIGN
     CALL SUBROUTINE MATCH
     IF (KWATE − 30) 15, 15, 20
20   KKK = 0
     END
```

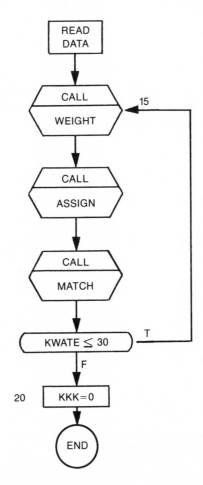

FIGURE 4. Flow chart for main program.

Subroutine WEIGHT

This subroutine weights criteria and calculates qualifications (see Fig. 5).

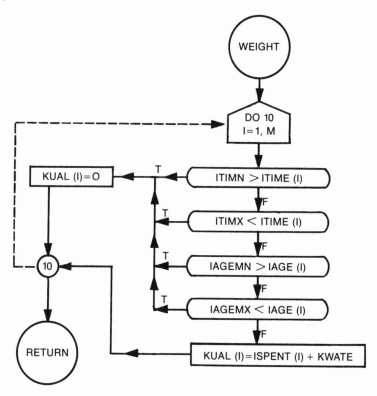

FIGURE 5. Flow chart for subroutine WEIGHT.

```
SUBROUTINE  WEIGHT
COMMON  KUAL, IGETZ, ITIME, IAGE, ISPENT, IGOT,
        M, ITIMX, ITIMN, N, IAGEMX, IAGEMN, KWATE
DO 10 I = 1, M
    IF (ITIMN – ITIME(I) ) 1, 1, 5
1   IF  (ITIME(I) –ITIMX) 2, 2, 5
2   IF  (IAGEMN – IAGE(I) ) 3, 3, 5
3   IF  (IAGE(I) – IAGEMX) 4, 4, 5
4   KUAL(I) =  ISPENT(I) +  KWATE
    GO  TO  10
5   KUAL(I) = 0
```

```
10  CONTINUE
    RETURN
    END
```

Subroutine ASSIGN and Function IBIG

Subroutine ASSIGN picks the top N of M individuals as rated by qualifications calculated above (see Fig. 6). The flow chart for Function IBIG is pictured in Fig. 7.

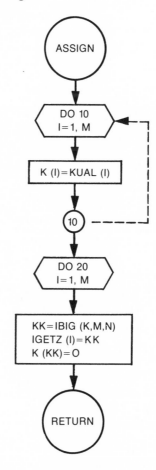

FIGURE 6. Flow chart for subroutine ASSIGN.

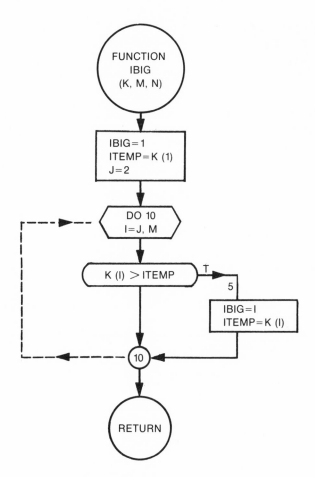

FIGURE 7. Flow chart for function IBIG.

SUBROUTINE ASSIGN
COMMON KUAL, IGETZ, ITIME, IAGE, ISPENT, IGOT,
      M, ITIMX, ITIMN, N, IAGEMX, IAGEMN, KWATE
DIMENSION K (30)
DO 10 I = 1, M
K(I) = KUAL(I)
10   CONTINUE
DO 20 I = 1, N
KK = IBIG (K, M, N)
IGETZ(I) = KK
K(KK) = 0

```
20  CONTINUE
    RETURN
    END

    FUNCTION  IBIG (K, M, N)
    DIMENSION  K(1)
    IBIG = 1
    ITEMP =  K(1)
    J = 2
    DO 10 I = J, M
    IF  (K(I) −  ITEMP) 10, 10, 5
 5  IBIG = I
    ITEMP =  K(I)
10  CONTINUE
    RETURN
    END
```

Subroutine MATCH

This subroutine checks to see if selection matches the actual data.
If not, it kicks out and returns to main program. (See Fig. 8.)

```
    SUBROUTINE  MATCH
    COMMON  KUAL, IGETZ, ITIME, IAGE, ISPENT, IGOT,
        M, ITIMX, ITIMN, N, IAGEMX, IAGEMN, KWATE
 1  FORMAT (43 H△△△THE  WEIGHT  USED  FOR  THE
        ASSIGNMENT  WAS △△, I 2)
    DO 15 I = 1, N
    DO 10 J = 1, N
    IF (IGOT(I) −  IGETZ(J) ) 5, 15, 5
 5  MISS = J
10  CONTINUE
    IF (MISS −  N) 15, 25, 15
15  CONTINUE
    PRINT 1, KWATE
    DO 20 I = 1, N
    K = IGETZ(I)
 2  FORMAT (10X, I4, 4X, I4)
    PRINT 2, (IGETZ(I), KUAL(K) )
20  CONTINUE
    GO  TO 30
```

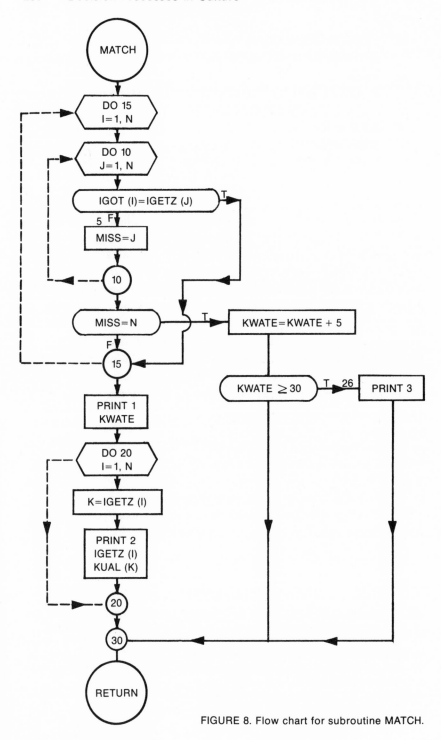

FIGURE 8. Flow chart for subroutine MATCH.

```
25   KWATE = KWATE + 5
     IF (KWATE − 30) 30, 26, 26
26   PRINT 3
3    FORMAT (48H GO DIRECTLY TO JAIL, DO NOT
        COLLECT 200 DOLLARS)
30   KKK = 0
     RETURN
     END
```

CONCLUSION

The program raises the important problems of replicability and predictability. The culturally relevant mobility criteria suggested by an ethnographer may be matched quite easily with individual career histories in the subroutine call/match (replicability); and criteria may be reweighted, or new criteria simulated to obtain a relative equality between IGOT and IGETZ. Once criteria are adequately quantified, the program may be of some utility in prediction.

We have been primarily concerned with reducing social relations (individual mobility, economic and political manipulation, etc.) to simulated intellectual processes, and in this respect we have followed a methodological path suggested by Lévi-Strauss (1962).

The interested reader may grasp some of the relations between the game theory, graph theory (Atkins and Curtis, Livingstone) and linear programming methods presented in this volume by consulting Luce and Raiffa's demonstration (1957:408–23), employing the duality theorem, that the general linear programming problem can be interpreted as a two-person zero-sum game, as well as Berge's (1962:71–85) graph-theoretic solution of a classic linear programming problem (maximum flow in a transport network).

REFERENCES

Atkins, J. and L. Curtis. 1968. Game Rules and the Rules of Culture *in* Game Theory in the Behavioral Sciences, ed. Ira R. Buchler and Hugo G. Nutini. Pittsburgh: U. of Pittsburgh Press.

Berge, C. 1962. The Theory of Graphs. New York: Wiley

Buchler, I. R. 1967. La Organización Ceremonial de Una Aldea Mexicana. América Indigena 27(2):237–63.

Camara, F. 1952. Religion and Political Organization *in* Heritage of Conquest: The Ethnology of Middle America, ed. S. Tax. Glencoe: Free Press.

Cancian, F. 1964. Some Aspects of the Social and Religious Organization of a Maya Society. Actas y Memorias, XXXV Congreso Internacional de Americanistas, Mexico, 1962 1:335–43.

———. 1965. Economics and Prestige in a Maya Community. Stanford: Stanford U. Press.

Carrasco, P. 1961. The Civil-Religious Hierarchy in Mesoamerican Communities: Pre-Spanish Background and Colonial Development. American Anthropologist 63:484–97.

Gale, D. 1960. The Theory of Linear Economic Models. New York: McGraw-Hill.

Hymes, D. (ed.) 1965. The Use of Computers in Anthropology. The Hague: Mouton.

Lamb, S. and A. K. Romney. 1965. An Anthropologist's Introduction to the Computer in The Use of Computers in Anthropology, ed. D. Hymes. The Hague: Mouton.

Lévi-Strauss, Claude. 1962. La Pensée Sauvage. Paris: Librairie Plon.

Luce, R. D. and H. Raiffa. 1957. Games and Decisions: Introduction and Critical Survey (Appendix 5, Linear programming and two-person zero-sum games). New York: Wiley.

Nash, M. 1958. Political Relations In Guatemala. Social and Economic Studies 7:65–75.

Naylor, T. H. and E. T. Byrne. 1963. Linear Programming: Methods and Cases. Belmont, Mass.: Wadsworth.

Shubik, M. 1964. Game Theory and the Study of Social Behavior: An Introductory Exposition in Game Theory and Related Approaches to Social Behavior, ed. M. Shubik. New York: Wiley.

Wolf, E. 1962. Sons of the Shaking Earth. Chicago: U. of Chicago Press.

CHAPTER **11**
John R. Atkins
Luke Curtis

Game Rules and
the Rules of Culture

THE initial stimulus for this study was a desire
to examine the possible pertinence for anthropology of a single, limited
aspect of game theory. We wished to investigate how game theorists
represent formally the rules of games, on the hypothesis that the particular kinds of formalism chosen by mathematicians to model game
rules might be relevant to the task of constructing adequate formal
ethnographic models of cultural rules. By "game rules" we mean here
game-defining rules, in the sense of those sets of relatively fixed conventions by which particular games are given their basic structure or
constitution. Such rules of necessity come to the attention of the game
theorist at the very beginning of his search for "solutions," "decision
rules," "strategies," and the like, since one must ask first how a given
game is played—that is, how it *must* be played—before posing the
further question of how it may be played intelligently.

Once we had chosen to study the general manner in which game
theorists respond to the first of these two questions, it was our expectation that the present paper would be devoted primarily to a straightforward report of our findings on this topic. Along the way, however,
the research departed from plan, with the result that the following
presentation no longer conforms to the shape that was intended for it.
Game rules *sensu strictu* are discussed at the outset only, and the treatment is sharply selective as well as condensed. We then offer a tentative
formulation of "rule structure" in general terms, which is followed by
an illustrative ethnographic analysis. The final and longest portion of

The work reported in this paper was supported in part by Training Grant NU–5004
from the Public Health Service, U.S. Department of Health, Education, and Welfare
(Nurse Scientist Training Program).

213

the paper outlines a further development of the notion of rule structure and introduces a series of measurement proposals.

GAME RULES

Following Berge[1] (1962, p. 59), any game G may be viewed formally as "a 'structure' [imposed on] an abstract set X," where X is
interpreted as the set of all possible *positions* of G. The game theorist
tends to regard the specific character of the individual positions $x \in X$
as uninteresting, or at least as more or less unproblematic. By contrast,
the anthropologist who is interested in characterizing particular sets
of possible analogues of game positions in culture generally (whether
these be taken as "situations," "states of affairs," "social categories,"
or entities of some quite different sort) tends to regard the construction of an adequate descriptive specification of such units as a central
and challenging task.

We suggest that one useful way of representing a set X of "game
position analogues" is to define a finite vector space S of dimension k
—ideally both orthogonal and of smallest possible cardinality—such
that the k discrete variables that coordinate S can be shown to be
adequate, collectively, to distinguish each $x \in X$ from every other (cf.
Berge's schematic treatment of chess positions; *ibid*). Each "position"
of X may then be located uniquely in S by means of an ordered k-tuple,
the respective components of which are particular values of the variables (coordinates) by which the space is defined. In general, some
or many of the points of S will not represent any element of X (i.e., the
space may generate invalid as well as valid or "legitimate" game
positions), even if S is orthogonal and of the smallest dimension adequate to its task. Thus if an analysis of what might be called *position-
defining rules* were to utilize a finite vector space S or some similar
construction, it would be one formal task of the analysis to specify X
as a particular subset of the point-set S or, equivalently, to specify a
partition of S of the form $X,\overline{X}$.

In the formulation of Berge (1962, pp. 58, 220), the *moves* of a game
G are represented by a multivalued function Γ that maps X into X.
(With neither loss nor gain in generality, the phrase "multivalued
function" may be replaced by the terms "mapping," "correspondence,"
or "dyadic relation.") The Γ function denotes the set of all and only
those *ordered pairs* of positions x,y such that an immediate or one-step
move to position x from position y is a *legitimate* move in G. The pairs

x, y belong to the set X^2, which is the Cartesian product of the (position) set X with itself—that is, the set containing *all possible* ordered pairs in which both the first-listed and second-listed members of each pair are elements of X. The function is concerned with the distinction within the set X^2 between (1) pairs of game positions from X that satisfy, in the order in which the members of the pair are listed, the relation "__ may immediately follow __ in G" and (2) pairs of positions from X that do not, in the order listed, satisfy this relation. The gamma function may be said to specify a game's *move-defining rules* by replicating the contrast between allowed and disallowed moves as a dichotomous partition Γ, $\bar{\Gamma}$ of the set X^2 (i.e., the division of X^2 into two disjoint or mutually exclusive subsets which jointly exhaust this set of pairs). Equivalently, the function may be said to specify move-rules by identifying $\Gamma \subseteq X^2$ as a "privileged," or G-legitimated, subset of one-step transitions $X \rightarrow X$, chosen from all of the logical possibilities for direct transitions from one position $x \epsilon X$ to another.

However, it should be made clear that a function such as Γ is simply a list of ordered pairs; it specifies move-defining rules only in the sense of summarizing, extensionally, the net effect of the latter. For each possible game position, Γ indicates to which position (if any) the game may next proceed. It therefore gives a handy answer, so to speak, to an often complex question, as the answer given must take into account all G-rules that bear on move legitimacy—and in any concrete game there may be a considerable number of separately stated rules of this kind. To the degree that Γ simply summarizes descriptively the collective effect of a number of more particulate rules, the analyst may wish to explicate the structure of this function as, for example, an intersection or product of a corresponding number of more specific functions of the same general type.

An additional complexity arises in those games (and their cultural analogues) in which the legitimacy of a one-step move may depend, in part, on the moves that have gone before it. In such cases it seems preferable to consider the move-defining rule system as operating on multistep sequences, or *paths*, with the move-defining function(s) serving to differentiate valid or allowed paths from those which are disallowed. In order to cope with such "path-rules" as well as the simpler dyadic or one-step "arc-rules," Γ may be regarded as a subset of the set X^m, where $m \geq 2$, rather than as a subset of X^2.

Since games of interest to the game theorist typically involve two or more players, it is often necessary to deal not only with moves and

positions, but also with *turn of play*. Turn-defining rules may be said
to allocate positions to players, in the sense of assigning the right of
move-selection, at given positions, to one game-player rather than
another. If we assume that X and Γ have been defined without reference to player turns, the effects of turn-rules may be expressed by
introducing a suitable partition of the set X. For example, if the game
involves only two players, A and B, the set X may be partitioned on
the basis of turn allocations into the subsets X_A, X_B, X_0, where X_0 contains those positions in which it is the turn of play of neither player (i.e., the
terminal, or winning, positions of the game). Alternatively, the analyst
may choose to merge turn-defining rules with the rules defining positions, and hence moves, by incorporating one additional variable into
the specifications for the set X (for example, by increasing the dimension of S from k to $k + 1$).

Turn-rules find their most obvious anthropological interpretation in
cultural rules that assign the responsibility or privilege of decision-
making in specified situations to persons of designated statuses. Alan
Howard's "structural principles" are rules of precisely this sort, as
contrasted with his "cultural principles," which are analogous to move-
and position-defining rules; cf. Howard (1963, p. 410). Interpreting
turn of play along these general lines is likely to prove fruitful, but the
analyst may need to exercise care in drawing up the list of entities that
are to be considered the "players" of the game-analogue under study.
In certain contexts, for example, it might prove shortsighted to over-
look the possibility that Society, Tradition, and Nature (or the like) may
be among the more prominent "decision-makers," or turn-taking players,
in cultural games.

Although we have discussed only positions, moves, and turns, it is
possible to describe all other aspects of game structure by referring to
partitions of, or selections of subsets within, some basic collection of
entities (e.g., positions) together with such higher-order sets as may be
defined thereupon. "Preference functions," for example, may be viewed
as a player's partition of the set of game positions (and/or moves) into
as many subsets as are distinguishable on his scale of preferences;
"subjective probabilities" may be regarded as a similar partition on
either X or Γ ; "strategies" may be described as partial graphs, subgraphs, or partial subgraphs of the digraph of a game (which, in turn,
is simply a position set X together with one or more functions defining
partitions on powers thereof); and so forth. The game features of

greatest intrinsic interest tend, of course, to involve orderings as well as mere partitioning, but partitioning is basic.

All of the formal concepts employed or implied in the foregoing paragraphs stem directly from abstract set theory, or can easily be reduced thereto. It is our belief that anthropologists interested in the structural aspects of cultural rules will find a relevant, appropriate, and useful set of cognitive tools in the elementary notions of set theory and closely kindred systems of mathematical thought. It is in this spirit that we present our own tentative first attempts to analyze rule structure.

THE FORMAL STRUCTURE OF RULES

Philosophers and laymen alike use the English word *rule* in several different senses, as Max Black's thoughtful discussion of the matter has made quite clear (1962, pp. 64–139). It is our impression that the word is employed by anthropologists in ways that are hardly less various, even when the quasi-technical term *cultural* is added as a presumably specifying modifier. However, we eschew here any attempt to survey anthropological meanings in this area, and no substantive definitions of either "rule" or "cultural rule" are undertaken here. Our interest in the rule concept is centered on its underlying formal structure or implicit logical syntax, rather than on details of empirical semantics. What we have to say is so basic or elemental in character that we expect it to apply (at least "in principle") to virtually anything that may reasonably be called a rule, cultural or otherwise. It is recognized that a general, abstract, and formal approach to the subject of rule structure can carry no advance assurance of useful results, but we think an experiment along these lines is worth trying.

Let us begin by postulating that rules of every sort share at least one common property: they all may be said to *rule in* something or other, while *ruling out* something else. This assertion does not report any startling empirical discovery, of course; it merely constitutes a proposal that attention be shifted from the abstract noun "rule" to the pair of verbs "to rule in (out)." We are claiming, in effect, that ruling in and out is what rules at minimum "do" and are at minimum "for," whatever else may be said of them. This is a purely heuristic characterization. Its ultimate cognitive utility must be assessed on pragmatic grounds.

Let R be any rule or rule system, and let the set S be the domain to which R applies. We require the set S to be finite, and we presume it to be composed of distinguishable entities of some sort—*all* entities, in fact, of the particular sort with which R happens to deal. Since the variety of kinds of entities to which rules may apply is very wide, it is important in discussing the general case to avoid an unduly narrow conceptualization of the nature of the elements of S. Perhaps it will not be too constricting to regard S as composed of a set of "conceivables" within the cognitive frame[2] of some observer, maker, or interpreter of rules. It seems reasonable to suppose that cultural rules deal always with conceivables, since there is little need for a society to rule out anything that its members find literally inconceivable or to require of its members anything to which they can conceive no alternative. Indeed, most rules of culture assume considerably more than this. What a cultural rule rules out, for example, is regarded usually as not merely conceivable but also possible, and perhaps not only possible but even probable—at least in the absence of whatever restraining influence the rules themselves are presumed to introduce.

If a rule or set of rules R is to be described as acting within its domain S in such a way as to both rule in *and* rule out, then it follows that this action must include the making of a distinction in S. Only if R succeeds in differentiating certain members of S from other members thereof may the former be identified as "In" and the latter as "Out," or vice versa. Hence we shall say that it is the business of any rule R to sort the elements of its domain into at least two disjoint subsets. In order to exclude rules that are vacuous and therefore trivial, we shall require also that these R-induced subsets be nonempty (and hence that S itself be nonempty). Thus what emerges in summary is a formal characterization of any nonvacuous rule or rule system as *partitioning* a finite and nonempty set S into subsets $X_1, X_2, ..., X_q$, where $q \geq 2$.

In much of our discussion we shall assume that $q \leq 2$ also, on the ground that binary division is probably the most important single case empirically (as well as the simplest case formally). However, our basic focus on partitions consisting of exactly two disjoint and nonempty subsets need not be viewed as a fatal restriction. When R must, in fact, be regarded as dividing its domain more finely than this—that is, when $q \geq 3$—the division in question may always be analyzed as the complex resultant of z dichotomizations, either simultaneous or successive, where $z \leqslant (q - 1)$.

Conceiving rules as if "essentially" they dichotomize, we shall speak of them as drawing lines in their respective domains which distinguish a *Yes* from a *No* or an *In* from an *Out*. The use of tags such as "In" and "Out" as labels for pairs of R-induced subsets is to a considerable extent arbitrary, but it is consistent with a frequent additional feature of the partitions created by man-made rules—the fact that not only do rules make distinctions, but often the distinctions they make are in some sense invidious. The difference between the paired sides of a rule-induced dichotomy may be expressed concretely in a variety of ways, depending on the specific details of content and context which are associated with particular rules or classes thereof. But often the distinction can be characterized in rather general terms as a contrast between the selected and rejected, the affirmed and denied, the admissible and inadmissible, the possible and impossible, or some other kind of Yes/No opposition. Symbolically, when $X_q = X_2$ we shall refer to X_1 as the "privileged" or P subset of S and refer to X_2 (the complement of P in S) as the subset $\bar{P}$ (not-P). Thus we propose for the general dichotomous case that any rule or rule system R be thought of as partitioning its domain of application S into the pair of mutually exclusive and jointly exhaustive subsets $P,\bar{P}$. The interpretation of the symbol P as "privileged" may be considered purely arbitrary in dealing with cases which do not exhibit clear-cut "invidious" or Yes/No features.

If a particular rule-induced dividing line happens empirically to be sharply drawn, and if further the domain itself is well defined, the rule which is responsible for this state of affairs is apt to be described as precise—in contrast to rules which are regarded as vague or ambiguous by virtue of fuzzy dividing lines, uncertain domain boundaries, or both. Yet the sphere of application of even the vaguest rule usually includes at least a few undisputed cases, in the sense of elements that fall without question into S and can also be assigned unequivocally to either P or $\bar{P}$. (Indeed, our earlier stipulations reflect a judgment that it is unprofitable to use the word *rule* at all unless some nonvanishing minimum degree of ruling in and out can be established.) One practical way of formulating the problem of hazy domain boundaries is to assume that R partitions the universe at large into three parts—consisting, respectively, of (1) entities that belong without question to the relevant domain S, (2) entities that clearly fall outside of S, and (3) entities with respect to which the applicability of R, and hence membership in S, is disputed or doubtful. The independent problem of gaps, overlaps, or general fuzziness in the internal division of S into P and $\bar{P}$ may be formalized as a further and similar trisection of either (1) or (1) plus (3).

What has been sketched in this section is a first approximation to an elementary formal framework within which various structural properties of rules may be considered. The framework does not pretend to be complete, as it touches on only those aspects of rules that concern us in the balance of the paper. At this juncture we are concerned less with the adequacy of our formulation than we are with its possible generality and its heuristic or suggestive value. We draw some encouragement as to its generality from our experience in examining how game rules are represented formally in game theory, for we see our proposals as basically consistent with the general manner in which mathematicians have dealt with rules of the game-defining and game-playing varieties.

The final section of this paper, which is concerned with rule-induced "constraint" and its measurement, builds further on the simple formal framework of the present section. However, we need first to provide a mildly ethnographic interlude.

TENEJAPA LADINO WEDDINGS

In order to provide a brief illustration of our formal approach to rules in a context that is specifically anthropological, we offer an analysis of a single small fragment of Tenejapa culture as described by Metzger and Williams (1963, pp. 1076–1101). The example has been chosen from the literature almost at random, since its only role is to serve as a vehicle for explicating methodological questions. We wish, nevertheless, to record our grateful indebtedness to the ethnographers who have supplied the example, for it is the quality of their reporting that has made our analysis possible.

The *fiesta de matrimonio* of the ladinos of Tenejapa may be described as a multistage ritual transition, or complex "mediating performance," through which a ladino couple may move from the status of *novios oficiales* (engaged) to that of *esposos* (married). The transition is effected through a series of n events, $n \leqslant 11$, which are either all of the named events of Table 1 or some permitted subset of this set.

TABLE 1. THE NAMED EVENTS A,B, . . . , N OF THE
TENEJAPAN LADINO *FIESTA DE MATRIMONIO* (compiled
from Metzger and Williams, 1963).

A = *Presentación* ceremony
B = *Presentación* fiesta
C = *Despedida* ceremony
D = *Despedida* fiesta
E = *Confesión* ceremony
F = *Comunión* ceremony
G = *Comunión* fiesta
H = *Casamiento* ceremony
L = *Casamiento* fiesta
M = *Tornaboda* ceremony
N = *Tornaboda* fiesta

The discussion to follow is limited entirely to an examination of two aspects of the structure of this ritual. The first of these is the question of the number of *combinations* of the events A,B,...,N (that is, subsets of the total set) that are accepted as culturally legitimate versions of the rite. We shall refer to this as the problem of *concurrence patterning*. The second aspect is the question of the way or ways in which the events forming legitimate versions of the rite are ordered in time, which will be referred to as the problem of *temporal patterning*. There will be no discussion of the many interesting variations in content which are allowed within the individual events themselves, nor of the various economic, religious, and other contextual factors that determine which one or more of the several permitted event-combinations is specifically appropriate for particular couples. We shall deal first with the problem of concurrence patterning.

Given a set of eleven events, there are 2^{11} or 2,048 possible subsets of such a set, where each of these subsets is a distinct unordered combination of *n* events, $0 \leq n \leq 11$. We must first ask how many of the 2,048 logically possible combinations of events of Table I form normatively acceptable versions of the Tenejapan *fiesta de matrimonio*. As we interpret Metzger and Williams, the culturally legitimate combinations are limited to the following eight:

(1) ∅
(2) E,H
(3) E,H,A,F,L
(4) E,H,A,F,L,B

(5) E,H,A,F,L,G
(6) E,H,A,F,L,B,G
(7) E,H,A,F,L,G,C,D,M,N
(8) E,H,A,F,L,B,G,C,D,M,N

The subset Ø, which is the null or empty set, is included to provide for the limiting case in which the rite in question does *not* occur—a combination that is permitted, we are happy to note.

Examination of the above list discloses that the pattern in which individual events are "in" or "out" of the rite does not exhibit independence of occurrence. For example, the event E occurs with or without the event A, but A cannot occur without E, nor B without A; E *must* occur with H, and H with E; and so forth. In order to allow a more efficient analysis of all such concurrence dependencies, we define the relation "___ must occur if ___ occurs" on the set U, where the elements of U are the events of Table I. Let this relation be represented by the symbol $\geq$. The incidence matrix M for the relation $\geq$ on U is shown in Fig. 1. (We have omitted the reflexive main-diagonal entries as irrelevant to our problem.)

$\geq$	A	B	C	D	E	F	G	H	L	M	N
A		1	1	1		1	1		1	1	1
B											
C				1					1	1	
D			1						1	1	
E	1	1	1	1		1	1	1	1	1	1
F	1	1	1	1			1		1	1	1
G		1	1						1	1	
H	1	1	1	1	1	1	1		1	1	1
L	1	1	1	1		1	1			1	1
M		1	1								1
N		1	1					1			

FIGURE 1. Matrix M: the relation $\geq$ defined on the set U.

It is possible to regard the matrix M as an "atomic reduction" of the formal structure exhibited by the concurrence patterning of events in the *fiesta de matrimonio*, insofar as this patterning deals with the presence or absence of events of type U. Let the individual entries of M be interpreted as representing the "unit rules" in our representation of this structure. Through pairwise comparison of these unit rules, analysis leads immediately to the identification of two kinds of rules at a next higher level: (1) equivalence rules, which establish connections in U that are transitive, reflexive, and symmetric, and (2) ordering rules, which establish connections in U that are transitive, reflexive, and antisymmetric. Let us proceed to examine these rules of higher order.

Inspection of M reveals that for certain pairs of events in U the relation $\geq$ holds symmetrically. For example, we have both $E \geq H$ and $H \geq E$, indicating that the ceremonial events E and H are always either both present or both absent (as a consequence, we assume, of it being "improper" for either of these events to occur without the other). It follows from this local symmetry of $\geq$ that the subset $\{E,H\}$ may be described as an *equivalence class* in U induced by the relation $\geq$. Other local symmetries of $\geq$ in the matrix M establish the subsets $\{A,F,L\}$ and $\{C,D,M,N\}$ as forming two additional equivalence classes of this same sort.

The practical significance of these equivalences is that certain of the events A,B,...,N are shown thereby to belong together, in the sense that they cannot be distinguished from one another on the basis of patterns of concurrence alone. Thus the set of eleven *fiesta* events may be dissected on this basis into five distinct parts, yielding the following set, U', as a partition of U:

$$U' = \left[\{E,H\},\{A,F,L\},\{G\},\{C,D,M,N\},\{B\} \right]$$

This reduction allows us to replace the 11×11 matrix M by a 5×5 matrix corresponding to the partition U', which results in the matrix M' of Fig. 2. The rows and columns of M' are identified by the letter-

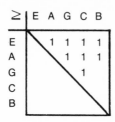

FIGURE 2. Matrix M': the relation $\geq$ on U'.

names of five single events, each chosen from the original set U as an arbitrary representative of one of the five equivalence classes. Although M', like M, is an incidence matrix of the relation $\geq$, in this new matrix the off-diagonal pairs that satisfy $\geqslant$ are strictly ordered in every case (i.e., they satisfy the relation $>$ as well as the relation $\geqslant$).

The only further simplification which seems possible in our concurrence analysis is to delete from M' all entries that are deducible from other entries therein by virtue of the transitivity of the relation $\geqslant$. When these deletions are carried out, we obtain the matrix M'', which is shown in Fig. 3.

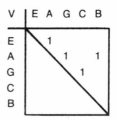

FIGURE 3. Matrix M'': the relation V on U'.

In order to facilitate a comparison of the information contained in the two 5×5 matrices M' and M'', let us exploit the intuitive advantages of diagrams by providing a corresponding linear digraph for each matrix (Fig. 4). The graphs G_1 and G_2 in the figure convey exactly the same information as the respective matrices M' and M'', since the members of each ordered pair of events linked by a "1" in M' or M'' are linked in the corresponding digraph by an arrow or directed line ($\rightarrow$).

An interesting issue is raised by the differences between the two digraphs of Fig. 4. It is possible to argue that the four indirect or

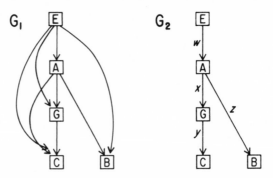

FIGURE 4. Graphs G_1 and G_2.

transitively derivable arcs which appear in G_1 but not in G_2 ought to be ignored in any representation of empirical reality that strives for simplicity, on the grounds that they are "superfluous" or "redundant" —and hence expendable. From this point of view, the graph G_2 would be preferred. However, that which is purely derivative logically may have an independent or nonderivative importance in the empirical situation itself. For example, the transitively derivable dependency of event C on event A may empirically have an independent force of its own that is separate, or at least separable, from the intervening dependencies of C on G and G on A. The critical test would be to see what would happen if the empirical equivalents of either or both of the latter dependencies were to be abandoned, to dissolve, or otherwise to disappear. Would the referent of the formerly "indirect" and "derivative" A,C linkage automatically disappear also? Or might it remain, as strong or stronger than before?

Although we lack the data that would be needed to resolve a question of this kind in the present case, in general it seems clear that the world does contain transitive empirical relations in which indirect connections would *not* be broken automatically by the severance of all intermediate linkages, just as there exist other transitive relations for which the opposite is true. So long as we think of cultural rules in static terms only, there can be little harm in omitting from our descriptions anything that is logically redundant; indeed, the resulting gain in elegance and economy of expression is very much worth seeking. But concern for dynamics may suggest a need to exercise some caution in wielding Occam's razor, for imprudent pruning is worse than none at all.

We may now summarize our treatment of the "concurrence patterning" exhibited by events of the Tenejapan *fiesta de matrimonio*. Consideration of the dyadic relation $\geq$ on the set U yielded a number of positive instances (shown in matrix M) of this relation, which we interpreted as the atomic or "unit" rules for a formal representation of the system at hand. These serve to differentiate the 8 combinations of elements of U that seemingly are allowed from the 2,040 combinations which appear to be *disallowed*. These unit rules were shown also to be interrelated in such a way as to form a set of equivalence rules (reflected in the partition U') and a set of ordering rules (depicted in G_1 and/or G_2).

The problem of temporal patterning may be treated much more simply. Let the relation T, with the meaning "__ is not preceded by __ ," be defined on U. It is clear from the Metzger and Williams description that the elements of U are completely ordered by the relation T. In other words, the T-induced equivalence classes are limited to the unit subsets only, since all distinct pairs from U satisfy T in one direction only. Given, therefore, the manner in which we have assigned letter-names to the various events of U, and given further the strict ordering of U induced by T, it follows that the one uniquely proper temporal sequence for any permitted combination of these events may be replicated by simple alphabetization.

CONSTRAINT MEASURES

The foregoing provides a basis for several possible lines of further inquiry into the structure of rules and rule systems. The present section is motivated by an interest in one of these lines of inquiry—the possibility of using certain elementary ideas from information theory to develop methods for analyzing rule structure quantitatively.

As suggested earlier, perhaps the simplest general statement that can be made about any rule is that it both "rules in" and "rules out." This phraseology leads in a natural way to thinking of rules as "constraint-inducing." We shall regard any rule or rule system R as imposing a *constraint* on its domain S to the degree that it relegates certain elements thereof to the "No" subset, $\overline{P}$—and thereby reduces both the absolute and the relative size of the "Yes" or privileged subset, P. What interests us here is the possibility of measuring and comparing degrees of rule-induced constraint, when constraint is conceptualized in this manner.

For ease of exposition, let R be a cultural rule that is conveniently precise and simple in its structure, and let $|S| = n$, where n is a known positive integer and $|S|$ is the cardinality or "size" of the set S (i.e., the number of its elements). For example, we may suppose that an emic description of S has disclosed that it consists (let us say) of n specifiably distinct "actions" which are "performable by persons of status X" in "situations of types Y and Z." Given that R exhaustively sorts the n elements of S into respective "Yes" and "No" subsets P and $\overline{P}$, it is clear that the cardinalities of both of these subsets are known if it is possible to ascertain the cardinality of either one of them, since

$$|S| = |P| + |\overline{P}| = n$$

and n is presumed given.

We shall want our numerical measures of degree of constraint to vary inversely with the ratio of $|P|$ to $|S|$. However, rather than employing the raw cardinalities of the sets P and S as immediate constituents of the proposed formulae, we prefer to use the base-2 logarithms of these numbers. Thus we put

$$p = \log_2 |P|$$

$$s = \log_2 |S|$$

and define the *absolute constraint*, C_a, introduced into a domain S by rule or rules R as

$$C_a = - \log_2 \frac{|P|}{|S|}$$

which becomes

$$C_a = s - p$$

The values of this measure will approach zero as p tends toward s and approach s as p tends toward zero; i.e., $0 < C_a < s$, where the fact that both limits are unattainable asymptotes is a result of our requiring that both P and $\bar{P}$ be nonempty as well as finite. The quantity s may be described in the language of information theory as the minimum number of binary digits, or *bits,* that would be needed on average to provide each element of S with a unique identification number in a binary $(0,1)$ numerical code. Since a similar interpretation may be applied to the quantity p with respect to the set P, we may say that the function C_a gives the number of bits theoretically "saved" if S were to be replaced by its subset P as the ensemble to be encoded. This may also be expressed as equivalent to the reduction in dimensionality of a finite binary vector space of cardinality $|S|$ that has been "shrunk" to cardinality $|P|$. We shall say that the units measured by C_a are bits.

It will be noted that the range of C_a depends on the size of S. Since we wish to be able to compare degrees of constraint among rules that may not have domains of equal size, we add a second function, C, in order to express the *relative* constraint introduced into S by R—and hence to measure constraint in a general or domain-free sense. This is taken as the ratio of C_a to s. Thus we have

$$C = \frac{s - p}{s}$$

which reduces to

$$C = 1 - \frac{p}{s}$$

The measure C yields values that are pure numbers (rather than numbers of bits). With S finite, its values will be restricted to positive proper fractions; i.e., $0 < C < 1$.

It is proposed further that the difference, ΔC, between two degrees of constraint C and C' be defined as

$$\Delta C = C' - C$$

where C and C' are values of our relative constraint measure for the rules R and R', respectively. (The corresponding domains S and S' may or may not be distinct.)

The difference ΔC will have the range $-1 < \Delta C < +1$. Its absolute value (i.e., ΔC without regard for sign) may be used to express the extent of difference between any two rules in the degree of constraint they impose (in the same or different domains).

The situation in which the algebraic sign of the measure ΔC assumes special interest is when R and R' represent two different versions of a rule system that is changing over time. If R' is the later version of the system, a positive value for $C' - C$ will indicate that constraint has increased, while a negative value will mean that a decrease, or *de-constraint*, has occurred.

In order to illustrate the arithmetic of the above measures, let us return briefly to the "concurrence rules" that were constructed earlier to replicate certain aspects of the Tenejapan *fiesta de matrimonio*. The domain for these rules is the set of all possible subsets of the set of events listed in Table I (i.e., all possible unordered combinations of eleven or fewer of these events). Thus we have

$$|S| = 2^{11} = 2,048$$

and therefore

$$s = \log_2 2,048 = 11$$

The equivalence rules that were used to reduce the 11×11 matrix M to the 5×5 matrix M' were shown to eliminate all but $2^5 = 32$ of the full set of logically possible combinations. If these were assumed to be the only rules operating to constrain S, we would have $|P| = 2^5$ and hence $p = 5$. This gives an absolute constraint of

$$C_a = s - p = 11 - 5$$

or 6 bits. (A careful examination of the structure of the partition U' will verify that this represents 2 bits of constraint for each nonredundant dyadic equivalence.)

The *relative* constraint due to these equivalence rules is

$$C = 1 - \frac{p}{s} = \frac{6}{11}$$

or approximately 0.55. This is the domain-free measure, since it uses division by s to "correct" C_a for the specific size of the domain in question.

It was shown earlier that the number of potentially legitimate *fiestas* was further reducible by the set of hierarchical ordering rules given in matrix M'. These fixed the final cardinality for the set P (the "privileged" combinations) at 8 or 2^3 allowed versions of the rite. Since the total absolute constraint now becomes

$$C_a = 11 - 3 = 8$$

we see that the number of additional bits of C_a which are imposed by the ordering rules—i.e., additional to the 6 already allocated to the equivalences—is 2. (This represents an average of 1 bit per nonredundant instance of $>$.)

It follows that the total *relative* constraint is

$$C = 1 - \frac{3}{11} = \frac{8}{11}$$

or approximately 0.73.

In order to illustrate the measure ΔC, let us concentrate on the simple system of graph G_2. Since this structure is based on the partition U', we shall take the set of all subsets of U' (rather than of U) as the domain that is relevant here. Hence $|S| = 32$ elements. Since the four arc-rules of G_2 eliminate all but 8 of these possibilities, the relative constraint imposed by these rules collectively is

$$C = 1 - \frac{3}{5} = 0.40$$

Each of the individual arcs or "unit rules" of G_2 makes its own contribution to this value of C. Are these individual contributions equal or unequal?

A useful way to assess the individual role played by any given arc is to imagine it deleted from the system. One may then count the number of combinations that would be permitted in its absence, compute a new value for C, and use Δ C to express the de-constraint effected by the imagined removal. If this procedure is followed for the arc w, for example, we obtain a Δ C of -0.16. This figure reflects the "degree of system destruction" which would be produced by the erasure of w. Its absence would allow 6 new event-combinations to be added to the privileged ranks of "legitimate" *fiesta* versions, boosting $|P|$ from 8 to 14. By contrast, only 2 new versions would be added to the original 8 if the arc deleted were z rather than w, since restoring w and eliminating z yields $\Delta C = -0.06$. (Intermediate values—4 new versions and a Δ C of -0.12—result from the choice of either x or y as the arc to be purged.) Thus our deletion test shows clearly that the various unit rules of G_2 tend to differ in their "criticality" to the system as a whole.

It is even more interesting to consider *sequences* of arc-deletions— that is, the progressive or cumulative subtraction of rules, one by one, beginning with any rule picked at random and proceeding along all possible de-constraint paths. The miniature system G_2 may again be used in illustration. As shown above, the first arc deleted will open up 2, 4, or 6 new possibilities, depending on which arc is chosen. Since the outcomes are better expressed in terms of *total* numbers of versions presumed to be legitimate, the results of the first step will be described in terms of the new cardinality of the set P; thus after one deletion we have $|P| = 10, 12,$ or 14.

As the de-constraint process reaches its *second* stage, once again there are three outcomes. The number $|P|$ becomes 16, 18, or 20. But it is at this stage that we discover—if the result was not anticipated— that the de-constraint paths for G_2 are nonlinear. That is, it is *not* possible to predict the net de-constraint effected by removing two given arcs solely from knowing how much de-constraint is produced by deleting each of them individually. The second-stage results are not simple linear combinations of answers obtained at stage one.

Note, for example, the behavior of rules x and y. These arcs were equivalent at stage one, in the sense that the erasure of either of them added 4 new elements to the P subset, giving $|P| = 12$. This was the intermediate first-stage outcome. If they are both removed together, $|P|$ becomes 16, which is *not* intermediate among the *second*-stage outcomes. Moreover, the effect of a second-stage annihilation that pairs one of these arcs with either w or z will depend on whether it is x or y that participates in the pairing. Thus the deletion of x with w or z yields $|P| = 18$ in both cases, while the pairing of y with w or z gives $|P| = 20$ in the first case and $|P| = 16$ in the second. According to the single-deletion test, the arcs x and y are strictly equipotent. Yet our more refined analysis reveals that these rules play quite different structural roles in the overall system.

Because of the small size of the structure G_2, the results at stages three and four of the de-constraint process carry somewhat less interest than those for the first two stages. At both the third and fourth steps of the process all difference between individual rules disappears. The de-constraint achieved by the removal of three arcs from G_2 is the same, at $\Delta C = -0.32$, no matter which three are deleted. This corresponds to a uniform $|P| = 24$ versions, which is all but 8 of the entire set of 32 possible subsets of the set U'. If all four rules are purged, there is, of course, no constraint at all; $|P| = |S|$ and ΔC achieves its maximum negative value at -1.00.

The total number of distinct orders in which arcs may be deleted serially from G_2 until all are gone is $4! = 24$. However, these 24 possible sequences produce only 9 distinct values for $|P|$—and hence for C and ΔC as well. Deletion-sequences which, though distinct, produce the same series of ΔC values may be grouped together as yielding a single "de-constraint path." There are exactly 8 distinct de-constraint paths (in this sense) for the system G_2. These paths are shown in graph G_3 of Fig. 5. Note that the dotted line in Fig. 5 indicates an *impossible* one-step change in C; if this transition were possible, there would be 9 distinct de-constraint paths (instead of 8) in this four-stage system.

In the systematic de-constraint of G_2, the question of which arc or set of arcs is selected for deletion at a given stage—for example, whether w or z is chosen at stage one—has been seen to affect the values of C and ΔC at two of the four stages of the process. Even at these two stages, however, the magnitude of this "selection effect" is

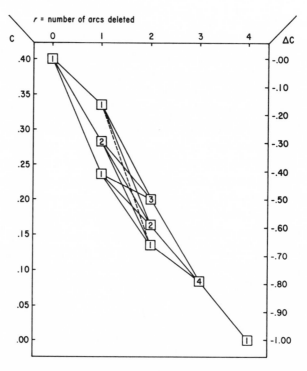

FIGURE 5. Graph G_3. Values of C (left) and ΔC (right) for all possible de-constraint paths of the system G_2. The integers shown within the small squares give the number of distinct ways in which the indicated values of C and ΔC can be obtained with r deletions of arcs.

subordinate to the influence of a more important factor, which is the number of arcs deleted. (This is the variable labeled r in Fig. 5. It is equivalent, of course, to "stage-number" in our arc-by-arc deletion process.) As the figure shows, the overall effect of variation in r dominates that due to variation in deletion choices at any given r; indeed, there is no overlapping of C-values as the process moves from any one stage to the next. This characteristic is not universal for systems of this general kind. For example, it can be shown that it does not hold for the more complicated system depicted in graph G_1 (under the assumption that the "redundant" arcs of G_1 may show existential independence empirically). In de-constraining G_1 a larger ΔC can be achieved by abolishing two arc-rules than by eliminating three—if the choices are careful in the former case, and careless in the latter.

It would be possible to demonstrate a number of other interesting facets of rule system de-constraint behavior through a detailed study of G_1 (or a structure still more complex, such as the matrix M of our *fiesta* analysis), but we shall forego further illustration of the matter here.

In all of the foregoing, there has been an implicit assignment of "equal importance" to each element of a rule's domain. The emphasis has been on counting such elements, and the operation of counting is inherently egalitarian. (The enumeration paradigm 1,2,3,..., may be thought of as a cumulative summation of the series 1,1,1,..., and by definition $1 = 1$.) More precisely, C_a and C are based on what might be called a double-standard democracy, for the egalitarianism is intra-caste only; the In-group members of P are treated equally and the Out-castes of $\overline{P}$ are treated equally, but the Ins and Outs receive differential treatment. In many applications it will be desirable to assign a multiplicative scalar or "weight," w, to each domain element in an effort to reflect the relative importance of the various elements within S—where "importance" is defined in any sense deemed both pertinent and measurable. Let $w_1, w_2, ..., w_n$ be a set of such weights, assigned, respectively, to the n elements of a given S. If it be stipulated

that $0 \leq w_i \leq 1$ and $\sum_{i=1}^{n} w_i = 1$, these scalars will have the formal struc-

ture of probabilities, even if there is nothing at all "probabilistic" about the particular weighting criterion chosen.

This point is important to a clarification of the relationship between our constraint measures and the basic measures of information theory. In effect, the syntax of C_a, C, and ΔC implies that each element of a rule domain may be assigned the same weight initially: let us say $w = 1/|S|$. But the subsequent metrical discrimination between Ins and Outs may be thought of as (1) increasing the weight for each $\{s \mid s \in P\}$ to $1/|P|$ and (2) shrinking that for each $\{s \mid s \in \overline{P}\}$ to $w = 0$. The typical information-theoretic measure is concerned with the distribution of probabilities over some ensemble of discrete alternatives (Shannon and Weaver, 1949). Assume that the probabilities for certain of the "alternatives" of an ensemble were zero and that the (nonzero) probabilities for the remaining elements were equal. Under these conditions the information theorist's *redundancy* would become equivalent, structurally, to our relative constraint measure C (with the probabilities of the former interpreted more generally as "weights"); similarly, the complement of *entropy* would reduce to C_a. With the same special

234   JOHN ATKINS and LUKE CURTIS

strictures, the cultural measures of *relative orderliness* and of *organization* proposed by Wallace (1961, pp. 156–57) also reduce to C and C_a, respectively.

We regard the investigation of constraint in rule systems and further study of the structural properties of de-constraint paths as potentially fruitful lines of inquiry. As a matter of strategy, it may be wise initially to focus research efforts in this area on relatively simple, well-described domains of manageable size, and to adopt the provisional fiction that all elements of a given domain are equally important. The level of analysis at which the functions C_a, C, and ΔC operate is metrically primitive, but the introduction of more sophisticated concepts is not likely to prove very profitable until a great deal more is learned at this humbler level.

NOTES

1. Berge's formulation was chosen for emphasis here because it exhibits a number of useful features. It is brief and clear; it is simultaneously set-theoretic and graph-theoretic (with obvious resulting intuitive advantages); and it is sufficiently general to accommodate zero- and non-zero-sum games of finite or infinite length, with perfect or imperfect information, and with no restrictions on the allowed number of distinct move-paths connecting any two given positions of a game.

2. We assume that this hypothetical "cognitive frame" is both idiosyncratically and culturally constituted. Although our use of the singular is not meant to imply that domain conceptualization is unshared socially, we do wish to allow for domain and rule conceptualizations that are unique to the cognition of a single individual—in part because we are at least as interested in the cognition of the anthropologist himself as we are in cognitions reported by or imputed to his informants.

REFERENCES

Berge, Claude. 1962. The Theory of Graphs and Its Applications, trans. Alison Doig. New York: Wiley; London: Methuen & Co., Ltd.

Black, Max. 1962. Models and Metaphors: Studies in Language and Philosophy. Ithaca: Cornell U. Press.

Howard, Alan. 1963. Land, Activity Systems, and Decision-Making Models in Rotuma. Ethnology 2:407–40;

Metzger, Duane and Gerald E. Williams. 1963. A Formal Ethnographic Analysis of Tenejapa Ladino Weddings. American Anthropologist 65:1076–1101.

Shannon, Claude E. and Warren Weaver. 1949. The Mathematical Theory of Communication. Urbana: U. of Illinois Press.

Wallace, Anthony F. C. 1961. The Psychic Unity of Human Groups *in* Studying Personality Cross-Culturally, ed. B. Kaplan. New York: Harper & Row, 129–63.

CHAPTER 12

Frank B. Livingstone

The Application
of Structural Models
to Marriage Systems
in Anthropology

ALTHOUGH the conference stressed the
application of game theory to the behavioral sciences, this branch of
mathemathics is but one of many that are being applied to structural
problems in the behavioral sciences. Many of these techniques are very
similar and even amount to the same mathematical model but begin
at a different point or have a somewhat different notation; and books
on graph theory contain game theory, linear programming, flows in
networks, and vice versa. Thus it is difficult for an amateur to know
where one stops and the other begins, or even to know which is which.
However, all of these mathematical models are addressed to problems
concerned with a set either of individuals or of groups and a particular kind of relationship between them and, in addition, may include
attempts to maximize the relationships in one way or another. For this
reason, it seems that a discussion of any one of them includes the
others; and since graph theory is the broadest of the aforementioned
fields of mathematics, it offers the best possibilities. The specific applications of these models to the anthropological problems with which
we are concerned also seem to be well suited for the concepts of graph
theory.

Any such discussion raises the question of the relationship between
mathematical models and the data of science. I don't think this is a
particular problem for the mathematical hipsters but it is one of the
continuing arguments within the field of anthropology. Furthermore,
there is a considerable body of anthropologists who seem to think that
mathematical models have no place in our science—if that is what it is.

For example, Murphy (1963) ends his critique of Lévi-Strauss with a cautionary quote from Hegel:

When mathematical categories are used to determine something bearing upon the method or content of philosophic science [read structural analysis], such a procedure *proves* its preposterous nature chiefly herein, that insofar as mathematical formulae mean thoughts and conceptual distinctions, such meaning must first report, determine and justify itself in philosophy. . . . The mere employment of such borrowed forms is in any case an external and superficial procedure: a knowledge of their worth and of their meaning should precede their use; but such knowledge results only from conceptual contemplation, and not from the authority that mathematics gives them.

I am not sure what Murphy means to convey by this quote, but in any case his use of it doesn't seem to indicate an enthusiasm for mathematical analysis. Similarly in another critique of Lévi-Strauss, Maybury-Lewis (1960:35) states:

This points a methodological moral. Social relations cannot be formally represented by symbols in the same way as mathematical relations can. Accordingly, sociological models are not manipulable in the sense that mathematical equations are. Conclusions drawn from such models or from a comparison of such models without a simultaneous consideration of the data from which the models were constructed run a serious risk of error.

In his reply to Maybury-Lewis, Lévi Strauss (1960) emphasized that to most social anthropologists structure or models thereof are part of empirical reality. As such, they are simply descriptions of reality, and with this point of view, theory in anthropology is just description and derived factual generalizations about reality. My colleague, Elman Service, uses as an example of Radcliffe-Brown theory the statement: "All lions have manes," and when the first female lion is discovered, the theory is proved false or invalid. Much of early twentieth century anthropology, following Boas, was devoted to the pursuit of such exceptions, and this "not so in Bongo-Bongo" attitude still pervades much of anthropology. This attitude results in a strict inductive approach to science. For years, anthropology was in the position of trying to record data on cultures that were rapidly disappearing, and an attitude that emphasized the primary role of data collection was an obvious concomitant of the job at hand. I do not mean to disparage this worthwhile objective, but just as a society has to place value on the necessary roles such as that of a fighter pilot in order to have these roles filled during this era of anthropology's history the collection of data was valued as the greater good. Associated with it, there was a disdain for "armchair anthropologists," and the idea arose that, somehow, true generalizations would emanate from the great mass of data. "What we need is facts and more facts" is an apt expression of this philosophy of science. But even with this attitude pervading anthropology, it can be said today that the appropriate data on which the models to be described in this paper are based have never been collected, or, as Needham (1956:108) said more than ten years ago "There is no adequate account anywhere in the literature of unilateral cross-cousin marriage." This indicates that data collection is obviously based on theoretical models.

In recent years the "all x are y" type of generalization in anthropology has evolved with the development of statistics to the "x tends to be associated with y" type with a X^2 proof appended. But still theory is the discovery of significant relationships among facts. For most statistical problems the 5 percent level of significance is the highest any competent statistician would use, but at times the absence of significant associations at this level have caused anthropologists to use the 10 percent level, which is almost a travesty of statistical theory. In addition, most of this statistical testing is an inductive approach since it is mainly an attempt to discover interrelationships between categories of data. These categories are considered facts, but many of them seem to suffer unduly from vagueness, and in many cases there is no operational definition that one can apply to ethnographic material in order to determine the facts. For example, crosscousin marriage is a very common phenomenon, but if one looks at monographs and tries to decide who has it and exactly what it is they have, the result is a great variety of interpretations, which are so much fuel added to the fiery controversies in anthropology. The flames are fanned by the fact that in most ethnographies there are no numerical data on who marries whom. Naroll (1956) has made an attempt to provide operational definitions for all his terms so that anyone else who attempts the same analysis should come to the same conclusions, but this kind of standardization is extremely difficult to apply to ethnographic materials. (Anthropologists would rather argue anyway.) This inductive approach has reached its zenith in recent attempts to correlate everything with everything else in the world ethnographic sample (Coult and Habenstein 1966) and to make a factor analysis of the result (Sawyer and Levine 1966).

In contrast to this inductive approach, a deductive approach based on models should be complementary to it and is a necessary part of any science. Deductive models have lagged in anthropology, to a great extent because anthropologists cannot agree on what models are. The preceding quotations from Murphy and Maybury-Lewis treat them as facts. For this reason Murphy finds enigmatic Lévi-Strauss' statement that "the term 'social structure' has nothing to do with empirical reality but with models that are built up after it." It seems obvious that Lévi-Strauss is describing a mathematical model as mathematics, and not as an application to science. In biology we talk about breeding isolates, organisms, and genes, but we can also have a mathematical theory which relates these concepts to one another. Obviously we still use words which refer to empirical concepts, but we could use some vague mathematical terminology such as sets, elements, and relations. Within the theory or model it is the axioms about these concepts and the theorems that can be derived from them that are important, not whether in fact there are things called genes and breeding isolates out there. The models in social anthropology discussed here also concern the distribution of genes in human populations. The distribution or movement of genes among human populations is associated with marriage, although the association is not complete. For many human societies, this movement within a population is the transfer of women between exogamous descent groups. Thus, our model of a society is a group of clans that enter into marriage alliances which in turn effect an exchange of women among these groups. This definition of society is not meant to delineate those human groups which act this way and those which do not. I emphasize this because most anthropological definitions are considered as labels. In this sense our society pertains to nothing in the real world, as Lévi-Strauss has said.

There is also some confusion when any particular model is applied to a particular society as to whether it should be applied to actual behavior, to the native's conception of what ought to happen, or to the ethnographer's idea of what ought to happen. The second is usually distinguished from the first as jural rules vs. actual behavior—for example, "Thou shalt not kill" vs. the murders, riots, executions, and wars of actuality. In our model it will be "Thou shalt not marry thy father's sister's daughter," but this happens and the society has rules to deal with this infraction of the rules. The third type of model tends to distinguish Lévi-Strauss from other structuralists. In his reply to Maybury-Lewis, Lévi-Strauss (1960) used as an example a jigsaw puzzle, for which he contended Maybury-Lewis would consider

the pieces and the way they fit together as the model, while to him it
is the regularities of the saw and its camshafts that cut out the puzzle.
Thus, the model has little to do with the actual reality, but when the
formula for the operation of the saw is known, one can predict the
behavior of the actual puzzle.

As an example of these different types of models, I will use the
Purum marriage system. The Purum are perhaps the most over-ana-
lyzed society in anthropology (Needham 1958; Livingstone 1959;
Needham 1960b; Ackerman 1964; Geoghegan and Kay 1964; Cowgill
1964; Wilder 1964; Muller 1964; Needham 1964; Ackerman 1965; and
Schneider 1965; Needham 1966; Muller 1966). This may be because
they possess a particularly simple marriage system, but it is also because extensive numerical data have been collected on their marriages.
First, the ideal or normative Purum marriage system can be constructed from a series of statements about marriage relations among
the five clans into which the actual Purum exogamous descent groups
are divided. As Needham (1958) has shown, these clans are not descent
groups, but the elicited system seems quite clearly to be the native's
conception of how the marriage system works. The Purum system has
been labeled prescriptive matrilateral cross-cousin marriage, but this is
a misnomer. Although the mother's brother's daughter may be
married, it is only because this relative also belongs to a wife-giver
clan. Instead of prescriptive marriage or even asymmetrical marriage,
either the term matrilateral marriage alliance or connubium would be
more satisfactory. As Schneider (1965:67) has said with reference to
this type of marriage system: "It is fair to say that what started out as
the study of cross-cousin marriage has made sense in proportion to the
degree to which we have gotten away from genealogical cross-cousins.
The more our terminology has clung to the traditional names, like
MoBrDa and FaSiDa, the more confused the problem has become."

The ideal Purum marriage system divides the society into five
patrilineal clans each of which regards the others as either wife-givers
or wife-takers. Thus, the five clans of Purum society and the relation
"gives wives to" constitute a complete, symmetric, directed graph or
digraph. As such it is the same, mathematically, as the peck right or
dominance relation in chickens, the results of the judging of paired
comparisons, or the outcomes of a round robin tournament. For these
similar mathematical systems, much analysis has been done. H. G.
Landau (1951, 1965), following A. Rapoport (1949), has developed

the score structure for the dominance relation and analyzed the outcome of the introduction of a new member on it; H. A. David (1963) has recently summarized the work on paired comparisons; and J. W. Moon (1963) and D. R. Fulkerson (1965) have extended Landau's theorem to round robin tournaments. So many theorems concerning the lattertype of tournament, balanced incomplete block designs, and other types of combinatorial analysis have been proven by mathematicians that I am sure there must be many of significance for problems in structural anthropology.

As Kendall and Babington Smith (1940) showed, any relationship like this can be represented by a matrix of 0's and 1's. When clan i gives women to clan j, the matrix entry $a_{ij} = 1$, otherwise it is 0. Hence all $a_{ii} = 0$, and if $a_{ij} = 1$, then $a_{ji} = 0$; so that for all i and j, $a_{ij} \cdot a_{ji} = 0$. The result is an $n \times n$ skew symmetric matrix, where n is the number of clans in the society. Since the row totals for the matrix are the number of clans to whom each clan gives women and the column totals are the number each clan receives women from and all clans have one or the other relation with all the others, $a \cdot_i + a_i \cdot = (n - 1)$ and

$$\sum_{i,j} a_{ij} = n(n - 1)/2.$$

For any such matrix the rows can be rearranged so that $0 \leq a_1. \leq a_2. \cdots \leq a_n..$

Although the mathematical model for all these phenomena is identical, the equilibrium or optimum for the Purum marriage system is the direct opposite of the others. For the dominance relation (or in round robin tournaments where the relation is "dominates" or "defeats," or for paired comparisons where it is "is preferred to"), the optimum situation is a complete order such that there is one dominant or winner who has defeated everyone else, a second who has defeated all but the winner, etc. For this complete order the row totals would be 0, 1, 2,..., $(n-1)$. There are also no cyclic triads, that is, A defeats B, B defeats C, and then C defeats A; whichever happened last is termed an upset. Similarly if a judge prefers A to B, B to C, but also C to A, then he is inconsistent.

For the marriage system, however, this complete order is an impossibility. And instead of tending toward such an order, if the system were in this state, it would break down. In this state some clan could not get wives and another clan could not give wives to any other clan. In fact this is true when any row total is either 0 or $n - 1$. It should be

reemphasized that the Purum five-clan system is an ideal, but in a
sense we can say that the ideal is consistent with the operation of the

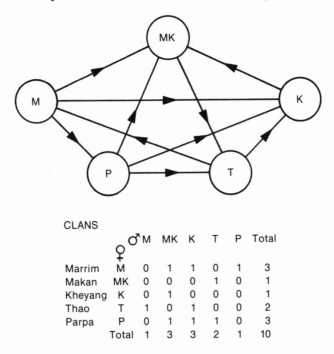

CLANS

	♂ M	MK	K	T	P	Total
♀						
Marrim M	0	1	1	0	1	3
Makan MK	0	0	0	1	0	1
Kheyang K	0	1	0	0	0	1
Thao T	1	0	1	0	0	2
Parpa P	0	1	1	1	0	3
Total	1	3	3	2	1	10

FIGURE 1. The ideal marriage relations among the clans of the Purum.

system (Fig. 1). However, the row totals or score structure for the
Purum is (1, 1, 2, 3, 3). If we assume equal numbers of both sexes,
then each clan would presumably give and take wives from an equal
number of other clans. At equilibrium, a five-clan system would thus
have a score structure (2, 2, 2, 2, 2), so that the Purum seem to be as
far from equilibrium as it is possible to be and still have a viable system.

For the Chawte, neighbors of the Purum, the structure is (1, 1, 2, 2)
for the system diagrammed in Lévi-Strauss (1949:329). But if one
separates the Thao clan and combines the relations in Shakespear
(1912) and the missing ones in Roy (1936), then the Chawte would
have a structure of (1, 1, 2, 3, 3). Even if either one of the two relations of the Thao clan that are missing from Shakespear is changed,
the structure would not change. However, let me emphasize that
Needham (1960a) has attempted to show that the best interpretation
of Shakespear's data is that they really refer to the Purum. In any

case, of the ten paired relations in the Chawte, five are like those of the Purum, but five are different or opposite.

For the score structure of a hierarchy, which is the same vector as our social structure, Landau (1951) has defined an index of hierarchy, h, and has obtained the expected value for this index. If the outcome of dominance contests is random then $E(h) = 3/(n + 1)$. The formula for this index is:

$$h = \frac{12}{n^3 - n} \sum_i \left(r_i - \frac{n - 1}{2} \right)^2$$

By what I think are legitimate mathematical manipulations, one can determine that $E(\Sigma r_i^2) = n^2(n - 1)/4$. For the Purum and Chawte structures this value is 24, while the expected value assuming random assignment of the relations is 25. The Purum and Chawte are as close to random as possible with a five-clan system, but the significance of this is difficult to ascertain. Perhaps it only means the answers to ethnographers' questions are random, which would have great implications for the study of social structure.

Although the Purum and Chawte seem to be very far from equilibrium, the ideal five-clan structure for Kachin society (Fig. 2) has the score structure (2, 2, 2, 2, 2). Since this structure is much more infrequent in terms of combinatorial possibilities than the others, it would seem that it is the ideal among the Kachin because it is the structure which works best. However, the Kachin comprise a great number of different autonomous societies in Northern Burma, and it would be extraordinary if all subscribed to this ideal. Furthermore, there are two different types of social structures in Northern Burma as outlined by Leach (1954) and this ideal structure fits only one of them, so the actual situation is obviously more complicated.

The situation is also more complicated because, in the actual social organization, exogamy is not based strictly on clans. In many cases, such as the Purum, the total clan seems to be almost exogamous, but the different subunits within the clan, the lineages, have quite different relations with the lineages of other clans. The localized lineage is the specific group that makes or breaks alliances with other lineages. In addition, the actual social organization must be more complicated in order to cope with the demographic changes due to chance which must occur in societies of this small size. In these societies the most rigid rule is the prohibition of giving wives to your own wife-givers or taking wives from your own wife-takers. Thus, for a society whose

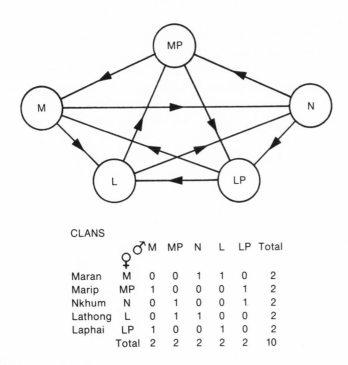

CLANS

| | ♂M | MP | N | L | LP | Total |
♀						
Maran M	0	0	1	1	0	2
Marip MP	1	0	0	0	1	2
Nkhum N	0	1	0	0	1	2
Lathong L	0	1	1	0	0	2
Laphai LP	1	0	0	1	0	2
Total	2	2	2	2	2	10

FIGURE 2. The ideal marriage relations among the Kachin. After Lévi-Strauss 1949:303.

clans and their marriage relations constitute a complete, symmetric digraph, any change in any relation would be a violation of their cardinal rule. In the Purum whose average exchange group or lineage has about twenty-five members, or in the Kachin village of Hpalang studied by Leach (1954), which has eight lineages with a range of one to seven houses per lineage, there must be continual realignment of the marriage relations among lineages. I have elsewhere (Livingstone 1959) attempted to show that if the ideal clan relations of Purum society are combined with the actual marriage statistics, then the assignment of the women of the clans as wives could not be attained within the rules of the system. This can be phrased as a problem in graph theory where the number of women marrying into the clan and those marrying out are the in and out degrees of the points of a digraph. The actual numbers for the Purum can constitute a strongly connected digraph; however, the realizability theorems for strongly connected digraphs (Hakimi 1965) are not so stringent as the conditions of a matrilateral connubium, since the marriage relations in such a society require that specific points be connected.

In any case, a complete symmetric digraph is much too rigid a structure for the functioning of a matrilateral connubium in these small endogamous societies, although Leach's group is not completely endogamous as the Purum were in fact. This problem is solved, or at least alleviated, by a reduction in the structure to a connected graph which is not complete (Fig. 3). For the Purum, Needham (1958) has shown that there are twelve alliance groups. Each clan is still exogamous, but the lineages within the clan have different alliance patterns.

	♂ ♀	M_1	M_2	M_3	M_4	MK_1	MK_2	K_1	K_2	T_1	T_2	T_4	P	Total
Ideal	M_1					0	1	0	0				1	2
	M_2					1	1	0	0	0	0	1	1	4
	M_3					0	1	0	0	0	0	0	1	2
	M_4					0	1	1		0	0		1	3
	MK_1	1	0	1	1			0		1	1	1	0	6
	MK_2	0	0	0	0			0		1	1	1	0	3
	K_1	1	1	1	0	1	1		0	0	0	0	0	5
	K_2	1		1										2
	T_1		1	1	1	0	0	1					0	4
	T_2		1	1	1	0	0	1					0	4
	T_4		0	1		0	0	1						2
	P	0	0	0	0	1	1	1		1	1			5
Total		3	3	6	3	3	6	5	0	3	3	3	4	42
Actual	M_1												4	4
	M_2					5		(2)	(2)				4	13
	M_3													0
	M_4							2					10	12
	MK_1	4			1				2	2	10	2		21
	MK_2							(1)	2		2			5
	K_1	3			(2)	18	2					(1)	(3)	29
	K_2	1			1	3		(3)					3	11
	T_1		2	4				3	4					13
	T_2		4					1						5
	T_4							4	1					5
	P					2		10	1	6	4			23
Total		8	6	4	4	28	2	26	12	8	16	3	24	141

FIGURE 3. The ideal marriage relations and the actual marriages among the Purum. Numbers in parentheses indicate marriages which are against the rules, while those underlined indicate marriages for which there were no rules.

Outside of the clans there are fifty-five possible relations between pairs of lineages of which forty-two are established; that is, the two lineages in question have an established wife-giver to wife-taker relationship. Among the Kachin, Leach (1954) states that in addition to the categories of wife-giver and wife-taker, there are two other categories into which other individuals or groups are placed, (1) relatives who are close enough to belong to the same exogamous group and hence are unmarriageable, and (2) "kissing cousins" who are considered to be relatives and therefore not enemies but are distant enough to be marriageable. Although for any lineage the entire society can be classified into these four categories, their composition is not stable. When a kissing cousin is married, the group then becomes a wife-giver or wife-taker according to the direction of the marriage. But, if one's group does not continue to marry this group, in the course of time it will fall back into the kissing cousin category. For the eight lineages of Hpalang of the twenty-eight possible alliances, only nine are wife-giver:wife-taker. However, there are eleven such alliances to lineages outside the village. The lineages are quite varied in size so that some have only one alliance. This implies that the lineage either could not give wives or could not take wives according to the present alliances.

If we restrict the class of connected digraphs that are permissible marriage systems to those with at least one in-directed line and one out-directed line at each point, then each point or lineage will be part of at least one cycle. The number of cycles or even triads that are cyclic triples is a good way of characterizing the connectedness of a graph. This number is also a distinguishing feature of our marriage model. This has also been stressed by Ackerman (1965). Just as the number of cycles is a measure of upsets or inconsistencies of judgment in round robin tournaments and paired comparisons, respectively, the number of cycles is also a measure of integration of a marriage system. At equilibrium for the ideal structure which is a complete digraph there is a maximum number of cycles. But when the digraph is not complete as in our second model, the relationship of cycles to the number of groups and their relationships is more complicated. However, the number of cycles would still seem to be a good measure of the integration of such a society, and, if we had the data, it would be possible to determine how much integration is necessary for a society to remain a unit.

With regard to complete symmetric digraphs, many theorems have been proven about these structures; the following are taken from Harary, Norman, and Cartwright (1965:ch. 11). The maximum wife-giver in a society is wife-giver, wife-taker, wife-giver of a wife-giver,

or wife-taker of a wife-taker to every other clan in the society. And
since our graph model cannot have a transmitter clan or one with no
wife-givers, there must be three clans with the properties of the aforementioned maximum wife-giver. With n clans and a score structure
$(r_1 \ldots r_i \ldots r_n)$, the number of cyclic triples is

$$c = \frac{n(n-1)(n-2)}{6} - \sum_i \frac{r_i(r_i-1)}{2}$$

and the maximum number of cyclic triples in societies with n clans are:
$(n^3 - n)/24$ with n odd, and $(n^3 - 4n)/24$ with n even, as was first
shown by Kendall and Babington Smith (1940). Since the society is a
strong digraph, it also contains a cycle of every length k where $k = 3,4,$
. . ., n. The n cycle is a complete path; so that any such structure must
practice marriage in a circle with all clans involved. Finally if the
difference between the number of wife-givers for any two clans is less
than $n/2$ or the number of wife-givers and wife-takers for all clans are
greater than or equal to $(n-1)/4$, then the society is a strongly
connected digraph or, in other words, the society is a realizable
matrilateral connubium.

We have assumed that our digraph model is complete, but if this
assumption is dropped and we assume, because of the equality of the
sexes in any clan, that each clan has the same number of wife-givers
as wife-takers, then the model is an isograph, about which one can
prove that every weak isograph is strongly connected (Harary et al.
1965:331).

The foregoing theorems indicate how much mathematical analysis
has been done on this kind of structure. It is only a small sample, but
there is also the question of its significance for our problems. Although they do give us some insight into the rigidity and perhaps
functioning of the structure, they are not the questions or answers
anthropologists would ask about this type of society. But with this
model we can ask significant questions, which to my knowledge
have not been answered. For example, for a given number of clans of
a given size, there must be optimum numbers or frequencies for the
three types of other clans, wife-givers, wife-takers, and kissing cousins.
With an equal sex ratio the first two would presumably be equal, but
what percentage of the other clans should be kissing cousins? This
would be similar to the classic problem of the Natchez social structure,
which can be shown to be unstable with certain assumptions (Goldberg

1958:238) but with different reproduction rates can be shown to be stable (Fischer 1964).

The preceding models have no strong status differential associated with the categories wife-taker and wife-giver. This is true in many societies in Southeast Asia but in many others, such as Kachin or the Northern Chin (Lehman 1963), there is such a status differential with the wife-giver as the superior. The egalitarian connubium is found among the Southern Chin with a democratic society, but among the Northern Chin there is a stratified society with differential statuses in the connubium (Lehman 1963). In this stratified society there is a rule that one cannot take wives from the wife-takers of one's own wife-takers, or that one cannot give wives to the wife-givers of one's own wife-givers. Thus, in Northern Chin society there can be no cyclic triples. This imposes much more restrictive limitations on possible structures and in addition would tend to make the system more hierarchical. For a closed society this structure would not be possible, but in Northern Chin society it seems that the highest castes of each community obtain wives from similar groups in other communities. This marriage system is almost the reverse of our previous model and at equilibrium would presumably be a complete hierarchy. This implies that some group would have no wife-takers or wife-givers, or in terms of network theory it would mean there was a source and a sink. As the wives flow through this network, there should be a continual buildup in the lower classes. This is similar to the Natchez problem or to the one raised by Salisbury's (1956) model of Siane marriage. It would appear to be an unstable system, but an unequal sex ratio or greater numbers of female infants would make it workable.

So far we have only discussed matrilateral systems, but Salisbury's (1956, 1964) model is of a patrilateral marriage system. In contrast to matrilateral systems, the relationship of wife-giver:wife-taker is not constant and always in the same direction but changes with every marriage. The system works as an exchange directly of women between two groups. When a woman goes in marriage from one group to another, the latter is then in the category of wife-ower to the first. Any clan can thus divide neighboring groups into wife-owers, and wife-owed. In this system every clan is more or less independent, so that there are no cycles of any meaning since the relations between clans are continually changing. But just as only two categories seem to be too rigid a structure to function with demographic changes in the matrilateral system, in this system there seems to be another category, with whom direct exchanges of "sisters" are made and the transaction is thus completed immediately. These patrilateral systems of obligatory marriage seem to be widespread in New Guinea. The marriage statistics in Gajdusek and Reid (1961) and Meggitt (1958) indicate how the marriages are contracted with surrounding communities and decrease in frequency with distance from the community. And Bateson's (1932) Iatmul demonstrate the categories, husband-men and wife-men, as Bateson called them. The clans from which one gets wives are also translated as father's mother's people. In the first ascending generation father's sister or women went as exchange to these clans, so that now they owe women to ego's clan. There is also the relation between clans of sister-exchangers. Although the graph model for this type of system is not identical to the matrilateral model, they seem to present many of the same problems of analysis.

Finally there are two further complications of the basic model for which mathematical techniques have been developed to some extent and for which game theory is relevant. First, there is the problem of variability in clan size. Most of the models assume rather static clan sizes with little variation among clans in size. But in these societies, the lineages or alliance groups are continually changing in size due to random factors but also due to the fact that larger lineages get larger and smaller lineages tend to get smaller. Part of the reason for this tendency seems to be the fact that lineages try to make alliances with larger rather than smaller ones. The continual changes that are occurring in the specific lineages and their composition are the result of fusion and fission of the lineages. For a given mean or optimum lineage size it should be possible to determine how fast the system will have to change in order to cope with just random factors. A review of the data on primitive societies in the Amazon, the Matto Grosso, or New Guinea seems to show that there is a marked clustering around the optimum clan size. This seems particularly marked in areas where there is still primitive warfare, and where alliances still serve a vital part of their function.

Second, there is the complication of other valuables in addition to women or other rights and privileges associated with these alliances. In very primitive societies, such as that of the Australian aborigines who are totally self-sufficient, the only resource from outside which the exogamous group needs is women. In these societies, marriage is either by direct exchange of women between groups or there are marriage systems, such as among the Murngin where more than two groups are involved and which are some form of indirect exchange. There is no warfare among the Murngin over other resources such as land (Warner 1937), but there is considerable fighting over women who are owed to one group but marry into another. This fighting is among relatives who belong to the same moiety. Similar kinds of marriage systems are found among the Ge of the Matto Grosso, another uncontrolled area with predominantly hunting and gathering groups.

With the development of agriculture and greater interdependence among groups, other valuables become involved in these exchanges. At this level brideprice in cows, cowries, or cash is paid for the women, but in almost all cases if no children are born of the marriage the brideprice is refunded. Although the introduction of money leads to the individualization of marriage choice and the subsequent break-down of alliances based on marriage, in many middle range societies the whole clan or lineage antes up the brideprice, so that the transaction is still a group decision. Each group is attempting to maximize its return from the exchange of its women. These returns can include women, who will provide the next generation of the clan, but they also include peace and allies. With evolution other resources such as steel axes, cows, land, water, or money can be involved in the returns. The maximization process could probably be described by game theory, but for the whole society with a number of such groups, the organization and its maximization seems quite similar to the modern economic problems which have been solved by linear programming methods.

REFERENCES

Ackerman, C. 1964. Structure and Statistics: The Purum Case. American Anthropologist 66:53–65.
———. 1965. Structure and Process: The Purum Case. American Anthropologist 67:83–91.
Bateson, G. 1932. Social Structure of the Iatmul People. Oceania 2:245–91.
Coult, A. D., and R. W. Habenstein. 1966. Cross-Tabulations of Murdock's World Ethnographic Sample. Columbia: U. of Missouri Press.
Cowgill, G. L. 1964. Statistics and Sense: More on the Purum Case. American Anthropologist 66:1358–65.
David, H. A. 1963. The Method of Paired Comparisons. New York: Hafner.
Fischer, J. L. 1964. Solutions for the Natchez Paradox. Ethnology 3:53–65.

Fulkerson, D. R. 1965. Upsets in Round Robin Tournaments. Canadian J. of
    Mathematics 17:957–69.
Gajdusek, D. C. and L. H. Reid. 1961. Studies on Kuru, IV. The Kuru Pattern in
    Moke, A Representative Fore Village. American J. of Tropical Medicine and
    Hygiene 10:628–38.
Geoghegan, W. H. and P. Kay. 1964. More on Structure and Statistics: A Critique
    of C. Ackerman's Analysis of the Purum. American Anthropologist
    66:1351–58.
Goldberg, S. 1958. Introduction to Difference Equations. New York: Wiley.
Hakimi, S. L. 1965. On the Degrees of the Vertices of a Directed Graph. J. of the
    Franklin Institute 279:290–308.
Harary, F., R. Z. Norman, and D. Cartwright. 1965. Structural Models: An Intro-
    duction of the Theory of Directed Graphs. New York: Wiley.
Kendall, M. G. and B. Babington Smith. 1940. On the Method of Paired Compar-
    isons. Biometrika 31:324–45.
Landau, H. G. 1951. On Dominance Relations and the Structure of Animal
    Societies. Bull. of Mathematical Biophysics 13:1–19, 245–62.
———. 1965. Development of Structure in a Society with a Dominance Relation
    when New Members Are Added Successively. Bull. of Mathematical Biophysics
    27:151–75 (special issue).
Leach, E. R. 1954. Political Systems of Highland Burma: A Study of Kachin Social
    Structure. London: G. Bell.
Lehman, F. K. 1963. The Structure of Chin Society. Urbana: U. of Illinois Press.
Lévi-Strauss, C. 1949. Les Structures Élémentaires de la Parente. Paris: Presses
    Universitaires de France.
———. 1960. On Manipulated Sociological Models. Bijdragen tot de taal-, Land-en
    Volkenkunde 116:45–54.
Livingstone, F. B. 1959. A Further Analysis of Purum Social Structure. American
    Anthropologist 61:1084–87.
Maybury-Lewis, D. 1960. The Analysis of Dual Organizations: A Methodological
    Critique. Bijdragen tot taal-land-en volkenkunde 116:17–44.
Meggitt, M. J. 1958. The Enga of the New Guinea Highlands: Some Preliminary
    Observations. Oceania 28:253–330.
Moon, J. W. 1963. An Extension of Landau's Theorem on Tournaments. Pacific
    J. of Mathematics 13:1343–45.
Muller, E. W. 1964. Structure and Statistics: Some Remarks on the Purum Case.
    American Anthropologist 66:1371–77.
———. 1966. Critique of Ackerman. American Anthropologist. 68:524–25.
Murphy, R. F. 1963. On Zen Marxism: Filiation and Alliance. Man 63:21.
Naroll, R. 1956. A Preliminary Index of Social Development. American Anthro-
    pologist 58:687–715.
Needham, R. 1956. Review of G. C. Homans and D. M. Schneider, Marriage,
    Authority, and Final Causes: A Study in Unilateral Cross Cousin Marriage.
    American J. of Sociology 62:107–08.
———. 1958. A Structural Analysis of Purum Society. American Anthropologist
    60:75–101.
———. 1960a. Chawte Social Structure. American Anthropologist 62:236–53.
———. 1960b. Structure and Change in Asymmetric Alliance: Comments on
    Livingstone's Further Analysis of Purum Society. American Anthropologist
    62:499–503.

————. 1964. Explanatory Notes on Prescriptive Alliance and the Purum. American Anthropologist 66:1377–86.

————. 1966. Comments on the Analysis of Purum Society. American Anthropologist 68:171–77.

Rapoport, A. 1949. Outline of a Probabilistic Approach to Animal Sociology. Bull. of Mathematical Biophysics 11:183–96, 273–81.

Roy, R. C. 1936. Notes on the Chawte Kuki Clan. Man in India 16:135–55.

Salisbury, R. F. 1956. Asymmetrical Marriage Systems. American Anthropologist 58:639–55.

————. 1964. New Guinea Highland Models and Descent Theory. Man 64:213.

Sawyer, J. and R. A. Levine. 1966. Cultural Dimensions: A Factor Analysis of the World Ethnographic Sample. American Anthropologist 68:708–31.

Schneider, D. M. 1965. Some Muddles in the Models: Or, How the System Really Works in The Relevance of Models for Social Anthropology (A. S. A. Monographs No. 1). New York: Praeger.

Shakespear, J. 1912. The Lushei Kuki Clans. London: Macmillan.

Warner, W. L. 1937. A Black Civilization. New York: Harper & Row.

Wilder, W. 1964. Confusion Versus Classification in the Study of Purum Society. American Anthropologist 66:1365–71.

M. Shubik

A Bibliography
with Some Comments

THIS somewhat diffuse bibliography provides references to the applications of game theory, gaming, and related approaches to many fields. The comments that accompany some of the references are not reviews; they are intended merely to call the reader's attention to features of particular works that are of unusual interest.

Two informal types of classification have been used for all books and articles (bibliographies have not been classified). The letter *S*, *M*, or *P* following a reference indicates:

S—primarily for social or behavioral scientists
M—primarily for readers with a relatively advanced mathematical background
P—a popularization

The second type of classification (the abbreviation following the hyphen) indicates the general subject area of the book or article:

Psy—Psychology and social psychology
Soc—Sociology and anthropology
Ec—Economics
Pol—Political and military science
S—Behavioral sciences in general
M—Mathematics or statistics

For example, *Games and Decisions* by Luce and Raiffa is classified as *S & M-S*. This indicates that it is written primarily for behavioral scientists, although it will also be of interest to those with a relatively advanced mathematical background, and its subject field is behavioral sciences in general. *Fights, Games and Debates* by Rapoport is classified as *P & S-S*, indicating that it can be read by the intelligent layman but that it can be read with benefit by the behavioral scientist, and that it is devoted to behavioral sciences in general. Braithwaite's *Theory of Games as a Tool for the Moral Philosopher* is classified as *S & M*—but further classification of this particular work is left to the reader.

BIBLIOGRAPHIES

Brody, R. A. 1960. Deterrence Strategies: An Annotated Bibliography. J. of Conflict Resolution IV (December), 443–57.

Cragin, S. W., Jr., et al. 1959. Simulation: Management's Laboratory. Dept. of Harvard University. (April; Mimeographed.)

Deacon, A. R. L., Jr. 1960. Selected References on Simulation and Games. Report of AMA's First National Forum on Simulation, May 16-18, 1960. Saranac Lake, N.Y. (Mimeographed.)

Hellebrandt, E. T., and W. D. Fleishhacker. 1959. General Business Management Simulation. College of Commerce, Ohio University. (Mimeographed.)

Malcolm, D. G. 1959. A Bibliography on the Use of Simulation in Management Analysis. Santa Monica: System Development Corp., SP-126. (November; Mimeographed.) Also published in Operations Research 8 (March-April) 169–77.

Minsky, M. 1961. A Selected Descriptor-Indexed Bibliography to the Literature on Artificial Intelligence. IRE Transactions on Human Factors in Electronics 2 (March) 39–55.

Pierce, A. M. 1959. A Concise Bibliography of the Literature of Artificial Intelligence. Bedford, Mass.: Air Force Cambridge Research Center. (September; Mimeographed.)

Riley, V. and J. R. Young. 1957. Bibliography on War Gaming. Chevy Chase, Md.: Operations Research Office, BRS-7, The John Hopkins University. (April; Mimeographed.)
  A valuable 94-page compendium with the first reference dating back to 1824. Comments and annotations are supplied for many of the modern war games.

Shubik, M. 1960. A Bibliography on Simulation, Gaming, Artificial Intelligence, and Allied Topics. J. of American Statistical Assoc. 55 (December), 736–51.

BOOKS

Arrow, K. J. 1951. Social Choice and Individual Values. New York: Wiley.
  S–Ec & S

Blackwell, D. and M. A. Girschik. 1954. Theory of Games and Statistical Decisions, New York: Wiley. M-M

Boulding, K. E. 1962. Conflict and Defense: A General Theory. New York: Harper & Row. S-S
  A broad and provocative discussion of many aspects of conflict. Boulding stresses the different manifestations of conflict in various organizations. He contrasts behavior of individuals, groups, formal and informal organizations, and he discusses economic, industrial, and international conflict, as well as ideological and ethical conflict. The book is more valuable for general ideas than for detailed analysis.

Braithwaite, R. B. 1955. Theory of Games as a Tool for the Moral Philosopher. Cambridge: Cambridge U. Press. S & M

Buchanan, J. M. and G. Tullock. 1962. The Calculus of Consent. Ann Arbor: U. of Michigan Press. S-Pol

Chamberlain, N. W. 1955. A General Theory of Economic Process. New York: Harper. S-Ec

Dahl, R. 1956. A Preface to Democratic Theory. Chicago: U. of Chicago Press. S-Pol

Douglas, A. 1962. Industrial International Peacemaking. New York: Columbia U. Press.   *S-Ec*

Hertz, J. H. 1959. International Politics in the Atomic Age. New York: Columbia U. Press.   *S-Pol*

Kahn, H. 1962. Thinking About the Unthinkable. New York: Horizon.   *P-S*
   This is a popularization of many of the ideas contained in Kahn's On Thermonuclear War. Regardless of one's emotional reactions to the contents, Kahn presents an analysis and discusses "some strange aids to thought," which make a case for this approach to the study of political and military affairs.

Kaplan, M. A. 1957. System and Process in International Politics. New York: Wiley.   *S-Pol*

Kemeny, J. G., H. Merkil, J. L. Snell, and G. L. Thompson. 1957. Introduction to Finite Mathematics. Englewood Cliffs, N.J.: Prentice-Hall.   *S-S*
   An excellent elementary introduction to mathematical methods of use in the behavioral sciences.

Kuhn, H. and A. W. Tucker, eds. 1950. Contributions to the Theory of Games. Vol. I. Annals of Mathematics Studies, No. 24. Princeton: Princeton U. Press.   *M-M*

————. 1953. Contributions to the Theory of Games, Vol. II. Annals of Mathematics Studies, No. 28. Princeton: Princeton U. Press.   *M-M*

Kuhn, J. W. 1961. Bargaining in Grievance Settlement. New York: Columbia U. Press.   *S-Ec*

Leites, N. 1959. On the Game of Politics in France. Stanford: Standford U. Press.   *S-Pol*

Luce, R. D. and H. Raiffa. 1957. Games and Decisions. New York: Wiley   *S & M-S*
   This is a first-class exposition of many of the concepts of the theory of games in relation to the behavioral sciences. For serious work in the application of game theory, it is important to have mastered most of the contents of this book. To those not trained in mathematics, the writing may be somewhat austere, but it is certainly rewarding.

McDonald, J. 1953. Strategy in Poker, Business, and War. New York: McGraw-Hill.   *P-Pol & Ec*

McKinsey, J. C. C. 1953. Introduction to the Theory of Games. New York: McGraw-Hill.   *S & M-M & S*

Morgenstern, O. 1959. The Question of National Defense. New York: Random House.   *S-Pol*

Phillips, Brig. Gen. T. R., ed. 1955. Roots of Strategy. Harrisburg: Military Service Publishing Co.   *S-Pol*

Rapoport, A. 1960. Fights, Games, and Debates. Ann Arbor: U. of Michigan Press.   *S & P-S*
   A stimulating and easy-to-read introduction to the construction of models of social processes. It contains an excellent exposition of the theory of games as well as a discussion of war, arms races, and other epidemics, based heavily on the work of L. F. Richardson. In the third part, debates are contrasted with fights and games where changes in the value systems of the participants do not take place.

Richardson, L. F. 1960a. Arms and Insecurity. Chicago: Quadrangle Books.   *S & M-Pol*

————. 1960b. Statistics of Deadly Quarrels. Chicago: Quadrangle Books.   *S & M-Pol*

Riker, W. H. 1962. The Theory of Political Coalitions. New Haven: Yale U. Press
    S-Pol
    This is a direct attempt at applying certain aspects of *n*-person game theory to
    political behavior. The book is written for the political scientist and not for the
    game theorist. Much of this type work must be done by political scientists be-
    fore game theory can be modified to suit their purposes. The mathematically
    inclined game theorist might argue that much liberty has been taken with the
    various concepts of solution employed here. It is evident that Riker's work calls
    for dynamic elements that are not yet sufficiently developed.
Schelling, T. C. 1960. The Strategy of Conflict. Cambridge: Harvard U. Press.
    S-Pol & S
Shubik, M. 1954. Readings in Game Theory and Political Behavior. New York:
    Doubleday. *S-Pol & S*
————. 1959. Strategy and Market Structure. New York: Wiley *S & M-Ec*
    An application of game theory to the study of oligopoly, with several chapters
    on the role of information and the construction of dynamic games. These chap-
    ters are of more general interest than to economic theorists alone.
Siegel, S. and L. E. Fouraker. 1960. Bargaining and Group Decisions-Making. New
    York: McGraw-Hill. *S-Psy & Ec*
Simon, H. A. 1957. Models of Man: Social and Rational. New York: Wiley. *S-S*
Snyder, R. C., H. W. Bruck, and B. Sapin. 1962. Foreign Policy Decision-Making.
    New York: The Free Press. *S-Pol*
Snyder, R. C. and J. A. Robinson. 1962. National and International Decision-
    Making. New York: Institute for National Order. *S-Pol*
    This report is more or less an encyclopedia of projects for the development of
    knowledge of the behavioral sciences that is necessary to providing understand-
    ing about the major problems of war and peace. It contains a very useful
    bibliography.
Thibaut, J. W. and H. H. Kelly. 1959. The Social Psychology of Groups. New York:
    Wiley. *S-Psy*
Thrall, R. M., C. H. Coombs, and R. L. Davis. 1954. Decision Processes. New York:
    Wiley. *M & S–M & S*
Tucker, A. W. and P. Wolfe, eds. 1957. Contributions to the Theory of Games, Vol.
    III. Annals of Mathematics Studies, No. 39. Princeton: Princeton U. Press.
    M-M
Ulmer, S. S. 1961. Introductory Readings in Political Behavior. Chicago: Rand
    McNally. *S-Pol*
von Neumann, J. and O. Morgenstern. 1953. Theory of Games and Economic
    Behavior. 3d ed. Princeton: Princeton U. Press. *M-M & Ec*
Williams, J. D. 1954. The Compleat Strategyst, Being a Primer to The Theory of
    Games. New York: McGraw-Hill. *P-S*
Zeuthen, F. 1930. Problems of Monopoly and Economic Warfare. London:
    Routledge. *S-Ec*

ARTICLES

Arrow, K. J. 1951a. Alternative Approaches to the Theory of Choice in Risk-Taking
    Situations. Econometrica 19: 404–37. *S-Ec & S*
————. 1951b. Mathematical Models in the Social Sciences *in* D. Lerner and H. S.
    Lasswell eds., The Policy Sciences. Stanford: Standford University Press,
    129–54. *S-S*

Atkinson, R. C., and P. Suppes. 1958. An Analysis of Two-Person Game Situations in Terms of Statistical Learning Theory. J. of Experimental Psychology 55: 369–78.   *S-Psy*

Barth, F. 1959. Segmentary Opposition and the Theory of Games: A Study of Pathan Organization. J. of the Royal Anthropological Institute 89: 5–21. *S-Soc*

Barnard, J. 1950. Where is the Modern Sociology of Conflict? American J. of Sociology 61: 11–16.   *S-Soc*

———. 1954. The Theory of Games of Strategy as a Modern Sociology of Conflict. American J. of Sociology 59 (March), 411–24.   *S-Soc*

Brody, R. A. 1961. Political Games for Model Construction in International Relations.
Dept. of Political Science, Northwestern University. (June; Mimeographed.) *S-Pol*
This article contains a useful summary of several political gaming exercises and references to them.

Caplow, T. A. 1956. A Theory of Coalitions in the Triad. American Social Rev. 21:489–93.   *S-Psy & Soc*

Dahl, R. A. 1957. The Concept of Power. Behavioral Science 2 (July), 201–15. *S-Pol*

Deutsch, M. 1949. A Theory of Cooperations and Competition. Human Relations 2:129–52.   *S-Psy*

———. 1958. Trust and Suspicion. J. of Conflict Resolution II: 267–79.   *S-Psy*

———. 1960. The Effect of Threat upon Interpersonal Bargaining. J. of Abnormal and Social Psychology 61:181–89.   *S-Psy*

Deutsch, M. and R. M. Krauss. 1962. Studies of Interpersonal Bargaining. J. of Conflict Resolution VI (March), 52–76.   *S-Psy*

Dresher, M. 1961. Games of Strategy: Theory and Applications. Santa Monica: RAND Corp. (May; Mimeographed.)   *M & S*

Edwards, W. 1953. Probability Preferences in Gambling. American J. of Psychology 66:349–64.   *S-Psy & S*

———. 1962. Utility, Subjective Probability, Their Interaction, and Varian Preferences. J. of Conflict Resolution VI (March), 42–51.   *S-Psy & S*

———. 1964. The Theory of Decision-Making. Psychological Bull. 51:380–417. *S-Psy & S*

Ellsberg, D. 1959. The Theory and Practice of Blackmail (Lowell Lecture). Santa Monica: RAND Corp.   *S–Pol*

Fagen, R. R. 1961. Some Contributions of Mathematical Reasoning to the Study of Politics. Amer. Pol. Sci. Rev. LV (December), 888–900.   *S-Pol*

Faxen, K. O. 1949. The Theory of Games, Expectation Analysis, and Trade Agreements. Nationalokonomisk Tidsskrift (Denmark) (November). *S-Ec*

Flood, M. M. 1954a. A Stochastic Model of Social Interaction. Trans-actions of the New York Academy of Science 16: 202–05.   *S-Psy*

———. 1954. Game-Learning Theory and Some Decision-Making Experiments: Environmental Non-Stationarity in a Sequential Decision-Making Experiment *in* R. M. Thrall, C. H. Coombs, and R. L. Davis, eds., Decision Processes, pp. 139–58, 287–99. New York: Wiley.   *S-Psy*

———. 1958. Some Experimental Games. Management Science 5:5–26.   *S-Psy & S*

Foster, C. and A. Rapoport. 1956. Parasitism and Symbiosis in an *N*-Person Non-Constant Sum, Continuous Game. Bull. of Mathematical Biophysics 18: 219–31. *S-S*

Frank, J. D. 1941. Recent Studies of the Level of Aspiration. Psychological Bull. 38: 218–26. *S-Psy*

French, J. R. P., Jr. 1956. A Formal Theory of Social Power. Psychology Rev. 63: 181–94. *S-Psy*

Gamson, W. A. 1961. A Theory of Coalition Formation. Amer. Social Rev. 26: 373–82. *S-Soc*

Glasser, G. J. 1958. Game Theory and Cumulative Voting for Corporate Directors. Management Science 5: 151–56. *S-Ec*

Goldhamer, H. and E. Shils. 1939. Types of Power and Status. Amer. J. of Sociology 45: 171–82. *S-Soc & S*

Harsanyi, J. C. 1956. Approaches to the Bargaining Problem Before and After the Theory of Games: A Critical Discussion of Zeuthen's, Hicks' and Nash's Theories. Econometrica 24: 144–57. *S-Ec & Pol*

————. 1961. On the Rationality Postulates Underlying the Theory of Cooperative Games. J. of Conflict Resolution V: 179–96. *S-Ec & Pol*

————. 1962a. Bargaining in Ignorance of the Opponent's Utility Function. J. of Conflict Resolution VI (March), 29–38. *S-Ec & Pol*

————. 1962b. Measurement of Social Power in N-Person Reciprocal Power Situations. Behavioral Science 7 (January), 81–91. *S-Ec & Pol*

————. 1962c. Measurement of Social Power, Opportunity Costs, and the Theory of Two-Person Bargaining Games. Behavioral Science 7 (January) 67–80. *S-Ec & Pol*

Haywood, O. G., Jr. 1950. Military Decision and the Mathematical Theory of Games. Air University Quarterly Rev. 4 (Summer), 17. *S-Pol*

————. 1954. Military Decision and Game Theory. J. of the Operations of the Research Society of Amer. 2: 365–85 *S-Pol*

Hoggatt, A. C. 1959. An Experimental Business Game. Behavioral Science 4: 192–203. *S-Ec & S*

Ikle, F. C. and N. Leites. 1962. Political Negotiation as a Process of Modifying Utilities. J. of Conflict Resolution VI (March), 12–28. *S-Pol*

Kalisch, G. K. 1954. Some Experimental N-Person Games *in* R. M. Thrall, C. H. Coombs, and R. L. Davis, eds., Decision Processes, pp. 322–28. New York: Wiley. *S & M-S & M*

Kaufman, H. and G. M. Becker. 1961. The Empirical Determination of Game-Theoretical Strategies. J. of Experimental Psychology 61: 462–68. *S-Psy*

Koo, A. Y. 1959. Recurrent Objections to the Minimax Strategy. Rev. of Economics and Statistics XLI (February), 36–43. *S-Ec*

Kort, F. 1957. Predicting Supreme Court Decisions. American Political Science Rev. LI (March), 11–12. *S-Pol*

Kuhn, H. W. 1953. Extensive Games and the Problem of Information *in* H. W. Kuhn and A. W. Tucker eds., Contributions to the Theory of Games, Vol. II, pp. 189–216. Annals of Mathematics Studies No. 28. Princeton: Princeton University Press. *M-M*

Lieberman, B. 1960. Human Behavior in a Strictly Determined 3×3 Matrix Game. Behavioral Science 5: 317–22. *S-Psy*

Loomis, J. L. 1959. Communication, the Development of Trust, and Cooperative Behavior. Human Relations 12: 305–15. *S-Psy*

Luce, R. D. 1954. A Definition of Stability for N-Person Games *in* H. W. Kuhn and A. W. Tucker eds., Contributions to the Theory of Games, Vol. IV, pp. 357–66. Annals of Mathematics Studies, No. 40. Princeton: Princeton University Press. *M & S-Psy*

————. 1955a. ψ-Stability: A New Equilibrium Concept for N-Person Game Theory. Mathematical Models of Human Behavior, Proceedings of a Symposium, Stanford: Dunlap & Assoc., 32–44.   *M-M & S*

————. 1955b. K-Stability of Symmetric and Quota Games. Annals of Mathematics 62: 517–27.   *M-M & S*

Luce, R. D. and E. W. Adams. 1956. The Determination of Subjective Characteristic Functions in Games with Misperceived Payoff Functions. Econometrica 24: 158–71.   *M*

Lutzker, D. R. 1960. Internationalism as a Predictor of Cooperative Behavior. J. of Conflict Resolution IV: 426–30.   *S-Pol & Psy*

Maccoby, M. 1961. Social Psychology of Deterrence. Bull. of the Atomic Scientists 17: 278–81.   *S*

March, J. G. 1955. An Introduction to the Theory and Measurement of Influence. American Political Science Rev. XLIX: 431–51.   *S-Pol*

————. 1957. Measurement Concepts in the Theory of Influence. J. of Politics 19:202–26.   *S-Pol*

Marschak, J. 1950. Rational Behavior, Uncertain Prospects, and Measurable Utility. Econometrica 18: 111–41.   *M & S-Ec & S*

McDonald, J. 1948. Poker: An American Game. Fortune 37 (March), 128.   *P*

McMurry, R. W. 1955. War and Peace in Labor Relations. Harvard Business Rev. (November-December 1955), pp. 18–60   *S*

Minas, J. S., A. Scodel, D. Marlow, and H. Rawson. 1960. Some Descriptive Aspects of Two-Person Non-Zero-Sum Games. II. J. of Conflict Resolution IV. 193–97   *S-Psy & S*

Morgenstern. O. 1949. The Theory of Games. Scientific American 180: 22–25.   *S*

————. 1960. Effective and Secure Deterrence: The Oceanic System. Royal Canadian Air Force Staff College J.   *S-Pol*

Nash, J. F. 1950a. Equilibrium Points in N-Person Games. Proceedings of the National Academy of Science 36: 48–49.   *M-M*

————. 1950b. The Bargaining Problem. Econometrica 18: 155–62. *M & S-Ec & M*

————. 1951. Non-Cooperative Games. Annals of Mathematics 54: 286–95.   *M-M*

Osgood, C. E. 1960. A Case for Gradual Unilateral Disengagement. Bull. of the Atomic Scientists 16: 127–31.   *S-Pol*

Pruitt, D. G. 1962. An Analysis of Responsiveness Between Nations. J. of Conflict Resolution VI (March), 5–18.   *S-Pol & S*

Quandt, R. E. 1961. On the Use of Game Models in Theories of International Relations. World Politics 14:69–76.   *S-Pol*

Raiffa, H. 1953. Arbitration Schemes for Generalized Two-Person Games *in* H. W. Kuhn and A. W. Tucker, eds., Contributions to the Theory of Games, Vol. II, pp. 361–387. Annals of Mathematics Studies, No. 28. Princeton: Princeton University Press.   *M & S-M & Ec*

Rapoport, A. 1957. Lewis F. Richardson's Mathematical Theory of War. J. of Conflict Resolution I: 244–99.   *S-Pol & S*

Rapoport, A., A. Chammah, J. Dwyer, and J. Gyr. 1962. Three-Person Non-Zero-Sum Non-negotiable Games. Behavioral Science 7 (January), 38–58. *S-Psy & S*

Rapoport, A. and C. Orwant. 1962. Experimental Games: A Review. Behavioral Science 7 (January), 1–37.   *S-S*

Riker, W. H. 1959. A Test of the Adequacy of the Power Index. Behavioral Science 4 (April), pp. 120–31.   *S-Pol*

Riker, W. H. and D. Niemi. 1962. The Stability of Coalitions on Roll Calls in the House of Representatives. American Political Science Rev. LIV (March), 58–65.   *S-Pol*

Sakaguchi, M. 1960. Reports on Experimental Games. Statistical Applied Research, JUSE 7:156–65.   *S-S*

Schelling, T. C. 1957. Bargaining, Communication, and Limited War. J. of Conflict Resolution I:19–36.   *S-Pol*

———. 1961. Experimental Games and Bargaining Theory. World Politics 14:47–68.   *S-Pol*

Schubert, G. A. 1958. The Study of Judicial Decision-Making as an Aspect of Political Behavior. American Political Science Rev. III:1007–25.   *S-Pol*

Seligman, B. B. 1952. Games Theory and Collective Bargaining. Labor and Nation 8:50–52.   *S-Ec & S*

Shapley, L. S. 1953. A Value for *N*-Person Games *in* H. W. Kuhn and A. W. Tucker, eds., Contributions to the Theory of Games, Vol. II, pp. 307–17. Annals of Mathematics Studies, No. 28. Princeton: Princeton U. Press.   *M-M*

———. 1962. Simple Games: An Outline of the Descriptive Theory. Behavioral Science 7 (January) 59–66.   *M-S & M*

Shapley, L. S. and M. Shubik. 1953. Solution of *N*-Person Games with Ordinal Utilities. Econometrica 21:348–49.   *M-Ec & M*

———. 1954. A Method for Evaluating the Distribution of Power in a Committee System. American Political Science Rev. XLVIII (September), 787–927   *S-Pol & S*

Shubik, M. 1952. Information, Theories of Competition, and the Theory of Games. J. of Political Economy LX (April), 145–50.   *S-Ec*

———. 1954. Information, Risk, Ignorance, and Indeterminacy. Quarterly J. of Economics LSVIII: 629–40.   *S-Ec*

———. 1955. The Uses of Game Theory in Management Science. Management Science 2 (October), 40–54.   *S-S*

———. 1956. A Game Theorist Looks at the Antitrust Laws and the Automobile Industry. Stanford Law Rev. 8 (July), 594–630.   *S*

———. 1959. Simulation and the Theory of the Firm. Proceedings of the Conference on the Western Data Processing Center Dedication, U. of California at Los Angeles, January 22–27, 1959.   *S-Ec & S*

———. 1960. Games, Decisions, and Industrial Organization. Management Science 6 (July), 455–74.   *S-S & M*

———. 1962. Some Experimental Non-Zero-Sum Games with Lack of Information about the Rules. Management Science 8 (January), 215–34.   *S-S & Psy*

Shubik, M. and G. L. Thompson. 1959. Games of Economic Survival. Naval Research Logistics Qtly. 6 (June), 11–23.   *M-M & Ec*

Singer, J. D. 1958. Threat-Perception and the Armament Tension Dilemma. J. of Conflict Resolution II: 90–105.   *S-Pol*

Sjoberg, G. 1960. Strategy and Social Power. J. of Conflict Resolution IV (June), 163–78.   *S-Pol*

Snyder, G. H. 1960. Deterrence and Power. J. of Conflict Resolution IV (June), 163–78.   *S-Pol*

Snyder, R. C. 1955. Game Theory and the Analysis of Political Behavior *in* Stephen K. Bailey et al., Research Frontiers in Politica and Government, pp. 70–103. Washington: Brookings Institution.   *S-Pol*

Solomon. L. 1960. The Influence of Some Types of Power Relationships and Game Strategies upon the Development of Interpersonal Trust. J. of Abnormal and Social Psychology 61:223–30.   *S-Psy*

Stone, J. J. 1958. An Experiment in Bargaining Games. Econometrica 26:286–96. *S-S & Ec*

Thomas, C. J. and W. L. Deemer. 1957. The Role of Operational Gaming in Operations Research. J. of the Operations Research Society of America 5 (February), 1–27.   *S-Pol*

Ulmer, S. S. 1960. The Analysis of Behavior Patterns in the United States Supreme Court. J. of Politics 22 (November), 629–53.   *S-Pol*

Vinacke, W. E. and A. Arkoff. 1957. An Experimental Study of Coalitions in the Triad. Amer. Social Rev. 22:406–14.   *S-Soc & Psy*

Willis, R. H. and M. L. Joseph. 1959. Bargaining Behavior I: "Prominence" as a Predictor of the Outcome of Games of Agreement. J. of Conflict Resolution III:102–13.   *S-Psy & Pol*

Wilson, K. V. and V. E. Bixenstine. 1962. Forms of Social Control in Two-Person Two-Choice Games. Behavioral Sceince 7 (January), 91–102.   *S-Psy*

Zellner, A. 1962. War and Peace: A Fantasy in Game Theory? J. of Conflict Resolution VI (March) 39–41.   *S-S*

Index